D1389849

CONFESSIONS OF A
POLITICAL MAVERICK

CONFESSIONS
OF A
POLITICAL
MAVERICK

AUSTIN MITCHELL

Biteback Publishing

First published in Great Britain in 2018 by
Biteback Publishing Ltd
Westminster Tower
3 Albert Embankment
London SE1 7SP
Copyright © Austin Mitchell 2018

Austin Mitchell has asserted his right under the Copyright, Designs and Patents Act 1988
to be identified as the author of this work.

All rights reserved. No part of this publication may be reproduced, stored in a retrieval system
or transmitted, in any form or by any means, without the publisher's prior permission in writing.

This book is sold subject to the condition that it shall not, by way of trade or otherwise, be
lent, resold, hired out or otherwise circulated without the publisher's prior consent in any form
of binding or cover other than that in which it is published and without a similar condition,
including this condition, being imposed on the subsequent purchaser.

Every reasonable effort has been made to trace copyright holders of material reproduced
in this book, but if any have been inadvertently overlooked the publisher would be glad
to hear from them.

ISBN 978-1-78590-401-1

10 9 8 7 6 5 4 3 2 1

A CIP catalogue record for this book is available from the British Library.

Set in Adobe Caslon Pro and Trade Gothic

Printed and bound in Great Britain by
CPI Group (UK) Ltd, Croydon CR0 4YY

FSC
www.fsc.org

MIX
Paper from
responsible sources
FSC® C020471

CONTENTS

INTRODUCTION

ODD MAN IN

'All political careers end in failure,' said Enoch Powell. His did, so he exemplified the trend. But he was wrong. They end in a welter of excuses and protracted efforts to explain away apparent failures as real successes. This tendency is illustrated by the autobiographies of those who've struggled to the upper reaches of the greasy pole. They describe politics from the top down, embellishing their triumphs, glossing over failures and lauding their own achievements. This earns a nice retirement bonus and opens the door to a steady income from public speeches, singing for chicken suppers and substantial fees for doling out small portions of their view of history.

Mavericks are different. Their careers often begin in failure, go on through failures and usually end the same way. Battling against the trend and questioning prevailing orthodoxies is not the most popular thing to do in Britain's conformist, complacent politics.

Yet it is necessary, as are the efforts of those who labour on the back benches of politics. To ignore either camp is like writing the lives of the engineers who built Britain's canals without mentioning the navvies who did the work. That analogy holds for politics, because backbenchers are the parliamentary labourers, doing the digging while the mavericks argue about the route, while the fate of both is decided by decisions from the top, over which they have all too little influence.

Their efforts are mostly unheralded and unsung. The chronicles of the great mention them only when they become particularly revolting and difficult enough to threaten the policies leaders want to pursue. You'll find few allusions to the toiling masses of backbenchers in the authorised biographies of Margaret Thatcher, whose chariot they pulled. Nor does Tony Blair's book, *A Journey*, say much about those who trudged behind. Even the high-powered journalists who are omniscient and know more of what's going on than backbenchers leave them out of the story. Leaders talk all the time to the *pundittieri* and their media bosses, but not to backbenchers, and the pundits themselves only occasionally mention the workforce.

As for the first draft of history, the press usually mention those who do and die without knowing the reason why only if they're comic, caught in sex scandals or other traps, or ready to make fools of themselves. The chroniclers of the second draft, the voluminous volumes poured out by the Seldons, the Rawnsleys and the Shipmans, can detail the meals of the people of power down to the last pâté de foie gras, but they tell us little about the lads and lasses who peeled the potatoes and washed the dishes.

As for the backbenchers themselves, their writings are best ignored – and they usually are. They're Pooterish chronicles that overcompensate for the subordinate role of the writers by glorifying the party they toiled for, laying claim to victories that weren't really theirs and asserting a role in policy changes they merely voted for. Backbench biographies are fewer, shorter and frequently self-published. They're written as if explaining a mystic world to ignorant outsiders. Tory backbenchers generally make the more pretentious claims, their party having been in power for longer. Labour Members tend to write about rows, or offer humorous DIY manuals on how to become an MP. *Commons Knowledge* by Paul Flynn (1997) made the case for 'the active rigorous backbench MP'. Flynn had just won an award for 'Backbencher of the Year'.

A few inflate mythical achievements in securing changes in the law, winning a better deal for grateful constituents or bringing yet another supermarket to Little Binding on the Marsh. Some include a few jokes from the parliamentary joke book (a rebound copy of *Punch* for 1912), but most wrap Parliament in veneration and awe, extolling the majesty and the mystery of the institution that elevated the authors to their higher level of obscurity.

Little of this literary output is strictly honest. So, in this maverick's tale I've tried to give a more realistic picture of the mundane reality of the backbencher's life, its frustrations and failures, the constant pressures of the treadmill and the lack of the influence and power wielded in more glamorous and better-paid occupations. Like the chronicles of most political careers, this is a story of failure, but at a lower level than the cataclysmic fiascos managed by those at the top of the tree.

This is the life story of someone who failed to make history and now *is* history. It describes the best way a backbencher can endure political history: by being an independent-minded maverick. Conformity is the way to the top. Dissenting earns you relegation, but it is much more fun, although it's also frustrating and isolating. In Silicon Valley, mavericking can make your fortune. In politics, it's not the path to power, pelf or place. Just a different view: from the bottom up, rather than the top down, as one of the parliamentary proletariat.

I can only hope that all this makes the present volume more accurate and honest than the self-glorification and the genuflexions to ortho-doxy in the chronicles of those powerful enough to have something to hide. Just as the workers on the shop floor usually know well what's going wrong with a failing firm, so do those who are there to imple-ment the decisions of the great without having an influence on them. They endure the consequences, rather than achieving glory, power or repute on the political scene, because to fail at the power game is to be written out of history altogether.

The worm's-eye perspective is very different to that of those who have reached the top of the greasy pole, and even to those who have only managed to slither up to its lower reaches. But it is more realistic and therefore more critical. Viewed from below, the brave adventures of Prime Ministers and their acolytes can look like the ill-thought-out improvisations they all too often are. The 'triumphs' can be seen as follies and 'Great Leaps Forward' turn into backward steps. In that sense, it may be seen as more cynical. It isn't, though it does lack the sycophancy that most studies of Parliament find necessary to polish the wheels of power.

Those at the top take backbenchers for granted. If they mention them at all, they see them as the servants of their will, usually obedi-ent, sometimes troublesome, people to be taken note of only if they're revolting. Occasionally they become scared of them, as Blair was in his final days, or angry, as Major was with the 'bastards', but usually that's because they neither know nor understand them. The worker at the parliamentary legislative face is more inclined to see ministerial feet of clay, to view Parliament as an inefficient factory with creaking, out-of-date machinery, sidelined by the might of the media. They see party not as a crusade for better, but as a bitch goddess who shapes their lives, rough-hew them how it may. MPs are required to keep quiet about such heretical views, as a condition of membership. Omertà is the vow of politics. MPs are only released from it on ejection.

After four decades of parliamentary life, I've attempted to put both the self-aggrandisement of the top people and the veneration of the traditionalists in perspective against the harsher realities faced by the people who make the system work, and who occasionally get to tinker with it. The relationship is unbalanced. Parliament is over-lauded and overloaded. The backbencher's more mundane life is less well known. Witty Tories like Julian Critchley and Nick de Bois have managed to write elegantly about it, but all too little is known about the foot soldiers in Labour's more bedraggled army.

For me, it began as the conventional story of a lower-middle-class kid brought up patriotic, dutiful and naive, deferential and conservative, whose career was boosted by a post-war settlement which tilted the social balances towards the people, and particularly to people like me – an improvement I wanted to extend to everyone.

Britain had won the war and surely led the world. New opportunities opened up. Our house became populated with a washing machine, a fridge and, most amazing of all, a television, all far, far better than my grandmother's house with its outside lavatory, washtub, mangle and coal-fired stove. Every day and in every way, life was getting better. It took me to grammar school, then on to become the first of my family, unnumbered generations of weavers, to go to university, rather than into the dark satanic mills among which I grew up.

I did well and became keen to advance equality and affluence to improve the lot of everyone, opening up the opportunities I'd had to all. With that simple ideology I was catapulted into a new life as Member of Parliament for Grimsby, a junior member of Britain's political elite, the class with the power to change, lead and, I hoped, build an even better Britain as a humble recruit to a Labour Party trudging towards Jerusalem.

Too late. The post-war settlement was already falling apart as stop-go deprived Britain of the steady growth our competitors were enjoying, and the pressures of inflation produced an industrial unrest that made industry a battleground between capital and labour, rather than encouraging the cooperation rewarded by rapid growth elsewhere. But I still hoped that the damage could be repaired and the comparative decline stopped.

Hopelessly wrong. The trade unions effectively destroyed the Labour government with the winter of discontent, ushering in a Tory Party determined to dismantle the post-war settlement and shift the social balances back to wealth and capitalism. Keynes was buried, the unions broken, the welfare state cut back, redistribution replaced with incentives and progressive taxation, with trickle-down economics, as part of a grand plan to depose the state and replace it with the market. The whole ethos of government was reversed from boosting to disciplining.

This was more than a change of policy from benign betterment to malign retribution. It was a change in the ethos of society. Profit replaced service, greed weakened duty and a zero-sum competition for shares replaced cooperation. Any sense of the national interest, always weaker in class-divided Britain than in competitors who'd grown wealthy by pursuing it, was lost in a clamour of competing self-interests, confusing prescriptions and short-term improvisation. What was the national interest and what drove it? Industry, finance, ideas, investment, the state, the market, competitiveness, demand or supply, high wages or low costs? No one agreed. Every sector saw its own self-interest as sacrosanct.

My naive hopes for progress became a fighting retreat, and Parliament was transformed from the organ of improvement into the battering ram of the elective dictatorship, turning ideology into legislation and imposing a new settlement which punished rather than protected the people. My political career, begun in hope, turned to frustration. Until, as I retired, the people called a halt through the EU referendum. A peasant's revolt did what long years of toiling in the parliamentary trenches had failed to do.

My view of Parliament had been influenced by Harry Boardman's *The Glory of Parliament* and my ideas about the role of the MP by Josiah Wedgwood's impressive description in his history of Parliament, painting MPs as a noble breed – the envy of less adequate legislatures around the world – who retire with the dignity of having their names inscribed on a long roll of honour going back to the first parliaments in the thirteenth century. An alluring prospect, though by the time I retired, a rather different picture was being painted by readers on the *Grimsby Telegraph*'s website. One asked:

What has Austin Mitchell ever done for us? He has been leading, or rather hoodwinking, the people of Grimsby for thirty years. When I return to my beloved town I grew up in and was so proud of, the streets are neglected, the roads in need of repair. I see a lot of people wandering aimlessly. Where has our spirit gone? No thanks to you, Austin Mitchell.

The difference between these two attitudes can't be fully explained by the passage of time or the individual incompetence of the MP for Grimsby. It's the result of the decline of Parliament and its political parties. This has transformed MPs from valued, elite figures into less competent and less respected men and women struggling to do a job that's becoming too big for them. That's the story of the relationship between Parliament and me.

CHAPTER ONE

AN ACCIDENTAL MP

Most Members of Parliament are sharp-elbowed, highly motivated, clever-clogs show-offs with psychological high-vis jackets and enhanced egos. (Glenda Jackson commented after her twenty-three years in Parliament that the egos she saw there 'wouldn't have been tolerated for thirty seconds in the theatre'.) These anxious extroverts plot, scheme and fight their way into Parliament, a struggle that can take years of doubt, difficulty and effort. Even such powerful figures as Margaret Thacher and Tony Blair had trouble getting selected. Ann Widdecombe says, 'I must have been to a hundred interviews before I got a safe seat. You could paper a room with my rejection letters.' For the successful, this is a necessary toughening-up process to prepare them for the rough-house world of politics. For the rest, it's a test to weed out those who aren't tough or thick-skinned enough to get there.

No such problems for me. I glided into Grimsby, the best of seats and one of the safest, by invitation. I fought a campaign that was almost triumphal – and won. I wasn't God's gift to politics, but I was super lucky. An MP by accident.

Ken Livingstone hadn't yet told the world that anyone silly enough to want to go into Parliament (as he did) needs psychiatric help. Nor had the jokes been made about it being a fun factory, a palace of varieties or a parliament of whores. The glory of Parliament, evoked by Norman Shrapnel's *Guardian* sketches and the *Daily Telegraph*'s reverential reports, still lingered. I thought I was taking on a serious job where I could work to make Britain a better place, rather than gratifying my ego or furthering ambitions I didn't have. As a regional television personality, I'd had all the adulation any sane person could want. Whatever Kissinger said about power being an aphrodisiac, I knew that television was a better one.

I did, however, have one thing in common with other would-be MPs. I had no idea what the job was all about. Never have so many competed so desperately for a job about which they know so little. We all say we want to improve the world, stop the hospital's closure or get a better deal for the people – our own, someone else's, or all of them – yet few have much idea how to do that through Parliament. I certainly didn't. I wasn't even keen to play a role in the great battle of parties, though I was happy to have a ringside seat at the fight. I wasn't a political animal of either Oxbridge or the hurly-burly variety. I was nice rather than nasty, pleasant rather than pushy, and had never had to struggle for anything in a career that had been more of an upward drift than a fight to the top. Guided by luck not ambition – that's me.

I was Labour. I'd joined the party in 1956 over the Suez invasion, became active at university and then transferred to the New Zealand Labour Party. I went to New Zealand to teach because there were no university jobs going in Britain. In my long career of happy accidents, this was the happiest of all, because New Zealand is the best place on earth (outside Grimsby). It certainly made me happy. With the second highest standard of living in the world and unemployment so low the

Minister of Labour was reputed to know every unemployed person by their Christian name, it was the model of a good society. It was classless, with no inhibition on doing whatever you wanted, whether it was rising to the top or shearing sheep. In Britain, I'd have been a history lecturer defending my period of history against all comers. In New Zealand, I became a political scientist, author and television personality, as well as a political figure, rising much further, more quickly, than I'd ever have been able to in Britain. Confidence boosted, in the way that a nonconformist lad from the north should be, I returned to England to finish my DPhil. Everyone should have one. After eight years as a perpetual student, I was determined to get mine.

Going back to New Zealand with my doctorate secured, I fell into television fame, was offered the chair of politics at Canterbury University and was appointed to a fellowship at Nuffield College. There I met a great New Zealander, Geoffrey Cox, who invited me to join the brand-new Yorkshire Television. I left Oxford without regrets (but feeling some guilt), without being entranced by its pretensions, its phoniness, its proctors or its pedantry, to go back to my first love: television. I quickly became the presenter of Yorkshire Television's successful regional programme, *Calendar*. I was famous in my own backyard, which, looking back, is all I really wanted to be.

Having moved ever upwards by luck and accident, I didn't particularly want to move down into Parliament. Why would I have been so daft? As the Clown Prince of Yorkshire I had the best of jobs in the best of counties. I was a populist Tyke speaking to Yorkshire in its own language, well paid, well known and wrapped in all the divinity that doth hedge a television personality. I had no thoughts about the future beyond an expectation (which we were allowed back then) that the good times would roll on for ever. I should have realised that an interviewer is just another piece of technical equipment, like a camera or a lighting rig, and can be changed and got rid of just as easy. But, like most egomaniacs who appear on telly, I never thought that it could happen to me.

Parliament had never been part of my plans, so it's difficult to say why I accepted relegation to it. I was fascinated by politics, I'd taught it at university and I particularly enjoyed doing political programmes and interviewing politicians, though Joe Haines said my interviewing technique was throwing marshmallows at people – a hostility he'd developed when I interviewed Marcia Falkender in bed. Politics is an addiction. Fortunately, most people don't have it. I did.

I had tried for selection half-heartedly, but realised that quality doesn't count in the selection of MPs. The race may not go to the fast, nor the fight to the strong, but it's least likely to do so in the selection of a Labour parliamentary candidate. Particularly in those days, when unions bought Labour seats cash on delivery.

Having only a pretty face and good intentions, I wisely decided not to put myself through that humiliation again. I couldn't embark on the long training, preparation and manipulation necessary to get selected or nurse a seat for years. No party except the Liberals, who'll pick anyone, was likely to select a naive tyro. I'd been a Liberal when I was fourteen. Since then I'd put away childish things. I gave up.

My mind was changed by accident. The death of Tony Crosland in 1977 created a vacancy in Grimsby, a peripheral (and reluctant) part of the Yorkshire television viewing area. Labour was deep in inter-election do-do and desperate for a strong candidate. My friend Joe Ashton MP suggested that I should stand and began to engineer my candidacy. I was never going to be selected for a general election, but a by-election needs no such apprenticeship, and being on television gave me the advantage of being already known rather than having to be sold to electors in a four-week publicity blitz. If I failed, as everyone expected, I'd had the experience and could always go back to being fluffy and cuddly. It was one of those decisions that had to be made instantly rather than after long consideration. The train was leaving the platform. I either leapt on, with no time to think about where the train was going, or I stayed on the platform. I jumped.

The chairman of the Grimsby Labour Party (who'd clearly never heard of me, or seen *Calendar*) rang and asked if I'd stand. Joe persuaded me to give it a go and to Grimsby I went, undeterred by the welcoming sign 'Death to All Yorkies' painted in huge letters beside the road. The wind was in my sails rather than those of the hundred or so other kamikaze candidates. I was put on a shortlist of six (no women in those days) and selected. I slept uneasily that night, feeling as if I was falling, falling, falling without a parachute. As the song says, 'It happened so sudden that I didn't have a chance. The six guns was a-blazing and I went in to my dance.' Unlike Ed Balls's, mine lasted thirty-eight years.

I glided into Parliament. In by-elections, candidates are power-assisted rather than left to struggle on their own. Grimsby was crucial for the Labour government. Massive help was drafted in. Agents and professional staff flocked in from all over the country grumbling that where Geoffrey Robinson had paid for them to stay in the best hotels when he'd won Coventry, now they were forced to doss in tatty boarding houses in Cleethorpes. Assorted MPs who'd never met me came up for the day to say what a wonderful bloke I was.

Top ministers David Owen and Michael Foot came. Michael gave a brilliant speech at a huge meeting, marred only by the fact that in his deafness he assumed the rowdy hecklers were Tories and dealt with them accordingly, though in fact they were SWP and totally bemused by his accusations that they were Thatcherite fools. David Owen, five years younger than I, was much smoother. He gave a packed Grimsby audience an elegant defence of the common market, after my speech denouncing it. No one seemed to notice the difference. For three weeks, Grimsby was a place of pilgrimage for every political tourist and several nutcases. By-elections are a brilliant way to boost tourism. Almost as good as the Tour de France.

I was accommodated above a fish-and-chip shop, rather like George Orwell, who was housed over a tripe shop when he took the road to Wigan pier. Good cover, because my clothes began to smell appropriately. I was transported everywhere smiling and waving like the Queen. I was trundled out to speak, kiss any available babies (not babes) and shake endless dirty hands. My speeches and pamphlets were written by press officer Min Birdsall, brought in from Labour's head office. They were much better than I could have done. Famous journalist Marje Proops of the *Daily Mirror* was brought up to reveal me as a real person, almost human. Being known through television was a big help, not because people voted for a TV personality but because it broke down barriers. Candidates have to force themselves on people to give them a shot of politics and shake hands. I didn't like doing that, but I didn't need to. A face they knew meant that they were coming to see what I looked like in real life, rather than backing off.

My first reaction to being selected had been to panic. Daunted by the task and the tight timetable, I rang Labour's Chief Whip Michael Cocks and asked him to postpone the poll. This produced a loud roar of laughter: 'I've just moved the writ.' Gradually, however, I became confident that I could win. Immediately after the selection, a poll conducted by Bob Worcester was shown to me, illegally, by Labour's press officer, Percy Clarke. He told me it was in his desk for safe-keeping and went to the lavatory for a visit which lasted an hour (the plumbing in Labour's Grimsby HQ was very primitive). It showed that hostility to Labour in Grimsby was not as hardened as it had become elsewhere. A town characterised by low pay had benefited from the £3-a-week income policy and the higher social spending Labour had introduced, and, more surprisingly, the loss of Icelandic fishing and the laying up of the big fishing vessels then rusting on the North Wall of the docks was blamed on the owners, who were cordially disliked, not the government.

I realised then that I could make it despite the prevailing gloom. James Fenton (political correspondent of the *New Statesman*, later to become Professor of Poetry at Oxford) announced that the smell of defeat hung over Grimsby. National journalists brought their punditry down to Grimsby and quizzed me on my politics, IQ and class. They came, sniffed the air, talked to each other and concluded that I was heading for defeat. Grimsby, they predicted, was lost, and their interest turned to Ashfield, the other seat Labour was defending with a majority of almost 23,000. The question was not whether the Tories would win Grimsby but whether Labour would lose Ashfield too. So off they went to talk to the miners.

It poured on polling day. The exit poll said I'd lost. I went to the count with my loser's speech ready. As counting went on and moved into a recount, I started giving interviews about my regrets and my hopes to get my YTV job back. These moving pleas were interrupted by my wife Linda tugging at my jacket: 'Shut up. You're ahead.' I was – by 520 votes. A fall from Tony Crosland's 7,000, but a win. I was MP for Grimsby.

Anthony Trollope wrote:

It is the highest and most legitimate pride of an Englishman to have the letters MP written after his name. No selection from the alphabet, no doctorship, no fellowship, be it of ever so learned or royal a society, no knightship – not though it be of the Garter – confers so fair an honour.

That wasn't quite how it felt. But I'd got it.

It was also the end of my long life of happy accidents. On 2 May 1977, I took my seat and landed on the shores of Westminsterland, a very different place to both the Yorkshire and the New Zealand I loved. Dreams are supposed to fade gradually in Westminster. Mine didn't take long.

CHAPTER TWO

FINDING MY FEET

I arrived at Westminster in a blaze of publicity which turned out to be my last. The hero of the Great Grimsby by-election made a staged entrance, Canons to the right of him, Nikons to the left of him, and disappeared into the Westminster processing machine which turns mere mortals into Members of Parliament.

I was nervous and naive but not unusual for parliamentary raw material. Clever, conventional, a grammar-school product driven by Boy Scout instincts and ideals to make the world a better place and help people, particularly those at the bottom of the heap. I was neither socially nor ideologically well prepared. The Parliamentary Labour Party, though not the leadership, was then proletarian in its ethos and trade union in its attitudes. This was before the rise of feminism and identity politics. MPs were proud to assert their working-class identity. I was a different class, programmed to different instincts. In Labour, but not of it.

Class was, and remains, the hallmark of the British. I came from the great lower-middle class, and was conditioned to the instincts and ideology of those dutiful souls, the backbone of Britain, who sit between the workers with their solidarity and the possessing classes with their selfishness. My sociology sprang from my paper round. I delivered the *Mirror* to the council estate, the *Express* to the owner-occupiers (and our house), the *Mail* to the pubs and chip shops and the *Telegraph* to the big houses with their drives. A typology of class-ridden Britain. Now a neophyte nurtured by the *Express* was plunged into *Mirror* territory.

Education reinforces conditioning. Britain's 'public' (but in fact very private) schools educate the well-off to the confident pursuit of self-interest, which has replaced the confident pursuit of empire they formerly inculcated. Self-confidence is the key. It distinguishes the chaps born to rule from the rest of us, who are educated to lesser roles. British education is the great divider. It fails to skill or civilise those at the bottom and channels the middle class into an excessively academic curriculum, rather than building confidence.

Being one of Clegg's children at a West Riding grammar school which took 30 per cent of the local primary school leavers – unlike Bradford Grammar, which took 2 per cent, or Bingley Modern, which took the rest to train them as hewers of wood and drawers of water – I'd been processed to be a member of the solid, patriotic backbone of Britain. As Orwell had put it in the war, 'The patriotism of the middle class is a thing to be made use of. The people who stand to attention during "God Save the King" would readily transfer their loyalty to a socialist regime, if they were handled with a minimum of tact.' They'd done that in 1945, but when the Tories humanised themselves into Butskellism, they'd moved right to a Butskellite Tory Party.

I'd gone the other way. Easy to do because the '50s were a social democratic age. I disliked the class system as I saw it at university, and particularly at Oxford, and was critical of the old imperialism shown at Suez, which decided me to join the Labour Party. Most of all I was enthused by Tony Crosland's *The Future of Socialism*. For him, and for me, it was about equality, building a more equal society, which would come from growth raising all boats and making redistribution less painful. I agreed, particularly after my years in New Zealand, the very model of an equal, classless society where everyone could fulfil their potential without being inhibited or kept down by class. Rather than nationalise anything, or embark on trade union struggle, I wanted a fair, open society like New Zealand's in England's less green and somewhat less pleasant land. Soppy stuff, set to the music of Bob Dylan, but not too out of tune with the Parliamentary Labour Party (PLP), which I now joined.

Parliament is supposed to be the great moderator, dulling the edge of antagonism, requiring people to cooperate, and civilising the few dangerous radicals who manage to get elected. None of that was necessary with me. I had the necessary MP characteristics – being extroverted, an exhibitionist, a bit of a show-off and a clever-clogs, typical of the breed – except in one respect. I wasn't particularly bothered about getting on. My star had already twinkled. If others wanted it to twinkle some more, well and good. I was happy coming to a ringside seat to watch a game that fascinated me.

I started with a disadvantage. I came in alone, not as one of a group all elected at the same time to learn the job together. Immediately after the 2017 election, *The Times* published a collection of advice from incumbent MPs to the new chums coming in:

CONNOR MCGINN (LAB): 'Pick a spot in the chamber and stay there.'

Andrea Leadsom (Con): 'Focus on one or two things you really care about and try to influence direction.'

Anna Soubry (Con): 'Keep your head down and make a good thoughtful maiden speech.'

Michael Fabricant (Con): 'Pace yourself. Do not expect to be in the cabinet in a couple of years ... Try and take one weekend off in three or four or you'll burn yourself out before you start.'

Wes Streeting (Lab): 'Form a group with new MPs.'

Anna Turley (Lab): 'Don't get distracted or caught up in the bubble. There are so many things that could take up your time.'

Andrew Gwynne (Lab): 'If you're lost, don't be afraid to ask for help. The chances are, the person you're asking is lost too.'

Sound advice, most of which I ignored. I'd add something else I didn't do: befriend the whip who allocates rooms. A little sycophancy never goes amiss in Parliament and a lot of it is even better. The only other advice I'd offer now would be, 'Don't get elected at a by-election.' I couldn't have got in any other way but it's the worst of entrances, by the political back door. By-elections aren't real elections. Swings are often greater and go in a different direction to those in more serious general elections. Voters are sounding off rather than taking a decision about the future of the country. Some victors have only a zero-hours contract. David Austick and Sarah Olney were supposed to herald a new dawn, only to be ejected before it rose.

The victor of a by-election walks in alone. Winners at a general election come in as a group, feeling a sense of solidarity which endures. They are trained, helped and processed together to make them fit for parliamentary use. Some, like the Tory crop of 1979 and 2010, or Labour's of 1974 and 2015, are called 'golden'. I was a crop of one, joining 649 Members who were battle-hardened, appeared to know what they were doing, and were far too busy to help, advise or encourage a new chum. Indeed, in a world where it's each against everyone, others regard the new arrival as a competitor for the limited supplies of pelf and place. The eyes which look so friendly when you arrive are really weighing you up to assess how much of a threat you are.

As I said earlier, I arrived in a blaze of publicity, marching in through a swarm of cameras clamouring for pics of a handsome new face. Joe Ashton took my wife, my mother and I for our first (and last) free meal. The Labour benches cheered their support (though it was really a cry of relief) as I took the oath. Prime Minister Jim Callaghan welcomed me personally (but briefly) and neighbouring MPs showed me round places I've never been to since. Tory MPs were very friendly, though I discovered later that this was mainly because they were desperate to pair with me so that they could spend more time out of Parliament.

Labour's two tribes, Tribune on the left and Manifesto on the right, each welcomed me in their newsletters as an addition to their ranks and a supporter of their views. A little premature. I didn't know the policies of either and preferred the Mitchell Group, or, as I later called it, the Gang of One.

End of glory days. I'd seen my victory as the turning of the tide which would save Labour, but found that the Lib–Lab pact had done that already. The bubble of excitement burst. The slog of struggling on with a tiny majority resumed and I was left to get on with it, plunged into Parliament's initiation rituals with no idea what to do, or how to do it, among MPs far too busy to show me.

Within two weeks I was being bawled out by my whip for coming into Parliament in jeans. 'This is the mother of parliaments, not a fucking garden shed.'

'Don't be such an anal neurotic,' I replied, only to receive a volume of abuse to which I wasn't accustomed after the adulation of my TV days. My son was stopped from coming in on his skateboard. Then I was conned into sitting on the Finance Bill Committee, which was sold to me as the path to promotion but turned out to be the parliamentary salt mines. The task of government members is to sit there silently, vote when told and keep their bloody mouths shut – which I was happy to do. I didn't understand a word of it.

Television personalities have to be smart, appear to be in control and constantly ask questions. In politics you have to answer them, a distinction I'd first become aware of in the election. Down on the fish dock at three in the morning, a fish lumper had started shouting at me that Enoch Powell was the only man with a solution to Britain's problems. I'd encouraged the tirade, thinking it made marvellous telly, until the producer pushed me, whispering that I was supposed to answer him.

This was a transition to another, very different, world. TV personalities are subject to adulation; politicians to suspicion. TV presenters are almost loved and looked up to as twinkling stars. Politicians are neither trusted nor believed but seen as party hacks. In television you work as a team dedicated to immediate objectives. In politics the objectives are long-term; it's every man for himself and the devil take the hindermost. In television it's all immediate, with constant excitement and pressure. Politics has huge *longueurs* punctuated by brief bursts of activity. In television you set your own agenda. In politics it's shaped for you by the party leadership and enforced by a collection of brutal thugs called whips, who in those days were all-powerful as they struggled to keep the flock together almost awake and ready to vote.

I soon began to realise that the biggest difference was in the satisfactions of the two trades. Television is instant. Instant triumph or failure, instant excitement and, if all goes well, immediate satisfaction and a feeling of achievement. Politics is a process, an art of juggling and trade-off as one objective is diluted or changed to make progress with another. It is a process of compromises and deals which rarely results in total satisfaction and which in some cases is never completed. It's not for the impatient. I was never the most patient of characters, and years in TV's instant land had accustomed me to thinking that a clear argument well put would always win the day. In politics, with its trade-offs, its deals and its vested interests, that rarely happens and you've got to learn the sideways shuffle of a crab. In short, my skills as a teacher and lecturer were no training for politics. I loved lecturing, but it's the art of telling people what you think is the truth and then leaving it up to them to act on it. It varies by varsity, from Oxford, where fellows in tutorials pretend to be thinking on their feet then repeat the spontaneous performance for the next victim, to what Oxbridge would see as the lesser universities, where you tell them what you're going to say, say it, then sum it up in the hope that something sticks. Not so in politics, where audiences are less likely to listen, often don't want to hear what you've got to say, and then go away and forget it. Certainly the argument doesn't produce the action, which has to be pushed home by a lot more persuasion, cajoling, bonding and deal-making to get anywhere. I was badly prepared for politics, with my assumption that telling the truth produces the result. It took a long time for me to realise that it doesn't. It's no use thinking you're the way, the truth and the light, even though I felt I came closer to it than most. In the political clash of perversities, others don't see it quite that way.

As I came into the game, politics was still becoming a profession and a career, though a lesser one – like teaching, but with none of the satisfactions of that job. Unlike other professions, such as the law, accountancy, business or the media, it was paid for out of the public purse and therefore underpaid. I can't remember whether I knew what pay I was fighting for when I first stood in Great Grimsby, but Harold

Wilson hadn't dared to raise it to £8,000 as recommended by an independent review. I got £6,000, around a third of what I'd been earning before. This didn't worry me. Dosh wasn't particularly important as long as I could always afford a clean shirt at M&S. My motivation was duty rather than money. That's easier to say when you've got a working wife, though it wasn't an augury of great riches to come.

The first problem at Westminster is building a nest. I was offered nowhere to work, not even a locker. So I colonised an empty desk in the cloister, dumped my pile of congratulatory mail on it, along with my typewriter, and worked on it for a few days, only to have Robert Kilroy-Silk come in, claim it was his and throw all my stuff on the floor. Not exactly a welcoming gesture.

The next problem was whether or not to move wife, family and home to London. Instead of the fake hieroglyphics that adorn the river front of Parliament, Pugin should have carved 'Abandon Home All Ye Who Enter Here', because families are placed under enormous strain when parents work in two different places and home is not where they want it to be, but where the job requires. The problem can never be solved in a satisfactory way. Its consequences are marital differences, divorces and kids deprived of a proper family life, occasionally leading to drugs or suicide.

I neither thought through the potential problems nor consulted my wife and family. The MP, I thought, should live in his constituency, share its life and send his kids to school there. Which was more than a little difficult for kids who liked it where they were in Yorkshire, and a wife whose job was three hours away in Manchester, with Granada Television.

So to Grimsby we went, buying a house that Roy Hattersley described as a palace. As a result, my kids had to face rows at school about their dad's politics, and Linda had to change to a job in London, leaving the twins, aged nine, with a housekeeper in the constituency during the week. I deprived my son and daughter of a normal family life with full-time parents. Thank God they've grown up well and good despite this, but I missed out on the greatest pleasure (and responsibility) of family life: seeing my kids grow up. I was far too distracted by work and absence for that, and now regret the sacrifice I made with such insouciance then.

However, I had the advantage of having somewhere to live in London, a house I'd bought when I worked on *Twenty-Four Hours*. My sister-in-law and her husband had shared it, but they decided to go back to Australia and asked me to sell it. I sold very, very, very slowly, comforting them with the news that the market was rising. Better to wait than sell soon. So the greatest problem faced by new MPs from outside London had been solved as easily as it would have been by a wealthy Tory. Peter Walker advised Tories to 'make enough money to be independent before you become an MP'. I hadn't done that, but on a Labour scale I was a made man, well enough off to provide for myself and not be dependent.

A house was all I needed at that stage, not a metropolitan existence around London's honeypots. The joys and excitements of the Great Wen escaped me. Linda loved the theatres, and the opportunities. I never wandered outside the bubble and didn't particularly want to. As a result, I wasn't part of the network of MPs living near each other in London. It hardly bothered me. London was a place of exile, not the great focus of the nation. Grimsby was what I was about.

I had had to work at getting to know Grimsby, trying to understand the town and put down roots there. I read the histories (there isn't a good one) and talked to everyone I could find in fishing, trying to get to grips with a divided, quarrelsome industry. The hardest part of the job is trying to fit all the pieces together like a jigsaw, only to find that it's never complete. Pieces change, people die, industries fail, organisations fold and estates are built. Most difficult to understand was fishing, an industry divided between owners (who'd ruled it like monarchs of the fish dock), merchants (who sold and distributed the fish), the skippers and fishermen (who caught it) and the lumpers (who landed it). When I arrived, the owners were pulling out with their money, the merchants were desperate for fish, and the lumpers were refusing to land it if it came from Iceland. Meanwhile, the fishermen had been abruptly demoted from three-day millionaires to beneficiaries looking for jobs because we'd lost Icelandic fishing at the end of 1976 and their vessels were rusting on the North Wall of the docks prior to being scrapped or sold.

I had to understand all of them. I read everything I could find about Grimsby and applied myself particularly to learning fishing. David Chatterton, a local fish merchant, took me under his wing like a foreign exchange student and I followed in the footsteps of my two Labour predecessors, whose first move on being elected was to go on a fishing trip. In their day, Iceland had been the main source of fish, so their trips lasted three weeks. By my time, all the big vessels had been scrapped or sold off, so I went out for six days on the North Sea in the *Alatna*, one of the small Danish seine-netters which were now the major part of the remaining fleet. I thoroughly enjoyed it, though it began mysteriously with a day of announcements about different departure times on different boats, finally ending at 2 a.m. the next day on the *Alatna*. The problem turned out to be finding a vessel with a WC. In those days people respected MPs. So the owners decided that they couldn't have the MP shitting over the side like the men.

Unfortunately, the WC was small, smelly and dark. Whenever I shut the door I was seasick. So I joined the crew in pissing over the side. Having done so, I could join the song Grimsby Town fans sang to visitors, 'We've peed on your fish', though my contribution had been at some dilution.

Life in both Grimsby and London was a survival exercise, but I struggled on, persuaded friends and former secretaries to help with the mail, and found a secretary in Grimsby who turned out to be a godsend, though on the day she gave up her old job I had a horrifying car crash driving back up the A1. I was carted off to hospital. *The Sun* speculated that Labour's majority was about to die in Bedford hospital. I was weeks in intensive care and recuperation. Don't tell me politics isn't a risky business.

Travel up and down was the worst part of representing Grimsby. I came to know the A1 backwards (though I never drove it that way). I got to know every ugly mile, the scenes of all my accidents, breakdowns and roadside diners. It was my lifeline. I hated it. But the rail service was little better and within three years British Rail took the direct connection off as unprofitable, forcing me to add a growing hatred of Doncaster railway station to my list of peeves.

Barbara Castle, who'd just been fired by Jim Callaghan, offered lots of good advice. When I asked her what I should do about all the mail with problems, she said simply, 'Send it to the civil service. It's their job, not yours.' She was absolutely right. Everywhere there were printed forms to send problems on to the civil servants with a request for a reply, which was supposed to satisfy the applicant. There were a variety of others: some telling people their question was a matter for local government; some asking them to bugger off; black-edged letters for those who had shuffled off the mortal coil; and little cards telling them their problem was receiving attention. I used none of them but wrote individual letters via my full-time secretary in Grimsby (whereas my predecessor had had a part-time one in London). Problems started coming in the day after my election and I began to feel that MPs needed their own surgery to help them find answers. I hoped to get my old friend Joe Kenyon to form a branch of his Unemployed Workers' and Claimants' Union in the town. He came, saw, and announced that he couldn't conquer. Grimsby didn't have the socialist instincts of Barnsley. But at least I had the nucleus of a local office which could be developed.

Things could only get better. Roy Hattersley made me a parliamentary private secretary in his Department of Prices and Consumer Protection. This allowed me to sit importantly behind him in debates, passing him notes from the civil servants which he never read. I also attended departmental meetings at which we watched the inflation rate fall, point by grudging point, each week, and I was allowed to make policy suggestions, which were then ignored. My fellow PPS Mike Noble and I agreed to colonise an empty room we found in Norman Shaw South, and moved our stuff, including his enormous rowing machine, into it. It was a bit primitive. All the money allocated had been spent on the upmarket Norman Shaw North so there was none left over for its neighbour, but it did have one supreme virtue: no one came along to contest our occupancy.

Parliament is designed to overawe. Like running a brothel in a cathedral, its processes are arcane, its decor intimidating. The responsibilities of MPs look weighty and impressive, but the facilities to fulfil them are less so. The Commons is like a tatty third-rate club, with a tea room designed to look like the station waiting room of *Brief Encounters*. Yet I was beginning to feel more confident and was beginning to look, even feel, like a Member of Parliament with prospects.

The feeling was false. Overconfidence, the curse of Cameron, is usually the prelude to disaster in politics. Ask Theresa May. It certainly was for me. It takes years, not the few months I'd had, to master the job. Even longer to learn the arts of politics and the arcane subtleties of Parliament. The processes of both are unpredictable, unmanageable and at times incomprehensible. I was a naive fool to think I'd achieved any mastery.

I did, however, find a few Members, mostly neighbours, happy to advise me on all the tricks and deceits of expense fiddling. Their efforts were pathetic, nowhere near the big-scale depredations revealed later. One Scot, now in the Lords, told me how to collect tickets from the travel office on a warrant, cash them in, then claim more. A northern MP told me to drive down with two or three or four other Members in one car, and claim the mileage for more. A Tory suggested that I should buy a big old car (preferably, he thought, a Jaguar or a Bentley) even if it wouldn't go, make my journeys in a smaller, more economical model but claim the expenses due on the bigger wreck. All this was petty and pathetic compared to the scale of expense fiddling at Yorkshire Television or in the print media by the journalists who were later to denounce MPs as venal and corrupt. It was also small compared to later MP claims for duck houses and moats, but it was an introduction to the mentality: get what you can out of a grudging machine.

My initial diffidence gradually wore off. I was learning the ropes, developing competence and feeling happier, less inhibited and less overawed than I had at the start. This wasn't so much a feeling that I was on my way to the top as a sense that I could do the job, which I regarded, then as now, to require a sense of duty rather than a lust for power. But duty, it seemed, would be rewarded. This produced a sense of satisfaction that I wasn't going to fail in what I saw primarily as a huge responsibility: to Grimsby, to Labour and to myself. Little did I realise that in politics, once you begin to feel all that, you're headed for a fall. Duty is no defence in a jungle.

The months between my arrival in May 1977 and the next election in April 1979 were a slow learning process, strenuous but exciting. I was even given minor responsibilities. David Owen sent two of us to Rhodesia to suss out the possibilities of compromise over Prime Minister Ian Smith's Unilateral Declaration of Independence. We sought them all over but found few, probably because our contacts were restricted to the white community, the military, the farmers and the security service. The only liberal white MP I met thumped me awake late at night to tell me he was leaving for South America. We made no contact with the black population, whose leaders were fighting a guerrilla war in the bush. We reported back that the war could not be sustained for much longer but we'd found no one ready to accept this idea. David Owen and his officials debriefed us but seemed to know it all already.

Back home I was saved by people more efficient and better organised than I could ever be. The first requirement was a surgery for people to bring their problems to the MP. Every MP should have one, though many didn't. Iain Macleod had never held surgeries 'because they attract loonies like bees to a honeypot'. They do. But they also attract real people with real problems and are an essential obligation which was then becoming more necessary. My predecessor Tony Crosland had held one every month on his visits to Grimsby, which always took him back to London in time for *Match of the Day*. I asked Matt Quinn, the agent, to organise one and he assembled a cast of insolvable cases to test me. I struggled on until I could find a secretary and recruited an excellent one, Anne Tate from Findus, who became my one-woman Grimsby staff and knew the benefit ropes better than I did – though we had to have her office, which was in my house, reshaped with a new exit when a constituent chased her round it.

This was the start of a constituency office which became my pride and joy. Now a constituency office is the norm, but then many MPs had their wives stay home and do the constituency work. I pioneered a full office service eventually, with three long-term staff, two of whom went on to university, one to breast augmentation surgery. Two died in service, one was with me all my career. I couldn't have done the job without them. It rapidly became clear that the most satisfying and effective part of the job is not declaiming in the chamber but using the power and status of the MP to get departments and the council to respond to people's problems. That role was to become increasingly important as both central and local government became less efficient.

In London, my former secretary from Yorkshire Television, who'd gone to work in a mission school in Rhodesia, brought order into my life. Her partner, Micky Chittenden, a former District Commissioner and public school chap, came in as my effective manager, bringing an immediate improvement in status, class and interest. He was the only man who could talk on equal terms with the formidable Miss Jean Frampton, who ran the Serjeant at Arms' services.

I also got a flow of American interns which began in 1978, bringing a series of able and attractive female students into the office for work experience. This produced envy from other MPs who lacked such blessings, and, being MPs, they imputed sexual motives. It became an embarrassment when I took one of the interns, a statuesque young Texan, the daughter of an Episcopalian archdeacon, to a post-programme lunch at Yorkshire Television during the 1979 election campaign. Margaret Beckett (then Margaret Jackson, MP for Lincoln) was the other Labour guest. When I extolled the virtues of American interns, she interrupted to say, 'Come off it, Austin, we all know what qualifications you wanted.' Old colleagues from YTV, who had a fair idea what these might be, encouraged her by asking, 'What were they, Margaret?' She replied, 'Big tits.' The archdeacon's daughter flushed. I choked. The room fell silent. The Americans were later replaced by interns from Hull University, each of whom came in for a year – a marvellous help which was invaluable in a Parliament prepared to rely on university charity to function.

I needed this support for my burgeoning constitutional responsibilities, but the little world I was building collapsed. The first stage of the fall from grace was the revolt of the trade unions. They'd saved the government by their incomes policy, which had defeated inflation. Government had fulfilled its social contract with them and kept in close touch, as I'd seen when a TV interview with Chancellor Denis Healey in his office was interrupted by a phone call from trade union leader Jack Jones. Denis responded, 'Yes, Jack,' 'No, Jack,' and almost 'Three bags full, Jack.'

The unions lost control of their members as the car workers muscled up for more, the drivers struck and the low-paid exploded in resentment. The result was a winter of discontent which effectively destroyed their government. Then, in March 1979, with the Labour government deprived of the Lib–Lab pact, which had expired in July 1978, it faced a Tory motion of no confidence. We'd become so adept at skating on thin ice that we'd managed to carry on skating six months after the ice had melted. Now we hoped to do so again – but we needed the support of some Northern Irish MPs. The whips persuaded the Irish Nationalist Member Frank Maguire to make a rare visit to support the government and flew him into Northolt. Roy Hattersley urged Jim Callaghan to offer Northern Ireland a gas pipeline to win a slew of Unionist votes, but when Jim refused, Roy delegated care of Frank to his two PPSs while he worked on a pair of sympathetic Unionist MPs.

Mike Noble walked Frank round for some hours. I was allocated a two-hour shift and took him to the family room to drink tea and watch telly, which was the most exciting thing to do in those days. But we couldn't keep him out of the chamber and he was deeply upset by a bitter attack from Gerry Fitt, leader of the Social Democratic and Labour Party (SDLP), for supporting a government which had imposed the infamous H Block prison cells and the deeply unpopular Secretary of State for Northern Ireland Roy Mason. Upset and humiliated, Maguire announced that he'd come over to abstain in person. He did. We lost two crucial votes: his and Alf Broughton's, who wanted to come but was too ill to move, and died five days later. Ann Taylor, then an assistant whip, pressed for him to be brought and, when told that the journey would kill him, is reputed to have replied, 'At least he'll die happy.'

At the last minute, it appeared we'd won. In a crowded chamber our whip got the count wrong and gave the Labour benches the thumbs up. We began to cheer, but the faltering 'Red Flag' died in our throats when the true figures were read out. The turkeys had voted for Christmas. The government had lost by one vote.

I shepherded the American interns out through a crowd of cheering Tories. A drunken conga line danced round the corridors and through the central lobby. Linda and I got drunk on red wine with journalist Llew Gardner from Thames Television, who could contain it better than me. The Labour government, which had saved the country from economic disaster, was out. Jim Callaghan was no longer Prime Minister. My apprenticeship as trainee for government was over. Eighteen long years of opposition had begun. I drove miserably back to Grims-by. It was the end of the Labour government and, as it turned out, of the social democratic post-war settlement.

Wise old Jim Callaghan realised the importance and the scale of the change. He remarked to his adviser Bernard Donoughue, who'd been in the Labour Club with me at Oxford but had more sensibly gone into the thinking side of politics rather than the party hackery-pokery I'd chosen, 'There are times, perhaps once every thirty years, when there is a sea change in politics. It then does not matter what you say or what you do. There is a shift in what the public wants and what it approves of.'

How right Jim was. But he never told me.

CHAPTER THREE

THE NEOLIBERAL BOUDICCA

The fall of the Labour government was a great dividing line, for me and the country. For the two years of my acclimatisation to the new world of politics, optimism had ruled. The media had moaned about weak government and dirty deals (they prefer strong Churchillian leadership even in the wrong direction), but I regarded Jim Callaghan's as a great Labour government, struggling to hold the rickety post-war settlement together long enough to inherit the flow of North Sea oil. Labour's frontbench financial spokesmen Joel Barnett and Bob Sheldon both assured me that this influx of wealth would open the way to the sustained growth Britain needed.

Callaghan's was a government whose measures I supported, whose compromises looked inevitable and whose leaders were big figures whom I trusted. They led a battle-hardened party whose toughness had brought it through five years of Tory assault and harassment. The Lib–Lab pact of 1976 had meant that the government would survive. My victory in Grimsby was a symbolic turning of the electoral tide, heralding better things. If only Labour could hang on.

It couldn't. A baying Tory Party, too long deprived of its rightful place in power by these unworthy socialists, came into office to change everything. Tory priorities are crude: power, power and more power. Labour's are more altruistic and confused. I didn't realise at the time, but, having got power, the Tories were going to use it to the maximum and hoped never to give it back.

I'd assumed that Margaret Thatcher's proclaimed policies – tax cuts when we needed to increase taxes; weaken the unions, whose pay policy had beaten inflation; and tighter money supply to push up a pound which needed to come down – couldn't possibly work. Margaret Thatcher's reign would be short. The country would see that growth and full employment were the only way forward, and Labour would resume its role as the new governing party. I was wrong.

Thatcher's honeymoon was, indeed, short because her economics were crazy. She'd been tutored in neoliberalism by Keith Joseph, who I already knew was the nicest man, but quite, quite mad. Every time I'd interviewed him on YTV he'd clutched a scarf like Linus's blanket, twisting and untwisting it round his fist until we took it off him, telling him it distracted from the brilliance of his argument. The essence of his economics was that no one in Britain was working hard enough so the answer was to take money from the poor to make them work harder and give it to the rich to incentivise them to do the same. Being less sophisticated (but more shrewd), Mrs Thatcher interpreted this in household terms. People should keep their larder well stocked (nymph in thy orisons be all thy tins remembered) and balance their budgets. Unfortunately, public economics don't work in the same way. In the household, borrowing is a burden; for the state, it's a boost, stimulating the economy and bringing in more taxes in a multiplier effect which the Tories neither understood nor wanted. On the other hand, debt in the household economy that the Lady was prescribing winds the economy down. Hers duly did so.

I'd forgotten a basic division in politics. Conservatives are born to confidence and marinated in it at their public schools. They know they're right even when they're at their most wrong, as they were for most of my time in Parliament. Labour, on the other hand, is more diffident. We want to be loved and have been educated to know our place. We crave respectability and are ready to conform to established norms to get it. So the Conservatives ploughed on boldly with their follies while we agonised about what to do, beginning by defiance but gradually lapsing into acceptance as neoliberal policies proved more popular than anyone had imagined. The class-divided English like discipline for those below them in the social scale. We weren't immune to that impulse, as the poor we should have served were transformed into scroungers, living in dependence on the charity and kindness of the *Daily Mail* readers they were holding back.

Following Margaret Thatcher's housewifely prescription, the Conservative government began with a massive shock dose of deflation. I saw no reason for it – there was none – but couldn't decide whether it was an accidental product of ignorance or a deliberate effort to discipline the unions and shake out overmanning and inefficiency. It did both by pushing unemployment up to Great Depression levels of over three million. This wasn't Schumpeter's 'creative destruction'. It was destruction pure and simple. Indeed, the only intellectual justification was the idea that phoenixes rise from ashes, so the more ashes that could be produced, the better the prospects.

I'd assumed the country would rise in revolt. Instead, it seemed resigned to the folly, accepting what was to become the perennial Tory excuse that unemployment was 'a price worth paying' (always by other people, of course). Much later, Norman Lamont blurted this line out, but deflating the economy and under-running it was implicit in Tory economics from the start. It reduced inflation, emasculated the workers and generated an exploitable hostility to the unemployed as scroungers who'd chosen a life of dependency. At the time, though, I merely realised that it demonstrated how much the intellectual tide had turned. Social democracy was no longer the norm. Social revenge was. The economy was to be managed for social discipline, not full employment.

It was also becoming clear that opposition was a different and less happy ball game. Everything changed, much of it for the worse. Parties are machines for winning and holding power. In a mass democracy, they bind society's chaotic multitude of views into some kind of unity. They are essential to getting elected: no one cometh to Parliament except through party. Which makes them both the rulers and the perverters of politics: loved because they're the path to power, hated because they dilute and distort individual desires and policies. Unity and discipline must be imposed to reach the promised land.

This Jekyll and Hyde duality creates the distinction between power and opposition. In power, party is a support team in a collective struggle with tangible results. In opposition, that bond is broken, differences emerge and argument builds about how to get back to the promised land. A defeated party falls apart, a propensity to which Labour is more exposed because it is defeated more often, is more heterogeneous in the range and diversity of its views, and is more divided between left and right, middle and working class than a Tory Party with a more defensive role. True to type, Labour in defeat embarked on civil wars in the early '50s, in 1970, in 1979 and again after 2010.

The turning of the tide in 1979 was the great pivotal point in British politics and my career. The struggle to shore up the benign post-war settlement and the welfare state was ended. Everything Labour had done was criticised and thrown up in the air. Draconian deflation was the new order. Members rode their own hobby horses in different directions, left and right urged different paths to power and career prospects were shattered. Promotion in power gives purpose, but with paradise lost, the struggle to rule in hell is less rewarding. Who knows when, or even if, opposition will be transformed into real power in office? I wasn't enthusiastic for the long haul, and ambition would have required long-term thinking and planning, whereas doing what interested me was more rewarding and more fun. This was a disastrous mistake, career-wise, though prescient given the fact that Labour was to be eighteen years in opposition. That made doing other things, such as writing, radio and television, far more interesting than struggling to get onto the bridge of a becalmed hulk.

For backbench MPs, opposition is fun but futile. Attack is easier than defence and criticism more enjoyable than the difficulties and compromises of formulating and selling policies. It's the opportunity to make a noise, establish a bold reputation, do what you want, and play the pirate rather than endure the disciplines of long-term planning. For the ambitious, it's less satisfactory, less purposeful, than playing a part, however small, in government. But that wasn't my mindset.

I fell enthusiastically into my new role. As a natural pedant, and one excited by ideas rather than the patient processes of construction, I was convinced that the government was wrong and I was right, so the duty of opposition was to make sure the people understood that. Being better at teaching than team work, I threw myself into what I initially assumed would be a short period of happy activity before the Thatcher folly failed and the country came to its senses. I little realised that Labour was embarking on a long fighting retreat against the new dominant ethos: neoliberalism. I assumed a few toots on Labour's trumpets would bring the walls of Thatcher's Jericho tumbling down;

I didn't have the sense to do what others soon did, and adjust to it. It was wrong, it wouldn't work and knocking it down would be easy. That misapprehension led to years of Labour crying in the wilderness through the '80s and then another period in the '90s when I continued crying but the party accommodated to the new reality, as power-hungry politicians must.

It was time, too, to think about my prospects. I didn't really fit into either of the two great categories into which MPs fall. Members can be insiders or outsiders, the ambitious who seek power and promotion, or the servers, content to do the job of MP and serve their constituents. Call the first group the ministrables, the second the foot soldiers. Or the players versus the spectators, or even the actors and the chorus. Both groups overlap to a degree. Governments have more posts than people of ability to fill them, so a few lunkheads get promoted. Real radicals like John Prescott, the Scargillite miners (who later became establishment ornaments) or Speaker Bercow, who started on the right but moved left to become an outstandingly fair Speaker, eventually compromise with power and get a share. Some relegated backbenchers will always be resentful because they haven't made it, usually for legitimate reasons which they interpret as malign, prejudiced or plain wrong.

Yet the distinction between the two groups is clear. Those who see themselves as men and women of destiny are different: aloof, preoccupied with the distracted, thoughtful look assumed by people of power, too important to have time for their old mates. That's the mien of junior ministers who disassociate themselves from the lumpen rumpers by becoming po-faced, distant and heavily serious, as if they carry the world's problems on their shoulders and know something everyone else doesn't. Beneath them swarm the hoi polloi of politics, assertive, clamorous and attention-seeking, noisily getting on with their lesser role. These are the Freds, Joes and Katies who keep the parties going, do the hack work and remain happy with it, if only because they've no alternative. Some occasionally feel paranoid because they've not got as far up the ladder as they deserve, but for most duty is a better driver than ambition, though the balance between them was changing in my time as career politicians replaced duty and service with a desire to get on.

I was less classifiable, but already drifting into the ranks of the outsiders. I did occasionally wonder why I wasn't being promoted while other less deserving cases whizzed up the ladder past me. Success had always come to me as a reward for ability in the past and I didn't realise that things don't work on that basis in politics. Most MPs think the Field Marshal's baton is in their rucksacks, and some who do reach the heights are seriously upset because they haven't got even higher – call it the Gordon Brown syndrome. But the basic problem was that I wasn't particularly bothered. I was happy with what I was doing. Ladder-climbing requires MPs to attach themselves to a rising star in the hope of being pulled up with them, but I never found anyone in politics inspiring enough to provide the tow or play the guru role that my friend Dr Erich Geiringer had been for me in New Zealand, my mentor Phillip Williams at Nuffield College in Oxford and Donald Baverstock, my inspiration in my television career. My heroes, Gaitskell and Crosland, were dead, Roy Hattersley was more interested in advancing Roy Hattersley, Peter Shore was too unconfident and diffident, Bryan Gould cautious and Austin Mitchell too good at seeing feet of clay.

As Margaret Thatcher consolidated and it became clear that she wasn't there just for Christmas, a shadow job in opposition looked more and more to be a waste of time and effort. If Labour came back to power, well and good. If I was good enough I'd get a job anyway, but I wasn't particularly keen to take on the heavy long-term burden of work and conformity, as a shadow with no substance, on matters I wasn't interested in. On a long-term basis this was a mistake, but relegation to the ranks didn't bother me then. Outsider life was more attractive, though I didn't expect to do it for eighteen years. In politics, you pays your money and you takes your choice. Then you suffer the consequences.

In fact, I was doing well. I'd been promoted to the Whips' Office after the election, a good place for learning the more sordid side of politics. I enjoyed handling committees, though the standing committees on privatisation and specifically that of British Aerospace, which I whipped, were a mess. Les Huckfield, the shadow minister, should never have been given a job in any sane party. He talked blithely of re-nationalising, if necessary without compensation, and refused to listen when I pointed out that we'd never be able to do that. So we ploughed hopelessly on, exuding enough hot air to power a new engine for BAe but having no effect whatsoever on the legislation.

On the other hand, the standing committees on finance bills, which I also whipped for Peter Shore when he was shadow Chancellor, were a joy. Our experienced Treasury team ran rings round the government and Bob Sheldon encouraged me to be a talking whip, making regular contributions, sometimes at inordinate length. Opposition's only weapon is to delay, and I'm good at prevarication.

The view of Parliament I had come in with, namely that it was the stage for the five-year election battle for control of the elective dictatorship, was broadly correct, but the revelation was how useless the debate was – more a parade of prejudices than a meeting of minds.

Labour, in my view, won the intellectual argument, but however many times we marched round the walls of Thatcher's Jerry-built Jericho, and however loudly we tooted our horns, the wall obstinately refused to fall. It actually got stronger.

The Parliamentary Labour Party wasn't what I'd expected it to be. Far from being a band of brothers and sisters (or, as we were then calling ourselves, comrades) working together to progress the cause of the people and create a fairer society, Labour was a scrum of competing egos and a scrabble of antagonisms and ambitions.

To win elections, parties must pose as a united team, if only because no one's going to elect a gang of squabbling prima donnas who can't even get on with each other. This is difficult, because in fact all parties are collections of jostling egos, all competing to get on and all holding different views of where they want to go. Far from being a united, like-minded team, Labour was a collection of ideologues and idiots, noblesse obligers and class warriors, ambitious, altruistic, radical and reactionary individuals, seeing each other as competitors for place, promotion and the love of the leader. This makes party a compound of dislikes, jealousies, even hatreds, in which all compete against each, and personal clashes and conflicts make united action difficult. The old joke about the young arrival being told that his opponents are in front of him, his real enemies behind, is true.

In New Zealand, I'd both written about and admired the party caucus as a pre-parliament: deciding the policies, vetting the legislation before it went to the House, electing and steering the Cabinet. The party caucus was all-important and I'd described the system in a book, *Government by Party* – only to find that it didn't apply here. In New Zealand, with party majorities anything just over half of a House of eighty (now 120) MPs, caucus is intimate, powerful and capable of formulating a collective view and influencing government. At Westminster, with the opposition caucus under 300 and the government caucus just over, this wasn't possible. Party meetings weren't, and didn't claim to be, a democratic machinery to control the leadership, but deferential bodies, useful for briefing Members and supplying them with speaker teams. Here, policy flows *de haut en bas*, rather than upwards from members, which makes the caucus a management tool, not management. In Labour's PLP committees, the leadership manages and guides the rank and file rather than vice versa, so the committees are nothing like the ministerial cabinets they should be. While backbenchers can sound off in party meetings, it's a safety valve, not a means of control – something ministers listen to but then ignore. The Conservatives do things better, by a process of osmosis from their 1922 Committee soundings up to the leaders, but both parliamentary parties are essentially sheep pens, not pre-parliaments. The result is to make the parliamentary parties less cohesive. Where parliamentary parties are involved in formulating policy, as they are in Australia and Canada, they are more likely to vote for it. Here, with larger caucuses having less influence, rebellion is the last resort of dissent.

To make matters worse, the Labour Party, which I'd found so impressive in power, fell apart. The left clamoured for revenge against the betrayals inevitable in government. The right defended its compromises, and enthusiasts pushed their barrows all over the place in what began to look like a civil war on wheels. To compound the problem, the great post-war generation of Labour leaders petered out. Jim Callaghan wearily gave up to the left's clamour for power. Denis Healey, the obvious alternative, had accumulated hatreds not devotees. Peter Shore was in decline, and Roy Jenkins was sulking in Brussels. The sentimentalists rallied to Michael Foot, a lovely man but no leader, who, for no reason I could understand, beat Denis Healey, the best leader Labour never had, for the leadership. I campaigned on Denis's behalf and received glowing thanks from his wife, Edna. Not a word from Denis, who withdrew into his hinterland as the party buried its head in the sand. Labour must be the only political party in the world unable to distinguish between principles and a death wish.

Tony Benn, who'd spent the previous decade selfishly telling twerps what they wanted to hear, came within a decimal point of defeating Denis for the deputy leadership. The Wembley conference rounded off the farce by splitting the party. I took my friend David Lange, the future leader of the New Zealand Labour Party, with me and watched him, like Alec Guinness in *The Bridge on the River Kwai*, come out muttering, 'This is madness.' It was, but it was a madness that had further to run. The Gang of Four, motivated by ambition, love of Europe, and big nuclear boots, backed by a clamour of media support which they mistook for substance, decided to flash in their own pan, taking a lot of good people and a number of dodgy MPs with them.

It was not only madness but a total contradiction of the political science I'd taught. It damaged the Labour Party irrevocably and entrenched a reactionary Tory government in power for eighteen disastrous years. The lurch to the left was compounded when Tony Benn swamped the policy processes for preparing the 1983 manifesto. I was on the PLP Media Committee. We developed what I thought a perfectly sensible policy, only to have a group of Tony's supporters come to the final meeting and make it both more radical and less possible. The same group had gone round the other PLP committees doing much the same thing. So we ended up with the longest suicide note in history, an unsaleable left-wing shopping list, and a vote-winner for Margaret Thatcher.

When the war against the left's takeover began, I joined Solidarity to take part, but it was becoming clear that Labour wasn't going anywhere for five or ten years. Neither was I. Why try to climb the shaky shadow ladder to power in a madhouse when there are more interesting things to do?

I never thought of leaving. To stay with Labour however daft it gets is a cardinal article of faith for me. I played my part in the fight for sense. But there were better things to do than wrestle in mud with loonies, so I sought relief in all the other opportunities for fun that were offered on the radio, on television and in writing. I wrote a book, *Four Years in the Death of the Labour Party*, prescribing many of the changes Tony Blair made a decade later. I found some relief in three speaking tours in America for the English-Speaking Union. Exactly the wrong course for an ambitious riser, but the right one for retaining a degree of sanity in a world going mad.

While I eased off, that world was changing. The old working-class/ trade union core of the Labour Party was shrinking. The paternalists and wets were dying out in the Tory Party, to be replaced by smaller-minded arrivistes and garagistes, as Julian Critchley called them. Career politics were replacing those of commitment, and neoliberalism eclipsed social democracy. The Tories swaggered with triumphant confidence, while a new generation in the Labour Party, the Blairs, Browns and Mandelsons, looked to change the Labour Party by making it an instrument of power rather than a collector of prickly principles. They urged conforming to the new ideology rather than replacing it.

I first realised the trend in 1989, when Gordon Brown agreed to launch a Fabian book of mine called *Competitive Socialism*. It was a good piece and on rereading it I think it stands up reasonably well today, with its prescription of expansion, rebalancing the economy to industry, and a competitive exchange rate, but Gordon endorsed it with all the enthusiasm of prescribing cyanide for headaches. He seemed to think that if he controlled the exchange rate it would free him to run the economy better. I knew it wouldn't, but, like other advocates of the free market, neither Brown nor Thatcher would let the market work on the exchange rate and both loathed the idea of devaluation, however necessary. A party which had never managed to understand economics echoed his views.

I was becoming out of tune. I saw neoliberalism as a betrayal of Labour's mission. It wasn't a smorgasbord from which you could pick parts, but a whole new diet, replacing the state with markets, public service with individual greed, and equality with meritocracy. All were the antithesis of Labour's ethos and ideology, but the party was beginning to see them as a necessary pathway to power. When Blair began his leadership with his great PR proposal to get rid of Clause Four, I didn't bother to oppose it, merely observing that if the leader wanted to jump off a cliff, the party had no alternative but to follow, though in fact it was the thin end of a nasty wedge.

Perhaps the triumph of neoliberalism was inevitable. The media endorsed it; the nation, weary of labour disputes and crises, accepted it. Business saw it as its victory in a class war that preoccupied them more than boosting Britain. Wealth and the City were delighted and, as the Labour Party began to compromise with diluted neoliberalism instead of offering an alternative, it became clear that Britain would continue a gallop down a dead-end street that an unthinking Tory Party and a malevolent media portrayed as a new dawn. Labour merely proposed to ameliorate the folly with a friendly smile and a dollop of compassion. What it would no longer offer to do was restore powers to the unions, boost the failing industries, charge the old taxes or reinstate the generosity of welfare. One by one, the policies of the '70s that I'd come in to support were dumped.

The party was already changing before Blair came to power. Neil Kinnock showed the way by shedding our two biggest and most unsaleable albatrosses, CND and EU withdrawal, but it was Tony's arrival in the leadership and then his triumph in the 1997 election that completed Labour's transformation from a simple social democratic party dedicated to tilting power to the people, into New Labour, dedicated to putting a gloss on the status quo. This changed everything. It changed Parliament by bringing in a flock of new enthusiasts, mostly Blairites on the make. It changed ministers by promoting middle-class meritocrats rather than lefties or the horny-handed sons of toil and the unions, and it changed the job of MPs by harnessing them to pulling the party chariot rather than influencing its direction. Charting the course was Tony's job.

The transformation produced more rebellions and dissent as Tony softened socialism and failed to use his huge majority to roll back Thatcherism. I'd voted loyally up until then, except on matters European, but in Tony's first parliament I rebelled on 3 per cent of the votes, not counting abstentions. In his second I rebelled on 5 per cent, making me one of the twenty most rebellious MPs, and in Labour's third term, which was also the parliament with most revolts, I rebelled on 7 per cent of the votes. In 2007, I led the first rebellion Gordon Brown had to face – before he'd even got back from the palace.

This radical shift changed constituency relations. After the departure of Michael Brotherton as my neighbour in 1983, I'd found a happier relationship with my new Tory neighbour in the newly created seat of Brigg & Cleethorpes, Michael Brown. North East Lincolnshire Council, the newly created local government unit that contained the two seats, had neither the influence of the numbers from the cities in Labour nor the pull of the Tory shires on the Tories but the combination of one government and one opposition Member provided a voice in both camps. With Michael Brown and, later, Martin Vickers, both of whom I liked and both of whom were dedicated constituency MPs, we worked well together for common purposes. In 1997, however, Shona McIsaac won Cleethorpes for Labour. The government/opposition dichotomy remained, but now the battle was within the Labour Party. Shona, dedicated to the party until she fell out with Gordon Brown, appointed herself as my care worker, stopping the old fool wandering off New Labour's road to the future.

The change in direction also reduced the power of MPs. Barbara Castle's advice to dump everything on the civil service became less relevant as the public service became less accommodating (and less efficient), means-testing replaced universal and accessible benefits, and functions were outsourced to organisations dedicated to profit rather than service. All this produced more problems for constituents and more work for MPs, but a diminution of their power. I could no longer get people council accommodation, loans, furniture or emergency finance. Debt problems multiplied and asylum and immigration cases became more difficult as well as more numerous. This rising tide of problems made MPs a nuisance in the neoliberal world, which responded by restricting their interventions and reducing their role to ringing departmental helplines to plead for aid that all too often didn't come.

At the same time, the parties were losing members, falling from millions in the 1970s to ageing memberships of less than half a million each by the new century. Financial problems accumulated, making Labour more dependent on altruistic donors who urged their interests in return for their dosh. Party staffing fell. Agents became extinct in the Labour Party, less common among the Tories. More work fell to MPs to keep their parties going and solvent. The Grimsby party that had been critical of my outside work now needed the income to pay its debts.

Labour sought to replace lost party staff with MPs. In 1997, it imposed a contract on new parliamentarians, committing them to meet monthly quotas on letter-writing, meeting members of the public and attending functions. This exhausting schedule quickly proved too gruelling for those who were keen to retain sanity and family life, and it had to be dropped before it could produce suicides or divorces, but it demonstrated what the leadership saw as the role of backbenchers: a pioneer corps kept in line and told what to do by pagers.

This attitude gave rise to a rare parliamentary joke: the Commons barber accidentally cut through the earpiece of a Labour MP, who immediately died. When inspected, the earplug turned out to be saying, 'Breathe in. Breathe out.' All this was a serious reduction in the role and the independence of backbenchers. It transformed them from tribunes of the people into party hacks, by-election canvassers and a chorus chanting slogans handed down from on high. Not exactly what Edmund Burke or Enoch Powell might have wanted.

Blairite ministers may have seen the backbencher's lot as hack work, but it was becoming harder. Constituents became more demanding. More of them had more problems, usually minor but often messy. Pressure groups learned the technique of getting local supporters to threaten vote withdrawal. As the benefit system changed from universal to means-testing, the mail bag grew, and more and more people came to surgery. The need for staff increased. Thankfully, I was able to keep things going with my outside earnings until the government responded by increasing staff allowances. I finished up running a small business, with three staff in Grimsby, where the problems were multiplying, and two in London to take the strain there.

The contrast with the past was striking. Roy Hattersley told me that when Sheffield MP George Darling had been made a PPS, his constituency party had agreed that he could visit even less than his previous six-monthly rota in the light of his onerous new duties. A Durham MP had told me that there was no need to answer letters. If the problem was serious, they'd come to his back door and his wife would deal with it. Joe Ashton left his wife Maggie to run the constituency from home. He told me, 'She knew every street and damn near everybody in it. Most of the time the voters say, "Don't bother with Joe, just ring Maggie and it will get done."' Eric Forth claimed never to do surgeries, but to make personal home visits to cases he deemed urgent. And he wasn't alone.

Neoliberalism, cuts and the rolling back of the state all required more and harder work, which could only be done by bigger and better staffs. Parliament became home to a growing number of enthusiastic young interns, advisers and researchers, all studying for Politics 101. Oldies grumbled. Julian Critchley accused me of running a harem (would that I'd been so lucky), but the influx of the staffers changed the whole nature of the place. They made Portcullis House more like a university in exile than the third-rate gentlemen's club of the old building. They improved the work and performance of MPs, kept Parliament in better touch with the world and the people, and improved the look of the place no end. I welcomed it and the only problem any of them caused me was the occasional tendency to treat the office as a doss house, resulting in early morning calls from Commons security, asking whether strange people found sleeping in my office were known to me.

Parliament was becoming a world of its own, corralling political enthusiasts into a Westminster bubble. Now, instead of being selected from among Britain's elite or big local figures, more MPs were being recruited from the ranks of these parliamentary researchers and special advisers, from unions, think tanks, parties, pressure groups and causes, all of them junior members of the political class already. Here was the political class breeding its own, prompting the question: what shall they know of England, who only politics know? Add in sons, daughters and other relatives of existing MPs – the Benns, the Gummers, the Kinnocks, the Armstrongs and the Burgons – and the political elite was becoming self-recruiting and self-perpetuating, rather like the aristocratic elite of the eighteenth century. Or the Long Parliament, where Cromwell had thirteen relatives.

Soon we all had our own staff and ministers had spads (special advisers) to tell them what to think and to provide a channel of communication for backbenchers. Most MPs had constituency offices and more lived in their constituencies. They sent birthday cards, congratulated constituents on getting married, having a baby or having the exquisite pleasure of moving into Slagville. Press statements poured out if a bus was late; fêtes, even those worse than death, were assiduously attended; and every goal by the local team was cheered, sometimes with glowing praise on Twitter and an Early Day Motion on the order paper. MPs were being transformed into social workers, local ombudsfolk, financial advisers and openers of last resort for fêtes and bazaars.

The work became harder, more detailed and inescapable. MPs from either side of the House remained two tribes but began to overlap, becoming more alike but more assertive about their differences. The one joy, which helped to bring us together and provided a degree of satisfaction no longer available in the chamber, was the new select committees, one for each area of policy, set up by Leader of the House Norman St John-Stevas with Mrs Thatcher's reluctant acquiescence. I managed, after some time, to get on the Treasury and Civil Service Committee. It was a delight and an education, two things that should always go together.

The committee became an effective critic of Chancellor Geoffrey Howe's deflation, monetarism and the stringencies of Tory budgets, because Labour Members, opposed to the whole caboodle, were able to drive a wedge between Tories, dividing the stern monetarists, who believed the government wasn't tough enough, from the wets, who thought it too tough. It was a wonderful education in economics at the hands of some of Britain's best economists, such as John Kay and Gavyn Davies. Our emollient chair, Edward du Cann, wasn't averse to criticisms of a government that had rejected him, and visits to America showed the damage done by the excessively high interest rates and high exchange rates resulting from Volcker's deflation.

This US visit was a whole new learning experience, though each morning we had to gather in Du Cann's state room and listen to him phoning Tiny Roland, as he did every day. The committee also educated me in Commons craftiness, when a draft report leaked to the press. I was responsible because I'd made an arrangement with a journalist to send him the evidence as it came in. In doing so, my staff had mistakenly sent him the draft as well, and all hell broke loose. 'What shall I do?' I asked Brian Sedgemore, who was a regular leaker to *Private Eye*. 'Just lie,' he advised. I told the enquirers that it wasn't me. Being gentlemen, they enquired no further.

The MP's role was becoming more work-a-day and stretched ever further. No wonder rising stars like Ruth Kelly, James Purnell, Matthew Parris, Ed Balls, Robert Kilroy-Silk, Sadiq Khan, George

Osborne, Alan Johnson, Alan Milburn, Patricia Hewitt, David Milib-
and, Archie Norman, Michael Portillo, Andy Burnham and Tristram
Hunt all decided after short parliamentary careers that there are better
– and more profitable – things to do than play Punch and Judy. Instead
of hanging around in the Lords, as ex-Prime Ministers used to do,
Blair and Cameron went immediately to till the money fields. This was
a higher rate of loss of top talent than in the past, and it symbolised the
failing prestige of Parliament and politics. An organisation in which
top talent leaves and top outsiders no longer want to come in is an
organisation in decline. Parliament certainly was, and the intellectual
level sank.

One of the departees, Andy Burnham, confessed, as he left to
become Mayor of Greater Manchester, that he was glad to be leaving
the trivia of politics, having grown fed up with it. I wasn't, but it was
certainly more mundane and less exciting. I was doing a different and
much harder job than the one I'd been elected for. Walter Bagehot
described Parliament as 'a big meeting of more or less idle people'. By
the time I retired it had become the inefficient, crumbling workplace
of a harassed body of overworked MPs, struggling to do a job which
was becoming too big for them. I still enjoyed it. I was better paid for
it than I had been in the early days, though nowhere near enough in
an age of exploding salaries. But it was no longer the undemanding job
generations of gentlemen had enjoyed and it certainly wasn't a chance
to build the better Britain I'd hoped for.

The rest of the Mitchell saga (Part One: The Rise Before the Fall)
can be briefly told. When Labour swept to power in 1997, I was clearly
too old to get any kind of job. I hadn't wasted my time struggling to
climb the shadow Cabinet ladder, beyond appointing myself as un-
official shadow spokesman on John Major's cones hotline, set up in

1992 so that members of the public could enquire about roadworks. I was too old for a job in Blair's bright new government of the next generation after me and had no desire to be a junior minister. Junior jobs had grown in number and are seen as a step up the ladder. In fact, they're usually a cul-de-sac for the junior ministrables, who are treated as apprentices relegated to unimportant work, touring local offices and boosting the boss. They get to ride in ministerial cars and don the mantle of importance, which distinguishes them from mere backbenchers, but the apprenticeship leads nowhere because the average tenure in any one job is just over a year and few reach higher because the top jobs are held by a coterie of trusties who are young enough to stay in for ever, and anyway their party usually isn't in power long enough for them to rise further. Which is probably appropriate, for in many of my submissions and delegations to junior ministers I found them to be nervous, inflexible and so lacking in real influence (and sometimes intelligence) that they were hardly worth pleading to. Some didn't even seem to understand the argument.

Even those dissenters who had risen in opposition, like Michael Meacher and Bryan Gould, were badly treated after the 1997 landslide, because they were insufficiently Blairite and blind to the charms of New Labour. Anyone not in the inner circle was relegated to the role of chorus singing Tony's praises. So, as Tony made his triumphal entry to Downing Street, shaking the hands of the party faithful brought in to cheer, rather than hang around waiting for the phone not to ring, I went on holiday to America and came back to watch from the back benches. I still didn't have any influence, but now I was sitting on the other side of the House, cheering the government on, rather than heckling it.

I was still on the Agriculture Committee. I chaired an excellent inquiry into fishing, only to have David Curry, the fisheries minister under Thatcher, come in at the last minute and veto all my proposals for government help on the grounds that fishermen were subsidy scroungers. In 2001, when the Agriculture Committee became the Environment, Food and Rural Affairs Committee and began to make exciting tours of Danish rubbish dumps, committee life lost its thrills. The election of a Labour government fulfilled some of my hopes and I cheered its achievements, but they weren't enough and I was critical of its failures, particularly in housing, which is basic to social provision but where we failed to build in the way every previous Labour government had. I was also dismayed by Labour's failure to rein in finance or regulate those risk-taking propensities that eventually produced the Great Recession.

I voted for Gordon Brown as Blair's successor. There was no alternative. He was the only candidate so everyone clamoured to nominate him, like a Scottish Putin, though many regretted it later and few expected him to walk the Blairite path in the devoted – albeit clumsy – way he did. I wasn't surprised when the Great Recession got us thrown out and brought in a Tory government that promised compassion but delivered austerity. This took everything back, full circle, to punishment as the path to growth, though now it was imposed with the support of the Lib Dems, who were so happy to be in power they didn't particularly care what they or it were being used for. Would Britain's elite ever listen? Would they ever learn?

CHAPTER FOUR

POPULIST SOCIALISM

If anyone had asked where the new MP for Grimsby stood on the left–right spectrum, the MP himself wouldn't have known, but the commentariat would probably have put him on the soft left – or 'centre left', as it was soon called to make it look more respectable.

I was certainly a believer in equality, comprehensive education and the mixed economy, and believed that the state had a part to play in the mix as the embodiment of the community, but I had an over-riding concern for the strength and power of the British economy as the only possible base for the good society. Essentially, my position was social democracy in one country: I felt that British national interests should always come first because the better society can only be built on a strong national economy, bettering the lives of the people and generating growth for government to distribute more fairly.

This view came from Tony Crosland's *The Future of Socialism*, which prescribed the kind of society I wanted. Socialism, Crosland argued, was about equality, and equality was best advanced by economic growth: raising all boats, generating the surplus and the public spending needed to improve society, and making redistribution less painful as everyone benefited. Growth was the key. That could only come from a more powerful British economy and a more vigorous one than the old boys' club that presided over the complacency of British industry in the '50s.

The way to invigoration, I felt, was pointed by J. M. Keynes in the 1920s, in a series of articles for the *London Evening Standard* (which George Osborne wouldn't publish today), which later came out as a book: *The Economic Consequences of Mr Churchill*. Keynes showed how British industry, particularly coal mining, had been crippled by Churchill's return to gold at too high a rate. This priced our exports out of foreign markets and produced an effort to cut costs which brought workers and bosses into conflict. Here was a sure indication that British industry would only flourish with a competitive exchange rate to make exports cheaper and imports dearer and allow us to balance trade in conditions of full employment and steady growth. This, I thought, was the obvious, logical solution.

I'd have done better to propose murder of the firstborn. Devaluation was the Great Unmentionable. Countries like France and Italy had thrived by using it to maintain growth, as did the new dragons now bursting onto the scene. Labour's two devaluations in 1949 and 1967 had boosted growth and improved the balance of payments, just as the Tory devaluations of 1971, 1992 and 2016 were to do, but Labour didn't want the taint of another. The Tories were obsessed with sound money. Inflation was the ultimate sin. No one seemed to realise that the previous devaluations hadn't boosted inflation seriously or that expanding the productive power of the economy was the only way to avoid overstraining the country's economic resources. Only Labour was likely to introduce the incomes policy or the industrial cooperation needed to check inflation, which made it paradoxical that we were the party most strongly opposed to breaking out of the deflationary trap and going for growth by devaluation.

Competitiveness was the key to growth, but Britain had opted for the opposite. After the Second World War, a succession of competitors starting with Germany and Japan (followed later by China and the Young Dragons) had begun with very low exchange rates, and used the boost that this gave to exports to build powerful exporting sectors and strong national champions, all benefiting from economies of scale and heavy investment (often generated by the state), and leading to upgrading and continuous improvement. Rebuilding with new and efficient factories made industry attractive to talent and kept the price of exports down to take on the world. Including us.

Britain was more complacent. Having won the war and made the world fit for British cars to break down in, it had settled back into a rentier role, rather than face up to the new challenges. Finance and the City were the dominant interests. They wanted a strong and stable exchange rate, the better to conduct their business and transact money around the world. The City became a replacement for empire, and the pound a national phallic symbol, making Britain proud when it was hard, but filled with post-imperial triste if it softened.

Unlike the City, industry didn't speak with one voice. It was divided, with the two sides – capital and labour – in conflict. Finance was concentrated in London; industry was scattered round the country and taken for granted. British industry failed to rebuild and modernise as war had forced Germany and France to do, and it became less attractive to talent, which was drawn instead into the media, the yap professions and the City. The industrial spirit died. British industry was content to rest on home and imperial markets, where the challenges were fewer. It was ever ready, as Bevan put it, to 'suck at the teats of the state' rather than compete in the world. No other country was as insouciant of its national interest and its industry as Britain, the great believer in free trade long after it had changed from an advantage for the first industrial nation to a threat to a deindustrialising one.

The result was slower growth and a steady loss of markets, first overseas, then at home. Industrial confrontation replaced cooperation as workers sought to improve a share that company prospects were failing to boost. Other nations grew steadily. We lurched from go to stop as each attempt to expand threatened the exchange rate and the government responded by raising interest rates, punishing industry and penalising production.

It was a sad record culminating in the failure of Harold Wilson's Labour government, the last attempt to build social democracy in one country. Everything that government promised was predicated on growth, but the great expectations and the national plan were both ditched because Wilson obstinately refused to devalue until it was forced on him, too little too late, in 1967. 'Let's Go with Labour' never turned into 'Let's Grow with Labour'.

All sorts of alternatives were then offered – a siege economy, tax incentives, industrial discipline, joining the common market, planning – but I was convinced that Labour's mission of maximising economic growth could only be achieved by strengthening the British economy. That required an industrial policy to boost investment and modernisation, a regional policy to spread growth around the country, cheap money and, above all, a competitive exchange rate to boost exports and hold the markets we were losing.

The exchange rate was the key and devaluation the need. I came into Parliament as an advocate of devaluation, supporting a Labour government that was doing exactly the opposite. Labour was determined to defeat inflation and Denis Healey was defending an exchange rate that was far too high for industry to be competitive by putting up interest rates and cutting government spending to suit the dictates of the IMF. I preached competitiveness from the start and at what must have been boring length. I might as well have been speaking in Urdu. The Labour Party wasn't interested in economics, micro or macro. A party without economics is a wagon without wheels but Labour was – and is – much more interested in giving marginalised groups like women the right to drive it or deciding what colour to paint it than in boosting the engine.

Such was my introduction to the paradoxes of politics. It's a process, not a crusade; moving crab-like, not forward; and always a choice of the lesser of competing evils rather than the implementation of some ultimate good. Its practitioners must move in zigzag fashion, and slowly, towards their objective and be prepared to slip back two steps for every three moved forward. Support what you don't want, in the hope of getting a little of what you do. No chance of implementing grand theories and little time to reflect on long-term purposes or develop new ideas. Attacking the other side is more important than serious thinking. British politics, like our legal system, works by confrontation. Its aim is to educate by conflict, but the process has a bias against understanding. It bemuses more than it informs and it precludes considered, consensual problem-solving.

As I came into Parliament, the benign post-war settlement that had given us decades of affluence was under huge strain, but I was convinced that it could and should be saved. Labour was holding things together by incomes policy to deal with inflation, and higher social spending to preserve living standards. The hope was that this would keep things going until the North Sea oil came on-stream to lift us out of the trough. Devaluation would have allowed us to do this without balance of payments problems. It would also have avoided the prospect of 'Dutch disease', so called because the discovery of gas pushed up the value of the guilder just as oil later pushed up the pound.

The hope of getting by until North Sea oil boosted the economy was killed by the winter of discontent, which brought the Tories to power in 1979 and allowed them to impose their nasty medicine: cutting spending, ending incomes policy, and imposing monetarism and neoliberalism, all aimed at rolling back the state and giving power to markets, which were considered so much smarter than government. The unions had gone on strike for their own decimation.

Thatcherite policies were the distillation of the accumulating grumbles of business in the good years. Business leaders had nattered on about 'freeing' enterprise, cutting taxes and regulations, slashing the welfare state and shackling the unions, and they had offered all this as excuses for their own failure. Now, to their delight, removing these 'barriers' became government policy. It was laughable in my eyes, but the laugh died as I realised that the Tories actually meant it. Business and the press greeted it as the realisation of their dreams. Britons are gluttons for punishment, when someone else is being punished. This collective ignorance deserved all that was predictably coming to Britain as the country was frog-marched down a dead-end street.

The inevitable result was decline and deindustrialisation. The welfare state was pruned, unemployment rose to record highs of over three million, Keynesianism was buried and the post-war settlement demolished. The great opportunity of North Sea oil, which Labour had hoped to invest in a national development fund as Norway had done, was thrown away, its money flow used to cover the consequences of failure by financing the import of goods Britain no longer made, and paying the taxes industry could no longer afford.

The rich took their revenge. Society became less equal, less fair and less employed. My ringside seat in Parliament allowed me to watch as the Tories celebrated their own folly. I joined the efforts of Bryan Gould, John Mills, Douglas Jay and Peter Shore to check it. We concentrated on demolishing the phoney medicine of monetarism. This easy answer to inflation was based on the myth that controlling the supply of money would bring down inflation. In fact, they could only control inflation by controlling the banks, which create 97 per cent of credit. Tories wouldn't do that, so instead they rationed money by high interest rates, which reward those who have it and penalise those who don't. The Tories also pushed up the pound, making Britain's industry even less competitive. This produced the highest rate of deindustrialisation in the advanced world. The medicine was killing the patient.

I glimpsed the consequences on my annual visits to the Caravan Show. Early on I sat next to the CEO of Caravans International. When I asked him how he liked Mrs Thatcher's medicine, he enthused, 'Marvellous. At last management has the power to manage.' Two years later, he wasn't there. His firm had gone bust after losing European markets because of sterling's overvaluation. The following year, I wasn't there either. The Grimsby caravan manufacturer had gone too.

It was frightening to watch it happen, even worse to hear the stupid chorus of approbation it brought from business. The woollen industry, where I'd tried for a job at the age of fifteen, was largely closed down, leaving it to the Japanese to develop new fibres and new uses for merino wool, in which Britain had once had a monopoly. The Morris Minor was a better car than the VW Beetle, but sold only 2 million where the VW sold 22 million, the latter being cheaper and continuously improved. The coal communities were ruined and fishing decimated, all in the name of progress. In no other country could such ruin and devastation be greeted as regeneration. At least not until the euro was invented.

We had one minor victory in demonstrating that the money supply is endogenous not exogenous, meaning that it couldn't be switched off like a tap but was sucked in like osmosis. The rigmarole of measuring the money supply and establishing targets for M_1, M_2 and M_3 was quietly abandoned. Thirty-five years later, the Bank of England admitted that the banks created and determined the money supply, a theoretical victory which came too late to stop Thatchernomics. Margaret Thatcher believed that the state, which Labour saw as the protector of people, should be replaced by the market, to set business and enterprise free. Unfortunately, this also empowered the strong and shackled the weak. The Tories didn't mind that.

Thatchernomics undermined the industrial base; shrank the basic industries, such as coal and steel; starved public services like health, education and housing; privatised utilities; and put three million people out of work. As Oliver Goldsmith put it, 'Ill fares the land, to hastening ills a prey, where wealth accumulates and men decay.' What was portrayed as an economic miracle was really a disaster, cushioned and concealed by North Sea oil.

We argued against the folly by every means at our disposal: books, pamphlets and speeches. But our hopes for better things from Labour faded. Peter Shore had seen that a devaluation was necessary and dared to propose one, but his successor, Roy Hattersley, proscribed it. Blair and Brown eventually accepted large chunks of the Thatcherite agenda in the hope of making Labour respectable.

Hopes of turning the situation around and generating the growth needed to boost the economy and maintain social democracy were inevitably centred on getting Labour to power, though I saw sense in the attempt to polish the image of the party and move it away from strikes, unions and nationalisation. This image makeover was undertaken by rebranding the party as 'New Labour', a young, modern, progressive party which would make a new start. For me, that would be a new start towards equality, a fairer society driven by a revived manufacturing sector to deliver the growth on which everything depended. For others, it was just better decoration and new wallpaper.

The progenitors of New Labour had something else in mind. I realised this as I met the new Members swept in by the 1997 landslide. I knew Chris Leslie from working together to defend our alma mater, Bingley Grammar School, but when I told him that, as an MP, he could stop talking the election rhubarb about freezing spending, balancing budgets and preserving fiscal prudence, he recoiled in horror: 'You don't understand. I really mean it.' I hoped that the arrival of young lawyers like Michael Foster, the newly elected MP for Hastings & Rye, and Hazel Blears, for Salford, would boost the campaign for better legal aid to protect the vulnerable, only to be dismayed when they attacked legal aid as inefficient and wasteful and our new Lord Chancellor defended every vestige of legal privilege. I wanted economic management to turn to Keynes to boost growth and bring back full employment, the best form of social security there is. Only economic growth can tilt the balances to the people, increase taxes and make them more progressive, boost spending and rebalance the economy. These new chums had more limited aims: to win power and hold it.

The gulf in economic policy became clearer with our two-year freeze on spending increases, our refusal to finance council house building and Brown's preference for prudence rather than growth. Blair took Labour's working-class base for granted. Though he represented a north-eastern seat, he was more interested in the views (and the company) of the metropolitan middle class, and those of the billionaires who always cluster around power, than the more basic needs of the people and the north. Tony dropped hard policies and any taint of socialism, and both he and Gordon accepted neoliberalism. Even worse, neither listened. I wrote, particularly to Gordon, as I had done to Tory ministers. They'd always replied, if only to dismiss my arguments, but writing to Gordon was like throwing letters into a black hole. He'd never reply and always delegated the job to junior ministers who didn't seem to understand what I was saying. I gave up. The Bank of England was consistently more open and helpful.

Their amazing first step of privatising the Bank of England (which Labour had nationalised as its first act in 1945) showed where their real intentions lay, because it was well calculated to hand power over interest rates to a financial interest which always likes them higher than manufacturing needs. Neither Blair nor Brown proposed to dismantle the Thatcher oeuvre, reverse the giveaway privatisations or get the pound down to competitive levels. They benefited from the 1992 Tory devaluation but allowed its benefits to run out as the pound rose, and they did nothing to rebalance the economy or rebuild the industrial base that paid the nation's way. That was their greatest failure. A government with a majority to do anything had prettied up the decor but let the house crumble.

Both welcomed globalisation; indeed, Blair preached it, though he failed to fulfil government's part in what should be a social contract. When globalisation threatens domestic jobs, the answer is not just to retrain workers for jobs that aren't there, but to move upmarket, to save production by investment and to sustain the hardest-hit areas, and to develop new industries. Instead, British governments actively encouraged globalisation as a way of giving the consumer what British industry no longer could, and compounded its impact by overvaluation and soft regulation; while failing to provide compensation and jobs for the areas of the country most disadvantaged by it.

This failure was fundamental and catastrophic. Globalisation damages local production and jobs, unless existing industries are helped to adjust. Germany's were. Ours weren't. Other nations helped their trading industries. Britain didn't because of a naive faith that the market would provide. When it failed to do so, the wreckage was sold off. We privatised council housing without building replacements for houses sold. We sold off government functions and utilities without adequate regulation to stop the new owners doing what they inevitably did: boost profits by firing staff and increasing charges to milk the consumer and British industry. So the costs of production grew, making industry even less competitive. We encouraged immigration without protecting British workers or boosting the social provision to absorb the influx of foreign labour. The social contract was effectively shredded.

The Labour Party didn't understand that its new commitment to neoliberal respectability ruled out methods of management used by previous Labour governments. Building large numbers of council houses had satisfied a major social need and stimulated growth; using Keynesian demand management had underpinned both steady growth and full employment; progressive taxation had furthered equality. In their place, the Blair government enthroned finance, 'reformed' public services (the new euphemism for paring back the state), passed housing over to private finance and relied on the market to regulate the economy. Instead of going for growth, we economised by not spending on infrastructure, by using private finance to fund public projects, and above all by not building houses, particularly not the social housing that previous Labour governments had deemed essential to welfare.

Labour did end the long-term disinvestment in health and education that Britain had suffered under the Conservatives, and used tax credits and the minimum wage to protect the vulnerable, but they set a cap on the welfare state, failed to regulate the privatised utilities effectively, and used the private finance initiative (PFI) to borrow more without putting it on the books. The public service didn't have the expertise to beat the teams of lawyers and accountants the private sector could mobilise. So the public got a series of bum deals in the sale of assets and in PFI contracts, which were much more expensive and imposed a future burden of debt on education and the NHS.

We demutualised the building societies to give them freedom to speculate, which eventually brought down Northern Rock, Bradford & Bingley and Halifax; relaxed regulation of finance and debt; and brought in pre-pack insolvencies, a fraudster's charter, and limited liability partnerships to make the big professional businesses happy. Labour was giving business a better deal than the Tories and making Britain 'a good place to do business', but at the cost of making it a less happy one for people to live in.

The pound, whose devaluation in 1992 had produced the growth Labour inherited, was allowed to rise – a reward to speculators which was then proclaimed as an indication of confidence in Labour. Debt rose, speculation became rampant. The result was a huge bubble, but Gordon, who revelled in being adored by the City, claimed to have created a new paradigm to banish boom and bust. This mixed bag of policies was certainly not a reconstitution of the post-war settlement. The post-war consensus had brought steady growth and full employment. Its replacement made way for the speculative bubble and the Great Recession that followed.

My interests widened during my brief tenure as a junior shadow minister in Trade and Industry, a job to which Bryan Gould had managed to get me promoted. Leading for the opposition on the Company Bill brought me in touch with Prem Sikka, an accountancy professor keen on reform of audit, corporate governance and tax policy. Prem saw that audit intended to give a true, fair and honest analysis of the company to investors was being discredited because the big four accountancy houses were using it as a market stall from which to sell more profitable services, such as tax avoidance schemes, personnel management services and even golf course design, to companies. This brought auditors into collusion with executives and led to softer audits to cement the relationship with their corporate clients. Such collusion was later to produce a series of collapses of companies which had been given sound audits, particularly by PricewaterhouseCoopers. But no one listened to Prem's warnings at the time. Audit and corporate governance were never top of the pops for Labour. The party was too keen to be friends with business and get approbation and support from the Big Four to see any need to regulate or inconvenience them in any way.

Short-term thinking and the drive for quick profits in a more competitive world had taken over the corporate sector. British business relied not on investment and continuous improvement, like the Germans, but on creative accounting to hype profits and executive pay, which was linked to profit. Financial jiggery-pokery and tax fiddles were more important than production. Industries grew by takeover and acquisition rather than investment or boosting market share. They preferred niches to competition. Shareholder value became more important than the company strength or market share, to which the big Asian conglomerates were dedicated. Foreigners bought up British assets in a great fire sale, bringing fat fees to the City. Shareholding, which the government was trying to spread by flogging off public assets to Sid, finished up with funds and institutions who took little interest in the strength of the companies, being more preoccupied with their own indices of profits and dividends. Workers, rather than being an asset, were treated as a cost, and constantly cut.

All this was a formula for disaster, not for the development of a powerful exporting economy like that of Germany. National champions, which had been built up and boosted by the state in Asian countries, were dismantled here. ICI, Leyland, Courtaulds and General Electric all went. Nationalised utilities, which had kept investment up and costs down, were sold off and the privatised entities then gouged consumers to boost profits.

The strong Mittelstand of family companies had been the engine of success for Germany, where they were cosseted and helped through difficulties. Here, small and medium-sized businesses thinned out as family firms closed down and family owners sold out to swap control for cash, preferring to become rentiers, landowners or names at Lloyds, rather than dirty their hands or shatter their cosy lifestyle with the struggle to keep underinvested firms going. Property developers could make more lucrative use of old factory sites as shopping centres, gyms and residential conversions than from the nasty struggle for production. Industry became obsessed with the short term and with speculative gains in the share price rather than with quality, investment and production.

German banks were regionalised and heavily invested in local industry. Ours were national and they starved industry to speculate or pour money into mortgages. Neither the British elite nor British governments had any idea of the national interest, having been educated to better pursue their own selfish interests rather than those of the nation. No one offered firm proposals to pursue the national interest as single-mindedly as our competitors were doing, because no one seemed to know what it was. When, later on, rebuilding became necessary, we had to bring in the Japanese to make the cars, the Germans to develop the railways, the French to replace our once world-leading nuclear industry and build our liners, and the Americans to provide our defence. Our merchant fleet still sailed big ships, none of them built in Britain and many of them under foreign flags. The Forth Rail Bridge had been a miracle of British engineering. The new bridge across the Firth of Forth, at Queensferry, was built by foreigners.

John Mills, Prem Sikka and I wrote pamphlets, speeches and letters to ministers and the Bank of England. We suggested reforms. I toured accountancy conferences and wrote a regular column for *Accountancy Age*. I'd have done better to go with the flow in a party that preferred not to think about either growth or the mechanics of production. After publishing one of our pamphlets, the Fabian Society held up the next indefinitely so as not to annoy Gordon Brown. We published at our own expense. *Accountancy Age* stopped the column when I joined a strike by their underpaid journalists. We made representations to the inquiries organised by the CBI. The chair of the first, Adrian Cadbury, accepted some of our ideas on audit committees, but the second inquiry merely guffawed at such strange ideas as workers on the board or rotation of auditors. We should have had a better response from Labour, but Gordon wouldn't even see us. Labour's company spokesman, Stuart Bell, was bought off by the accountants, and junior ministers showed all the enthusiasm of robots afflicted by rust. The job of the juniors was to act as a protective cushion, not a channel of information.

An example is the concession of limited liability partnerships to the big accountancy houses, who were anxious to protect their wealth, boats and houses from claims when they failed in their audit duty. The Big Six, which became the Big Five and then the Big Four, had grown ever more powerful and profitable. They needed controlling, not boosting, but Labour listened more to them than to the companies they fed on, and was persuaded to make this unnecessary concession. Limited liability partnerships made auditors more complacent and were partly responsible for the disastrous crop of audit failures, particularly by KPMG and PwC, after I'd retired. They made the big accountancy houses less controllable and less accountable, and opened the way for dodgy organisations to protect themselves as LLPs. But when the big audit houses bought, and wrote, legislation to legalise LLPs in Jersey, then threatened to divert their business there, Labour caved in. We went to Jersey to tell them they were being conned but were howled down. We warned ministers of the consequences, all to no avail. The most we could achieve was to delay the inauguration of limited liability partnerships for two weeks by threatening to prolong a filibuster on the bill, which would have delayed the minister's departure for Norway.

Treasury officials were very interested in our proposals on tax evasion and avoidance, both of which were becoming rife as the powerful tax avoidance industry became bigger, better paid and more skilful than the lumbering HMRC. Yet when we suggested that its power should be diminished, ministers weren't interested. Yvette Cooper listened impatiently, and did nothing. Labour lost its chance to tackle the issue, and the Tories later compounded the problem by turning a soft eye to the tax fiddles of the big boys. It all had to be exposed much later on by Margaret Hodge and the Public Accounts Committee, in the early 2010s. Hodge forced the Tory government to act, though, as usual, it was too little and too late.

By that time, little could be done. The EU insisted on free movement of capital, to the enormous benefit of Luxembourg and Ireland, which offered low-tax or no-tax deals, draining Britain of the social rent companies owed. The incoming Tory government compounded the problem by running down HMRC so that it couldn't keep up with the array of fiddles the tax avoidance industry developed. Even if their schemes were eventually caught out, the sellers of tax dodges faced neither sanctions nor fines.

As growth stalled and household incomes flattened, debt was the only way for government, companies and households to survive. Britain blew up a huge debt bubble, most of it to finance mortgages, car loans and speculation, rather than investment. I wrote regularly to the Governor of the Bank of England and to ministers to warn that if a thing couldn't go on for ever, it probably wouldn't. I wrote a powerful article for *Prospect* warning of the crash to come. They held it back for a year until I got it published in the *Political Quarterly* just before the inevitable happened. My reward was to watch a new Tory government repeating the old mistakes but with an added malevolence and the support of the Lib Dems, who'd disapproved so strongly of the first dose. Prophets are without honour in any party, not just Labour.

Hope became fighting retreat. Like bankers (and journalists), politicians think as a group and move as a herd. They don't admit error but always put its consequences on the people, the workers, the poor and any group with little power to resist. They'll gather rosebuds just as long as they can and clutch at any new way of doing so. When it fails, they lay the blame on someone else.

Complacency is a British disease. Having won the war, we had sat back while other nations built powerful trading economies. Our businesses preferred the comfort of the home market and saw little need to change or compete. Then, when the bubble inevitably burst, the incoming Tories adopted the wrong solutions and successfully shifted the blame onto Labour, by putting the resulting debt burden down to irresponsible spending rather than saving the banks. Being Tories, they let the banks off lightly. Instead, they punished 'scroungers', as if they'd been the cause of the speculative bubble. People on benefits were accused of choosing dependency, of wilfully leading a lifestyle of sloth propped up by the welfare state. Ministers painted moving pictures of hard-working families going to work in the morning cold, seeing the curtains still drawn next door, where their scrounging neighbours lay in bed, probably procreating, to produce more children to bring even bigger benefits.

In times of recession, Keynesian expansion and spending are the only way out. Obama took it with his big Recovery Act, which injected almost as much spending into the economy as Roosevelt's New Deal had in the 1930s. George Osborne did the reverse, calling it expansionary contraction, which meant cutting, freezing and deflating to cure a Great Recession that had hit Britain harder than most, because our overdeveloped financial sector had made the economy so lopsided.

Without growth, the fairer society becomes impossible. Hope is replaced by a zero-sum competition for shares instead of a steady expansion moving everyone up. In class-divided Britain, those who triumphed in this zero-sum game then blamed those who'd lost out. The rich got richer, the poor got poorer, society became harsher and the social balances were tilted towards wealth. The four horsemen of the new apocalypse – financialisation, globalisation, neoliberalism and austerity – galloped across the land. No longer the protector of the people or the regulator of excess, the state was viewed as the cause of failure and the enemy of business. 'Enrichissez-vous' became the new creed and Tory MPs showed the way by investing in cleaning companies, privatised utility shares, hedge funds – anything that offered a quick quid.

Nothing could stop the steamroller. Demonstrations were futile. Parliament had lost power to market forces, multinationals and the

EU. The Labour Party felt it had to accept neoliberal norms to win, and Blairite blandisers, who half-believed them and were determined to be nice to business, took over. The erstwhile defenders of the people – the unions, local government, the mutuals, the council estates and our divided party – were weakened.

As the counter-revolution triumphed, globalisation compounded the problems. Redistribution was replaced by incentives for the rich. Wealth was supposed to trickle down to a grateful people like horse manure, rather than being redistributed by the state. The aim of government was no longer to build a fair society but to make Britain a good place to do business.

This approach also made it a good place for business to do people. No government for the past forty years has accepted that capitalism cheats or that finance speculates and squanders, that companies fiddle, utilities overcharge and the market rewards the haves and punishes the have-nots.

Integrity has collapsed as honourable professionals and staid, honest banks have greedily diluted standards to boost profits. Foreign competitors, huge multinationals and the privatised utilities see 'rip-off Britain' as an easy market to exploit. The workers' share of the national income has fallen as shareholders' profits have risen. Manufacturing has shrunk from a third of GDP in the early '70s to 10 per cent today. It still produces 55 per cent of our exports but no longer enough to stop the deficit on traded goods rising to £120 billion, the highest proportion of GDP among advanced nations. This in turn has forced Britain to borrow overseas and sell assets and businesses to pay for its imports.

Such is the economics of the poor house. Britain is up for sale. Assets, utilities, property, land and businesses have been sold off to foreigners, losing the profit stream, the research capacity, the jobs and control. The sales, greater and faster than those in any other country, have pushed up the pound, further reducing our competitiveness and boosting imports to make the deficit worse.

The only way forward would have been to devalue sterling to a more competitive level, but no government would do this until, mercifully, it was forced by Brexit, and even then it was condemned by critics as an inflation disaster. Germany, which enjoyed the virtuous cycle of a competitive exchange rate (kept down by the euro's guy ropes), got growth and continuous improvement, and built up ever-growing surpluses. Britain was trapped in decline and faced growing deficits.

Which leaves us where we are today. The post-war settlement has been demolished. The market economy hasn't worked for the people. Austerity has delayed recovery. Finance has speculated, not invested. Banks have greedily grabbed companies instead of restructuring them. They pour money into the house-price spiral instead of production. Decades of deliberate underinvestment have left public services and infrastructure shoddy and have undermined the health service and education. The country is mired in debt. The EU has drained money, companies and demand. Globalisation and bargain-basement sales of assets have reduced national control of the economy. Business and the rich flaunt their triumph and fiddle their taxes. The poor suffer the consequences in cuts, uncertain labour markets and frozen income levels. All a bit different to either the glowing prospects held out for neoliberalism or the hopes of improvement I came in with.

Parliament has been no protection. The power of the executive dictatorship was used to carry out the counter-revolution. Softening the blows was the most it could do, but Conservative governments showed no desire to do even that. Labour, for its part, was in awe of money and too diffident to do anything about the overweening power and irresponsibility of big finance. It handed control of interest rates to finance, failed to check disastrous rises in the pound, did too little to stop the growth of tax avoidance, and slashed council spending, which was easier to cut than the central spending they directly controlled. They even declined to let local authorities build housing assets financed by local bonds to deal with local housing shortages.

When the Cameron government saw that the economy could be boosted by printing money, £375 billion of it, Labour was shocked. It could have developed a people's quantitative easing, used for public investment rather than allowing the banks to stuff it into reserves. Instead, it seemed so shocked by the breach of orthodoxy, it did no such thing. The City, with its pernicious financial orthodoxies, had never been stronger than under a Labour government, though that didn't stop them supporting and financing the Tories.

Britain is slow to change. Its politicians have little idea of the national interest. Governments and the political elite are remote from industry and the people. Only after three decades of Gradgrind economics, slow growth and flat living standards were the long-suffering people able call a halt and take their revenge by voting, in the opportunity an overconfident government gave them, to reject EU membership, which came to symbolise the whole of neoliberalism's futility even though it was only a part.

Britain's elite was shocked to discover that much of the country simmered with resentment rather than gibbered with gratitude for all that had been done to make it fit for neoliberalism. Instead, people felt they had been left behind by both parties. Both now face the problem of how to adjust themselves to the popular will. Depressingly, Labour – whose supporters had voted for Brexit while its MPs were more strongly for Remain – is finding the adjustment more difficult than the Tories.

CHAPTER FIVE

PRIME MINISTERS AND OTHER ANIMALS

The power of the Prime Minister and the vexed issue of whether he or she is *primus inter pares* or Britain's chief executive are much discussed by academics but of little relevance to backbenchers. The British Prime Minister is the most powerful political leader in any advanced democracy and as the PM has become more powerful the influence of backbenchers has become less. The American President runs a more powerful nation, but shares his power with the two separated powers of the American constitution, Congress and the Supreme Court. All threads come together in the hands of a British Prime Minister. In other countries, proportional representation brings coalition government, limiting the power of the Prime Minister. Here, the elective dictatorship makes the Prime Minister the boss.

As Britain has become less powerful, its CEO has become more so. Gladstone and Disraeli struggled to hold ramshackle governments together, but in a modern democracy, party discipline is greater. The media need to focus on a person, not a structure, so everything centres on the one at the top. After an initial honeymoon period, the media will become more critical, and there always comes a point at which they give up on a leader altogether. Yet in either mood the spotlight beams on the person at the top, a figure larger than life.

This is a distortion. Whatever their courtiers and the media think of them, Prime Ministers are human, almost ordinary folk writ large, usually too large. Their inadequacies can be concealed by acting skills, soft soap and media manipulation, but each one in my time was brought down by their human failings, which have been better disguised than was possible in the past. PMs are rarely alone. Like any comedy routine – Morecambe and Wise, Little and Large – they are partnerships. In Labour's, Blair sprinkled the glamour while Brown did the grunts. On the Tory side, Cameron did the boasting while Osborne the damage; Margaret rode the chariot, Nigel pulled it. Everything goes wrong if the partnership breaks down.

Prime Ministers are artefacts, the end result of a production line of advisers, press managers, PR people, speechwriters, joke writers and, in the case of some, makeup artists and hairdressers. These teams are usually so effective that it's possible to joke about the faking of the Prime Minister. It took teams to turn Margaret Thatcher into the new Boudicca and Tony Blair into the divine leader. They failed with John Major, and didn't even try with Michael Foot. But even the best teams can't eliminate the human failings that ultimately destroy their carefully polished artefacts. Which may be one reason why all PMs feel insecure. They know their own faults, Blair better than Thatcher, but all know that they can't live up to the confident, powerful image that is projected to the world.

Mortal characteristics emerge under the pressure of problems. They revealed Margaret Thatcher as domineering and socially prejudiced, Tony Blair as messianic, John Major as feeble and Gordon Brown as a nervous nail-biter. Only Jeremy Corbyn presents himself as himself, though he might have done better being someone else.

Perceptions depend on prospects. A leader who looks like a winner is adored, though always *pro tem*. One who doesn't is hapless and hopeless. Ask John Major or Theresa May. Yet people get tired even of winners, and those whom the media build, they can also destroy. Margaret Thatcher became increasingly strident as she turned her government into a one-woman band, loudly playing her own, increasingly discordant tunes. Tony Blair became the king of a sofa court. Cameron created a gang of posh mates, the Bullingdon boys in power, perhaps the dodgiest gang ever to hold it.

In the chamber, backbenchers see the backside of their leaders. They cheer in public but grumble in private. Most came away from meetings with Tony Blair and David Cameron with the feeling that the leader was on their side, though meetings with John Major or Gordon Brown made them feel like intruding nuisances. More usually, contacts are carefully managed. HR departments (*aka* the Whips' Office) try to maintain leader contact with the lower decks. Tony Blair rarely got down from his pedestal. David Cameron was too posh to mix with the hoi polloi, and Gordon Brown too much the sociopath to do it any better than a polite Dalek. Mrs Thatcher made imperial visits to the Members' dining room, where awed but honoured groups of chosen pols gobbled as she lectured them. Neil Kinnock ate while backbenchers told him how to run the party. Perhaps John Major dined with Mrs Currie. Jim Callaghan was more regular and a more natural mixer, but usually depressing.

Most leaders are cool to contemptuous about their parties. Tony Blair saw critics as troublemakers and the party as something to be dragged along behind him. Jim Callaghan grumbled about how irresponsible backbenchers had become, though his concern, like Harold Wilson's, was to hold them together. Mrs Thatcher disliked the wets and was uneasy with the traditional toffs. Gordon Brown mixed mainly with Scots. John Major hated the 'bastards' and Cameron feared them while pretending to be their mate. Theresa May seems worried by all of them, but keeps herself to herself, too cold to be loved.

Backbenchers form their own conclusions about the big cheeses before they begin to smell. Then realisation dawns that leaders aren't as smart as they seemed. I was disillusioned too quickly, but I'm a natural nit-picker, sniffing out faults like pigs find truffles. Must be my inner journalist, the kind of coldness at the heart which afflicts that profession.

The public follows some way behind, led by the *pundittieri*, the gossip columnists of power, constantly obsessed with who's up and who's down. They like change but can't build heroes without promptly knocking them down.

Jim Callaghan was more straightforward than his successors. As a result, he's been viewed more critically. He'd come to Nuffield College when I was a student and talked to us frankly as if we were intelligent adults, trotting out statistics to show that he was master of the situation at a time when he manifestly wasn't. He was less duplicitous than Harold Wilson but harboured grudges – witness his treatment of Barbara Castle. My by-election victory was a turning point for his government, helping it to carry on until better times. He showed no gratitude, though he did warn me, rightly, that I was getting too cynical.

Despite his reputation as a devious fixer, Jim was pretty straightforward. His PPS, Roger Scott, came back to the Commons every night exhausted while Jim worked on. 'Jim's a driven man,' Roger complained. But he was much closer to his party than his successors, the last Labour leader to dine fairly regularly with the troops. He preferred to deal with the old trade union party, rather than middle-class intellectuals, but he was always himself, rather than a creature created and glorified by a team of PR experts and advisers. He was usually right on minor issues but wrong on big ones. In October 1978, when he could have won an election, he postponed it, trusting the trade unions to hold the line on incomes policy until October 1979. They didn't. The winter of discontent brought Labour down. *Felo de se* by the labour movement. As a new MP, I supported Jim's decision, so I can't complain, though of course I do.

Assailed by ungrateful critics, and appalled by the subsequent follies in the rows that inevitably followed defeat, Jim gave up attempting to control the situation or the unions, which allowed the party to go into its second nervous breakdown. He compromised with the left's demands for control of policy and parliamentarians, then retired, to become Farmer Jim, caring for his beloved wife Audrey, who was dying with Alzheimer's. It was a sad end to a long career. But it made him a hero in my eyes.

I was less happy than I should have been with Neil Kinnock. He struggled well, though neither strongly nor quickly enough to drag the party out of its hole. In Michael Foot's brief leadership, Benn and the Bennites had imposed an unsalable set of policies in a 1983 manifesto, rightly called the longest suicide note in history. Militants had permeated the party and the left had boosted the power of conference. That and Mrs Thatcher's victory in the Falklands ensured Labour's defeat in the 1983 election, so Neil took over at a low point. He gradually weaned the party off its unelectable obsessions by dropping unilateralism and withdrawal from the EU. With the help of Gerald Kaufman and Bryan Gould chairing commissions to do the junking, Neil steered the party to more voter-friendly policies, while EC President Jacques Delors won over the trade unions to Europe with promises of the rights, the beer and the sandwiches Mrs Thatcher refused them.

Labour's leadership can never be left enough or right enough or even good enough to make all its members happy. Despite Neil's reforms, Labour lost the 1992 election, though not, as many claimed at the time, because of his over-exuberant performance at a Sheffield rally where he'd acted like a cheerleader rather than a statesman in waiting. Labour really lost because the Tory Party had wisely dumped Margaret Thatcher and her poll tax and replaced her with 'nice' John Major, who promised a safe new start. That turned the trick.

Neil disappeared into the mists of Europe, his achievement unrecognised, though he'd paved the way for successors to finish what he'd started and he'd enthused the party by his eloquence, though it was better in conference than in the Commons. He brought the party near to sense though not quite there, but suffered from a condition afflicting too many from the working class: he never felt quite up to it. Tories are bred to confidence. Neil was more insecure. Not a virtue in a leader.

Neil's departure paved the way for John Smith, the most popular, best loved and briefest Labour leader. I'd offended him by supporting Bryan Gould's mistimed decision to contest the leadership, but John commanded respect and was so canny and clever that he could even make me love a lawyer. He was brilliant in debate, boozy in a boozy party, but strong in the head, whereas the party's brains were in its heart. His own heart was in it but not up to it. His death brought great grief, a posse of weeping vultures to his funeral on Iona and Tony Blair to the leadership, with the good fortune of facing John Major at the despatch box rather than the formidable Margaret Thatcher in the weekly PMQs battle, which the Prime Minister usually dominates.

At this regular slugfest Margaret had been dismissed in avuncular fashion by Jim Callaghan when he was Prime Minister. When the roles were reversed, she trampled over him. Confident in her own ignorance, she was the antithesis of Jim. He saw the trade unions as partners; she hated them. He was emollient; she was abrasive. He agonised about the problems of a failing economy; she trotted out easy answers with excessive confidence. He kept social spending up to ease unemployment; she used unemployment as a weapon and cut spending to give tax cuts to the wealthy. He was the nation's uncle; she was its matron, ready to talk down to anyone. At first I didn't take her seriously. Too many easy answers: control inflation by managing the money supply, discipline the unions by legislation and unemployment, and hand powers to the market, which was a better manager than the state. It was all calculated to make a deteriorating situation worse. And it did.

The first duty of any Prime Minister is to be lucky. Jim wasn't. Margaret was. Her arrival in power coincided with the flow of North Sea oil. Had it not been for that, she would have been the most destructive leader since Genghis Khan. As it was, she became an oil-fuelled Boudicca. Weak public school chaps were excited by a strong matron. Others found her sexy, like Cecil Parkinson lying on the floor seeing a flicker of black knickers, or President Mitterrand describing her as having the eyes of Caligula but the mouth of Marilyn Monroe.

Her outfits, courtesy of Aquascutum and her dresser Crawfie, were always power dressing. Not for her the pantsuits of a Clinton or a Merkel. Her demeanour was always firm, even frightening. Her economics were those of a small shopkeeper but her follies were on a Chicago scale. They were welcomed by the right-wing media, by all who didn't suffer from them and by the more masochistically inclined among those who did. She disciplined the unions by closing the industries in which they were strong and by putting people out of work. She mobilised all the resources of the state against the miners, 'the enemy within'. Yet she was also firm on the Falklands and won where we'd have waffled. She was alienated from the common market (top marks), she tested the pompous and she encouraged argument. She even read my letters telling her how to run the country and wrote back graciously explaining to me how wrong I was. No other Prime Minister ever did that, so I felt a twinge of sympathy when she was forced out for being nasty to Europe, the victim of her own hubris.

Margaret was an artefact created from simple materials by Keith Joseph, who tutored her in neoliberalism; by Bernard Ingham, her press secretary, who wrote her scripts and put her thoughts better than she could; by Tim Bell, who styled her hair, modulated her voice down two octaves and taught her to talk to people as if their dog had just died; and by Christopher Fry, who wrote her jokes (both of them). She needed him because she had no sense of humour and couldn't understand why people laughed when she announced, 'I'm always on the job' or 'Every Prime Minister needs a Willie'.

Her successor, John Major, was more his own man, though not a big one. He was an honest man trying to do his best, and nice (in an English way), but neither commanding nor decisive. He suffered from a charisma deficiency and didn't have his predecessor's team to turn him into Superman. The real man shone through as boring, a touch petulant and pretty conventional. He was a man from a humble background who never quite made greatness. No one realised he was also a sexual tiger until Edwina spilled the seminal beans. That would have boosted his image had it been known at the time, though it said less for his taste.

John Major was a stop-gap and almost (but not quite) a gaping one. Having pushed the country into the Exchange Rate Mechanism (ERM), he was hapless in dealing with its collapse. It was Tea Room gossip in the Commons that he locked himself in the lavatory and left Norman Lamont (who'd never wanted to join the ERM in the first place) to face humiliation before being dismissed for his loyalty. John went on to commit Britain to the Maastricht Treaty to create monetary union. Euro-enthusiastic ministers claimed this as a 'game, set and match' victory, though it split the party and turned the rest of his period in office into a hapless struggle to counter the Tory hostility to the EU, which was growing as Labour became more enthusiastic about it. The subsidiarity that Major claimed to have won to reduce the powers of the EU proved to be a total myth.

John Major's failure brought God's gift to the Labour Party, Tony Blair, to power. Tony was Labour's saviour, the party's most successful election winner (he tells me) and the best figure to emerge from Labour's unpredictable PM production line since the Angel Gabriel. He even had some saintly characteristics: a nice public school lad, good-looking in a Bambi sort of way, eloquent in a verbless fashion, with a pushy wife (every politician should have one). Best of all, Tony had the skill Prime Ministers need: he was a great actor, with a barrister's ability to present any case and an eloquence that turned promises into aspirations rather than commitments. He shone in his own personal spotlight, which was permanently switched on to pick him out from a party in the shadows. He had youth and energy in a tired, middle-aged party, was a thespian among ploddingly sincere colleagues and projected himself as the future in a Labour Party laden down by its past. The art of political oratory is to say nothing passionately. Tony had it. Everyone came away from him believing that he was on their side, though they'd really had a sprinkle of stardust and a warm smile. His self-deprecating humour concealed a real *amour-propre*, which emerged when I called him Britain's Great Leader, the Kim Il Sung of Downing Street.

As he modestly proclaims, Tony won power for the party. His problem was that then he had no firm idea of what to do with it beyond a bit of 'modernisation'. He took the party on a journey but had little idea of the destination or the route, though he knew he wasn't going to drive on the left. He had few Labour instincts. The 'Blair Revolution' was in fact a public relations brochure for a mixture of modernisation, meritocracy and better public relations. Elections in our more middle-class society are won from the soggy centre ground, a land of soft, confused attitudes and ignorance. Sales there require diluting policies to avoid frightening anyone, particularly the wealthy and the media, and locking undesirable associates such as the trade unions and Michael Meacher as far away as possible. In the neoliberal era that began in 1979, conservatism and fear had taken power. Blair adjusted Labour's priorities to suit the new era, upsetting the party's rank and file, who wanted faster progress, harder policies and a slug of socialism. Instead, they got what Peter Mandelson called an 'overdose on reassurance' to prove the party so moderate and respectable that no one would notice a change of government. They were electing the sons of Thatcher.

Tony thought that things would 'only get better' because he was in power. He made some of the changes I'd urged in *Four Years in the Death of the Labour Party*, but to enhance the power of his leadership rather than reinvigorate the party. He certainly alleviated the problems caused by Tory parsimony and neglect, by spending more on education and the NHS, but, having done that, he wasted the growth he had inherited from Major's devaluation and failed to repair the welfare and economic structures Thatcher had damaged so badly.

Instead of boosting manufacturing, he boosted globalisation; instead of building houses, he reshuffled the stock; instead of rebuilding the regions damaged by industrial decline, he doled out peanuts; instead of controlling finance, he relaxed regulation; and instead of keeping the pound competitive, he encouraged it to go up. In short, he failed to seize the opportunity of the good years to shift the balances back to the people because he had no clear idea of what they needed and constantly looked upwards rather than down. With a huge majority and enormous goodwill he could have done anything. He did all too little. But made it glossy. Which made him the most successful Labour leader but the most tragic waster of opportunity.

He wavered and talked of hard choices but never made any, concealing his vacuity by clutching at every fashionable system of thought that came along, from stakeholder capitalism, to communitarianism, to triangulation to the Third Way, the kind of non-ideological ideology that appealed to people of vague aspirations and great goodwill, only to end up as the apostle of globalisation and the disciple of President Bush. This was Thatcherism with a smile, rectifying the failures of his predecessor at minimal cost and fighting little wars, all accompanied by lashings of the Euro-enthusiasm that seemed to have replaced socialism.

As a limpet in search of a rock, Tony never looked for it on the left, failed to find it in the Labour Party and ended up with Catholicism and George Bush's crusade to make the world fit for democracy. Sadly, the Iraq War this led to was based on lies and the settlement was bungled, forcing him to spend the rest of his life justifying the unjustifiable. This lost public support for Labour, though his greatest failure was that he failed to deliver the much-needed boost to Labour's heartlands in Scotland and the north, where Thatcher had done so much damage.

Parliament he used as an opportunity to show off. He gave news to *The Sun* before Parliament and preferred sofa courtiers to scruffy MPs. He didn't particularly like the party, the trade unions or the left and seemed to shudder whenever I mentioned the national executive to him. He wasn't too keen on the people, either, though he believed that they could be persuaded and that he could do it. It came as a terrible shock when first the media and then the people turned against him, and longer presence did not make hearts grow fonder.

Tony preferred to keep the Parliamentary Labour Party at a distance, where they could admire his good works, but Bruce Grocott, his loyal parliamentary private secretary, persuaded him to meet the troops. This didn't mean eating with us in the Members' dining room but trundling groups into the Cabinet Room in alphabetical lots (so the Bs knew they were among a lot of Bs). Each MP was allowed to ask a question. The Great Leader then summed up without answering any.

This wasn't consultation. It was showing off. Tony loved it, though he wasn't keen on the back-slapping style of politics. Mateyness was left to Gordon Brown, who did it clumsily. Blair was happier in his study and particularly dependent on Alastair Campbell, a renegade Yorkshireman and a tabloid journalist but a genius at putting over Labour's case and ensuring that ministers sang from the same hymn sheet and sang in tune. He made Tony's confused policies coherent, booted his enemies and the media, and intermittently dragged the leader out into the world. It was masterly, and the Labour lads and lasses sang along with it like a chorus. Until he went over the top by overegging the Iraq War. That made his role defensive and difficult, and the problems were compounded by friction with Mrs Blair and a war of attrition with Gordon that ended in Alastair's departure in

2004. It seemed as if the Prime Minister had lost his guide dog and shrunk into just another nervy politician.

What had begun as a glossy new government of eager meritocrats, with the left relegated to a ghetto out of harm's (and power's) way, was in the end a disappointment. Tony's was the central will, not the party's. His impulses could be confused, amounting to a restless drive to 'modernisation' for its own sake. His programme was not equality but meritocracy. Tony Crosland argued that the 'purpose of socialism is quite simply to eradicate this sense of class and create in its place a sense of common interest and equal status'. That was not Blair's aspiration at all. It may have been that of Gordon Brown, who did more than the Labour Party to hold Tony's dafter aspirations in check and certainly put himself forward as more Labour than Labour's leader.

This created a continuous conflict between Blair and his former roommate, in a relationship which began as Ant and Dec but finished like Dean Martin and Jerry Lewis. Having been 'promised' it, in the way Tony did of offering vague hopes without firm commitment, Gordon expected the succession. After five years he felt it was time to get it. The Great Helmsman had other ideas. The longer he stayed, the more indispensable he felt himself to be. So Gordon became obstructive, courting the unions and the left and claiming that only he was 'true Labour'. The argument flared in the row over joining the euro, which Blair was keen on but Brown wisely vetoed. It was carried on in the argument over student fees, in which Gordon threatened, right up to a last-minute climbdown, to lead his troops against the bill.

Much of this war at the top was hidden from the children, who never saw it with the clarity of commentators like Andrew Rawnsley and Matthew Parris. Each protagonist had his followers. The Scots inclined to Brown; the meritocrats clustered around Blair. The rest of us knew to communicate with Brown through Nick Brown or Jon Trickett; with Blair through his more numerous devotees and acolytes, such as John Austin, Peter 'Mandy' Mandelson for the upper classes, and Hazel Blears. For most purposes, though, and certainly for me, it was a policy argument. In this, Gordon, by projecting himself as the friend of the unions and true Labour, seemed the better option as Blair's histrionic faults glared. The row concealed Gordon's personal deficiencies so his faction emerged stronger.

The battle was more debilitating at the top than in the ranks because the party was happy with the dual leadership: Tony as the frontman, Gordon as the mechanic. In retrospect, however, it was more serious and particularly wearing for Tony, who ended up as a nervy, messianic prophet, wondering why the old sermons no longer seemed to work. He was slow-clapped by the Women's Institute, and eventually felled in a curious coup by a small coterie who represented themselves rather than the whole party. Tony, in his insecurity, took it as an overwhelming tide, gave up and allowed himself to be washed out.

For many, the Iraq War had been the last straw, though for me it merely added another straw to the bale. The war was Blair's personal responsibility. He backed it with an eloquence and passion that persuaded the reluctant. He gave Bush his full support too early and too unequivocally, when there was no need to do so. He ignored the views of European leaders, particularly Chirac, and he overstated the case for war. I abstained on the vote, and still feel that was cowardly but right. The regime was repellent but so were several others, such as Zimbabwe, and it wasn't our responsibility to clean up the world and make it safe for globalisation. For the public and for so many in the Labour Party, the Iraq War and the subsequent chaos marked the end of tolerance for Tony. His last years were sad, as realisation dawned that he'd got it wrong, distrust replaced devotion and Tony himself became paranoid about plots. His great ambition of becoming President of the European Union became impossible. It was a non-job for which he would have been perfect, given his skill in making beguiling promises without too much substance; exactly the kind of leadership an EU built on myths and kept going by the constant creation of new ones would have loved. Instead, they chose a bland bureaucrat, and Tony went off to a career of greedy money-grubbing, appearing in public mainly to defend his war in Iraq. Either the mighty had fallen, or the lost leader had found his true level, depending on your point of view. Either way, it was sad to see such a powerful politician devoting the rest of his life to justifying his position on a failed war.

Not having bred any successor to Tony Blair, the party had no alternative but to replace him with the last hope of Labourism, Gordon Brown. Gordon had assiduously projected himself as the real Labour alternative to Slick Willie, which wasn't too difficult, though he was a far worse actor than his predecessor. More surprisingly, after years of claiming to be real Labour, Gordon proved a better friend to the City of London and Big Finance than to the trade unions and the Old Labour malingerers he'd spent so much time courting. Backbenchers granted access discovered a big, growling bear of a man who would listen, sombre and silent, then go away, offering nothing much – usually a task force to handle redundancies or a training scheme to ease pain, but never any support for a failing firm, never any change in economic policy. Frank Field went to protest at the effects of ending the minimum rate tax band, only to be told, 'You've always been against me.' Gordon turned out to be Labour's Wizard of Oz: a remote figure, assumed to be all-powerful until the façade fell to reveal an indecisive, insecure man biting his nails.

Brown had built up a network of his own supporters in the departments. When Tony was finally forced out, Gordon came in unopposed to prove that the weaknesses about which Tony had warned his friends (but not the party) were all too real. Essentially a shy man, Gordon dithered, missed his chance of success by failing to call an early election, then denied he'd ever thought of it, and basked in the approbation of the City, to which he pandered so much that I thought they might affiliate to New Labour. Instead, they landed Gordon in the manure by their greedy irresponsibility. He'd boasted of having found a 'new paradigm' of perpetual growth to end boom and bust. It was really a bubble of debt and speculation, which burst, with disastrous consequences, in 2008.

Then Gordon came good. Very good, in fact. Tony would have failed because he couldn't 'do' economic crisis. Gordon could. He rallied the G20 to stimulus, but tarnished the achievement by announcing that he had 'saved the world'. He began the house-building programme he had long refused and turned on the money spigots in the best Keynesian fashion. It was right and effective, but it was too late. Unemployment rose. Banks crashed and had to be saved. The nation wasn't going to elect a tired government in a major recession, but nothing became Brown so much as his going, which was truly noble.

Gordon was a bigger man than those around him. He got the message and went. He left without a successor. Ed Miliband narrowly won a 'which twin has the Toni' election over his brother and set off down the road we'd all assumed Brown would follow.

Ed was clever, quick and bang up to date, but a wet tree with little empathy with real people and all the charisma of the butcher's lad put in charge of the shop. No presence. No rhetorical ability. No nous, and advised by a set of trendies who gave him ideas like the 'Ed stone' and the overuse of all-women shortlists. He couldn't inspire the party and preferred the triumph of the trendies. He ended shadow Cabinet elections, the last remaining power of the PLP, to appoint his own preferences and announced more left-wing policies without any ability to sell them. His worst decision was to boost Labour's declining membership by a cut-price offer to every passing lunatic. His aim was to make Labour a young, metro-trendy party, stuffed with women and fashionable young apparatchaps. This approach took it out of line with its working-class roots, its northern heartlands and his own Yorkshire constituency. Scotland turned to the SNP, the north turned to UKIP and the metropolitan trendies didn't turn out in adequate numbers. Labour seemed incapable of delivering. Ed sank without trace. So did the Ed stone.

Labour lost the 2010 election. Cameron didn't win but he had cleverly planned for the event, which Labour hadn't. His strategy was a deal with the Lib Dems, useful dupes who were so eager for office after being in opposition since 1916 that they'd accept almost anything to get there. Their Boy Scout patrol leader, Nick Clegg, fell for the bait, hook, line and sinker. Having already urged his party to neoliberal policies, Clegg was delighted to become Deputy Prime Minister, and the rest took turns to sit in ministerial cars. To get there, they dropped their liberal instincts, their pledges to resist student fees, and their opposition to Trident and nuclear power. They even abandoned their support for proportional representation, which had been a mainstay of the Liberal Democrats since they'd dwindled to an extra half-party in the two-party system. This commitment was watered down to the Alternative Vote, a weak alternative which was not proportional. They didn't even get that when the Tories cunningly sabotaged their referendum. So, tit for tat, they rejected the Tory reform of the Lords, where far more Liberals were preserved in ermine rather than in real life.

Exuding self-confidence, Cameron had few principles beyond staying in power, and for that he was prepared to change the few he had. He claimed his was the best of governments and was curing British ills when he was actually making them worse. He was impervious to criticism, better at hurling abusive responses and applying a knee to any available groin than giving answers. He successfully labelled the damaging improvisations of austerity as a 'long-term economic plan' and, once they had helped his government to survive, consigned the Lib Dems to the dustbin in 2015, a display of political duplicity almost as impressive as his economic illiteracy. Except that the Liberals deserved it; the country didn't.

Initially, Cameron had been persuaded by his adviser Steve Hilton to promote compassionate Conservatism, with himself as a better Blair. He urged his party to hug a hoodie or a husky. When this didn't go down too well in an obstinately right-wing party, he moved to the right, kowtowed to his septic Eurosceptics, fired Hilton and gave far too much credence to his Chancellor, a petulant know-all whose neoliberal policies were essentially the Thatcherite agenda of growth through suffering. As usual, the suffering was done by those lower down the social scale, and the growth failed to materialise because the policies were the exact opposite of those necessary to cure the Great Recession.

George Osborne called it contractionary expansion, telling the victims it was for their own good. Like so many of his ilk, he knew nothing of the life of real people but claimed to know what was good for them: work and austerity. He successfully seized the narrative by blaming recession not on the banks, who really were responsible, but on Labour, which had saved them. This con trick allowed the Tories to punish people on benefits, claiming they were lazy buggers who'd opted for the dependency culture and preferred to live the life of Riley on benefits rather than work at jobs that weren't there.

Dave was a laid-back CEO of the chums in a government of million-aire mates rather than their driver, perfectly happy to sit back, chillax and go on frequent holidays while ministers got on with it, whether 'it' was damaging the economy or throwing schools and the health service into turmoil. They could do pretty much what they wanted, and Cameron defended it all with a quick insult for Ed Miliband.

For understandable reasons, Dave didn't particularly like his party, though he gradually gave in to it for a quiet life, pandering to the Europhobe majority then attempting to pull the Harold Wilson trick of a pretend 'renegotiation' followed by a referendum to endorse his achievement. Unfortunately, he didn't understand either constipated Europe, where he demanded little and got less, or the electorate, which rejected the deal, the EU and Cameron himself. Like Blair to the last, he didn't stick around but went off to make money on an almost Blairian scale.

Dave, as he'd want me to call him, was my last Prime Minister. His demise brought in Theresa May, who started well, firing Osborne and promising a fairer society and justice for the JAMs (just about manag-ing folk). She proved better at proclaiming fairness than advancing it, though, and has carried on her predecessor's follies, like HS2 and the most expensive nuclear power station in the world at Hinkley, but she has begun to implement the electorate's decision to withdraw from the European Union. The daughter of a vicar, she is determined to do her duty, but she is a cold and 'difficult' woman without the luck Prime Ministers need, and she is far too weak to deal with the EU. Her honeymoon was short. Fearing worse difficulties to come, she ate her words and called an early election, offering 'strong and stable' leadership, and bungled it almost as badly as Ted Heath in February 1974, or Baldwin in 1929. As Zhou Enlai said of the French Revolution, it's too early to tell, but if I had to sympathise with any Tory leader, it would be her. Let's wait and see.

Wait, also, for a conclusion on Jeremy Corbyn, elected Labour leader on a surge of dissatisfaction at the old leadership, the old ways and the continuous compromises of Blair and Brown. A perpetual protester (no revolution was valid without Jeremy's endorsement and his invitation of its leaders to the Commons), he has had to take on the blander mantle of leadership. It doesn't quite fit. His appeal is that of an honest man of principle, something young electors like after years of easy promises and low performance, but his leadership gives rise to the basic question: can the principles remain pure, or will they be diluted by the imperatives, and the temptations, of power? Beatrice Webb said of Ramsay MacDonald that you cannot engineer an equalitarian state if you yourself are enjoying the pomp and circumstance of the city of the rich. Wilson, Blair and Brown had all enjoyed its delights, but Corbyn had devoted his life to the city of the people. This promised a new approach, though the transfer from the excitement of rebellion to the blandness of leadership is not going to be easy in a party quick to sniff out the first symptoms of the MacDonald syndrome.

It is not too early, though, to come to a conclusion on four decades of the prime ministerial breed. Prime Ministers are more human, and more fallible, than the supermen they're puffed up to be. In the end, they have all failed through their human inadequacies: Cameron's overconfidence, Blair's egotism, Thatcher's intolerance, Jim's bad timing. Most were hoist by their own petard: Blair by Iraq; Thatcher by her dislike of the EU; Cameron by his referendum. Only Harold Wilson made party unity central to his leadership, and only he enjoyed a smooth succession, handing over to an older man. The rest just chucked it all in and walked away – a trick also played by Ed Miliband, whose over-hasty resignation in 2015 left Labour in an even bigger mess than usual.

None told truth to the nation. Like Ian Smith in Rhodesia, who tried to sustain a white rule that could never last, successive British Prime Ministers told a country whose economy could no longer support both a world role and the good society of jobs and welfare that it was still great, assuring a diminished nation that it still led the world, the EU, the Commonwealth and possibly the Channel Islands. They fostered complacency rather than attempting the painful reforms that were becoming ever more necessary. Not one of them had any clear idea of what really needed to be done, because none had a clear vision of the national interest.

They lived in a protected enclave, surrounded by courtiers and visited by billionaires, financiers and newspaper editors. This made them increasingly out of touch with the real world and real people: Cool Britannia had little relevance in the backstreets of Rochdale. Prime Ministers came in fresh and promising but gradually became remote and out of touch, insulated in their own little world in Downing Street. All began to feel themselves indispensable. Most stayed on too long, until they had to be thrown out by the party or the people. Being top dog is debilitating. It drains Prime Ministers. It destroys the gloss and leaves them running on empty. Harold Wilson, the only one who recognised this, confessed that towards the end only brandy made the job bearable, but only he knew when it was time to go. The rest believed that the world, the party and the nation couldn't manage without them, though all would have benefited from the Churchill treatment: 'If he trips, he must be sustained. If he makes mistakes, they must be covered. If he sleeps, he must not be wantonly disturbed. If he is no good, he must be pole axed.' Labour is worse at poleaxing than the less sentimental Tories, but given the strain of modern politics it should be made compulsory by a fixed prime ministerial term. America has a maximum of eight years; France, a term of five. In Britain, where the Prime Minister is more powerful than either, six years is enough. More than enough for some.

CHAPTER SIX

ODDS AND A FEW SODS

The old slogan of the *News of the World*, 'All human life is here', applies to the House of Commons to only a limited degree. Most MPs are white, male, middle-aged and middle class, but within that limited universe there are many types: creeps, like Sir Desmond Swayne, who told the House he was 'a slavish supporter of this government'; super-creeps, like Mandy, the courtier who never became a king; pedants, like Robin Maxwell-Hyslop; academics, like Robert Rhodes James and John Mackintosh; frustrated artists, like Nicholas Ridley; amateur novelists, like Brian Sedgemore, Julian Critchley, Bob Marshall-Andrews and Robert Kilroy-Silk (mostly bad, unlike Edwina Currie, who can write); and thugs, like Tom Swain, who belted opponents but kicked the bucket in 1979.

MPs are a good crowd to be in: funnier than lawyers, happier than accountants and less boring than academics. They tend to be extroverts and show-offs. Politics is the showbiz of the ugly. Yet they're mostly likeable, some even lovable. They pose as, and mostly are, sensible and serious. They make jokes (but rarely now in public and never about women) and are gregarious behind their masks of respectability and high seriousness. The few who are prepared to demean themselves by playing the fool in public, as Jerry Hayes did when he appeared on TV dressed as a penis, or George Galloway pretending to be a cat, damage themselves. Most MPs drink more than the average amount of both tea and booze, which are the oil and the consolation of politics. (They're also something to do in the long boring waits for votes.)

MPs are good company, and interesting folk to be with. Not intellectuals, but a lively collection of idealists (real and pretend), creeps, social climbers, pillocks, twerps, over-energetic activists and a few who would be classified as certifiable if they were outside Parliament, though no monster raving loonies as yet. They're pretty conformist. A little creeping takes people a long way in politics. Then there are the exotic lifeforms, like Mickey Fab, the Brighton shock jock; Michael Green, the soothsayer; and Rory Stewart, the Afghanistan hitch-hiker; plus the apparently dead, like Dr Glyn, MP for Windsor, who always sat motionless in a near-death experience; along with urbane bon viveurs like Bob Marshall-Andrews; and humorists like former bus driver Stephen Pound, a man with a striking resemblance to Mr Punch, who, rumour has it, once tried to set the suit of a speaker in front of him on fire with his lighter. A shocking breach of the 'no smoking in the chamber' rule. Then there are the inactive sloths who add little to Parliament beyond their bulk, and the party hacks who will support their leader, right or wrong. They all dress drably, and until the women arrived only Gerald Kaufman and Leo Abse brought colour to a collection of dark-suited conformists, dressed like bank managers to sustain an image of virtue and respectability.

Parliament is a third-rate London club. As such, every fault and scandal among the Members is known and gossiped about. Once, I developed a project with Colin Seymour-Ure to show how the rumour mill worked, by tracing an invented rumour round the House, but the only rumour we invented – that I'd greeted an EU Commissioner under the mistaken impression that he was Demis Roussos, and congratulated him on his escape from a hijacking, to everyone's embarrassment – got me ridiculed in the *Times* Diary but reached no one in Parliament.

The substance of the gossip is usually political rather than sexual, though my wife kept warning me that 'they're all at it', something I put down to her working in television, where they were. In the early days, a few MPs would quietly step down after encounters in public lavatories or parks, though today the devoted researchers of the media broadcast the few scandals for the nation's delectation, creating the impression that sex throbs in the Palace of Westminster. It doesn't, though Sir Ronald Bell was reputed to have died screwing his secretary, and Alan Clark was a serial seducer, on a family-pack scale. Diane Abbott had a fling with Jeremy Corbyn (though not on his allotment), and Jonathan Aitken had a relationship with Mrs Khashoggi, who, he told me, was a meal and a half. Sex with Nicholas Soames was said to be like a wardrobe falling on the beneficiary with a protruding key; Peter Snape had interesting stories to tell about his conquests; and Stuart Bell wrote up his escapades from the '60s before he became God's representative in Parliament as Church Commissioner. But, on the whole, there's a lot of smoke and not much fire.

As the media abandoned politics for skin and sex, more scandals began to reach the public. Ron Brown's antics in the showers, Nigel Griffiths's discussion of Ugandan relations in his office, Ron Davies's moments of madness on Clapham Common, Brooks Newmark's aesthetic posing sans underpants and Simon Danczuk's sex addiction (illustrated by pictures of his ex-wife's cleavage) enlivened many tabloids. My friend Joe Ashton, elated by his success in giving the address in reply speech, called in at a Northampton massage parlour for debriefing on the way home. His number plate was noted by the cops in a raid and his career was damaged when his identity was revealed by a shocked cop who may have been either affronted by such immorality or just keen to make money by selling the story to the press. The bastard.

In fact, parliamentary sex is nothing like the bonanza showered on celebs and pop stars. Cherie Blair claimed that Tony was a sex machine. A whips' officer once told me he knew the name and telephone number of every MP's mistress and favourite brothel so he could call Members to vote, but, for most, sex is dull duty rather than an obsessive joy. Women MPs only allow touching by other women, though there's lots of that in today's kissy-kissy culture. Janet Fookes was rumoured to have a liking for Willie Hamilton, but cross-party dalliances are as rare as a romantic Yeti. There are political groupies, but they are few in number and are mostly middle-aged, neurotic and neither as nubile nor as enthusiastic as those who flock round more glamorous trades. MPs can't afford drug-fuelled sex bonanzas on a Frank Bough scale. Beer doesn't offer the same delights, though it can produce fights in the club bar, where the apparatchaps go. Illicit liaisons tend to be nasty, brutish and short. It's dangerous now to pat bottoms, embrace the opposite sex or kiss babies.

Accusations of paedophilia are occasionally raised, as they were against Cyril Smith and, posthumously, against former Speaker George Thomas and, more outlandishly, Ted Heath. Around the House they say at least two MPs have died of Aids. There are probably more homosexuals of both sexes in Parliament than in the real world. Statistics are lacking but boarding school toffs must have had a passing knowledge, which some may have continued at university, as Roy

Jenkins and Tony Crosland were rumoured to have done. Chris Smith was the first to announce he was gay. Matthew Parris has bravely, and movingly, come out, though only after leaving Parliament. Peter Mandelson went to great lengths to advertise his good fortune and conceal his homosexuality. Which was exactly the wrong way round for the Labour Party. Lib Dem star David Laws was forced to reveal his gay partnership when an expenses fiddle became public, but the Lib Dems' former leader Jeremy Thorpe had his ex-lover's dog, Rinka, killed to conceal his relationship with 'Bunnies', defying his party's commitment to animal welfare. Few flaunted it like Harvey Proctor, though Queen Victoria's denial that lesbianism could exist has been disproved by a few brave women MPs. Nowadays, though, it's more dangerous to criticise homosexuality than to practise it. No one claims to represent the LGBT 'community', though I once owned an MGB GT.

Since MPs got their own rooms, Parliament hasn't insisted on the old Oxbridge rule of never allowing people to work *solus cum sola*. This creates endless scope for rumours. There have been liaisons, even marriages with secretaries, though the numbers are quantified only by the *Daily Sport*, which isn't reliable. Probably the sexual habits and propensities of MPs can be assumed to be not too different from those of most people away from home, though perhaps more circumspect, given the potential for exposure in a national newspaper. It's no longer an expellable offence to be naughty, homosexual or lecherous. All that's left for that are treason and financial scandal, either through bankruptcy like Jeffrey Archer or through expenses fiddles.

MPs are ordinary and getting ordinarier, and as they become more representative they also become more like the rest of the world and less impressive. There are fewer peaks, whether measured by outstanding ability – top academics, top CEOs, Oxbridge Firsts – great wealth.

Fewer valleys, too, as measured by manual work, trade union service or poor origins. More are drawn from society's middle ranks, the base camps of the upper class, and from the political breeding ground of parliamentary or political research, which brings in outliers distinguished from real people by their abnormal interest in politics. Most of the population has other concerns.

Characters enliven the prevailing dullness. Some stand out as odd, but to call someone 'a character' really means they're no threat to the ladder-climbers but they make the Commons interesting. They provide something for the conformist mass to gossip about and occasionally make it laugh, as welcome as an oasis in a desert. The conformist crowd moves in herds and likes someone to look down on, while a lively Parliament needs troublemakers to leaven the lump. There can never be enough. Grimsby had more characters (and more awkward buggers) than Parliament. As the odds and sods of the Commons – people like Cyril Smith, Jeremy Thorpe, Tufton Beamish, Cyril Osborne, Gerald Nabarro or Michael (send a gunboat) Brotherton – faded out, the conformists took over.

I don't include Andrew Faulds, a former actor with no volume control who threatened to sue me when I claimed that sitting next to him was making me deaf. Nor do I count Dennis Skinner, who's now a national institution awaiting placement in the museum of Labour history. Dennis is a coal-black incorruptible. When he came to YTV for programmes, he would always refuse our hospitality and pay for his own food. On one occasion when he was persuaded to have a cup of coffee, he pushed sixpence across the table to Sir Richard Graham, the chairman of Yorkshire Television, to pay for it. Graham pushed it back and I assume the waitresses took it for a tip when we left the room. Dennis had no car and always insisted we bring him in a taxi, though on occasions when he came and saw an electrician's picket line he simply turned the taxi round and drove home without telling us.

Dennis was suspicious of me when I entered Parliament because I'd been critical of Clay Cross Council, which had been run by a Skinner family mafia, and I'd taken Dick Taverne, the Labour MP for Lincoln, who was dissatisfied with the party's direction and resigned only to win back his seat as an independent, to Clay Cross to criticise the council's defiance of the government. That was an unforgivable offence. As was Nicholas Soames's attempt to persuade Dennis to invite him to his council house for tea when he was on a shooting visit to nearby Chatsworth.

Dennis went round boosting the morale of local Labour parties and would brook no competitors in this pursuit. When I asked him about a speaking invitation, he urged me not to go, then did it himself. The Skinner road to socialism is paved with dead chickens. The mining industry died but Dennis fought on as spokesman for a traditional working class to become a national treasure: the rough trade alternative to Tony Benn, though he never played the media's *bête noire* as Tony did.

Tony Beaumont-Dark (satirised by *Viz* as Sir Anthony Regents-Park) was amiable to the point of affability. A Tory but not of the pitbull strain and wealthy enough not to care, he was occasionally inebriated and ever ready to gossip, criticise the government and give his views at some length. This made him the doyen of the rent-a-quote brigade, always glad to give a colourful quote to Chris Moncrieff, the Press Association representative, and happy to let Chris make one up for him if he wasn't available. He also had a virtue rare in Parliament. He was always ready to buy his round, particularly when the press were present.

Alan Clark was more a shameless self-publicising snob who'd managed to turn arrogance into a show-biz routine than a character. As a jumped-up aristocrat, he awed the Tory faithful and was arrogant to the plebs, but confident enough to dissent from the Thatcher government's policies, particularly monetarism, which he saw as destroying Britain's industrial strength. He even toyed with protection by import controls, but was less secure than he acted and could be touchy. In a standing committee when he was presenting the government's case arrogantly but badly, I congratulated him on raising the issue of import controls. He took this as an attack and immediately disowned the idea he'd been propagating only days before. Eventually he walked out of Parliament because no one loved him enough, then decided to walk back, though his second coming was a fade-out.

I include Spencer Le Marchant in the 'characters' category, though it may have been the booze talking. Spencer was at his most colourful when drunk, though his excesses were concealed inside the Whips' Office. They were transferred to our office on occasional visits, bringing champagne all round. This was a joy but no help in performing our duties (which could have been the intention). Spencer was amiable and happy to gossip with anyone, a pleasure denied most whips, who are professionally taciturn. He was a sad loss to the wine merchants when he died of alcoholism.

Morgan Phillips claimed that the Labour Party owed more to Methodism than it did to Marx. By the time I was elected, there wasn't much of either, though a non-conformist sanctimony still lingered. The Tories were always more accommodating of oddities, accepted as upper-class eccentricity or even the natural right of an MP. They were home to Peter Morrison, a paedophile; Cecil Parkinson, an adulterer; Jeffrey Archer, a fantasist; and various homosexuals, though they found difficulties with Nicholas Fairbairn.

Fairbairn's erratic behaviour, his series of affairs that made Don

Juan look like a castrati, and his swings from liberal politics to the extreme right, from homosexuality to repellent descriptions of homo-sexual relations, were attributed to mental instability. In fact, they were probably symptoms of the alcoholism from which he died. He posed, and dressed, as a Scottish grandee, bringing colour in tartan hues to the Commons. But he was always friendly to non-Scottish plebs like me and was certainly well tolerated by Mrs Thatcher, the Methodist ayatollah, though his rumoured advances to her were sternly rebuffed. It was a high-profile act that couldn't be kept going for ever. He died from it in 1995. No one since has brought as much colour and self-destructive folly to the Commons, though Eric Joyce tried hard.

Enoch Powell was a very different kettle of quirks. He stood out not so much as a character, more as a monolith, built in another age but perfectly preserved in Northern Ireland, where history lives on. He was a survivor from the age of imperialism and eloquence. Members rushed to the chamber when his name appeared on the annunciator. His contributions were compelling, as we wondered how his remorse-less stream of logic could always end with such daft conclusions.

Powell's great days were over when I arrived. He'd become a prison-er of the petty and prejudiced politics of Northern Ireland, but could still clear the mists from the dreary steeples of Fermanagh and Tyrone by brilliant speeches, and woe betide anyone who attempted to inter-ject or argue. I tried occasionally but was always chopped down. He was feared rather than loved, though I treasured a photograph of him jumping on a pogo stick in his homburg.

He was also mean. I knew from having interviewed him on television that he would always haggle about the fee before being interviewed, but when I expressed interest in his poetry he immediately sold me a book of poems, though fortunately at the publication price of some years earlier. Powell was a magic maverick. Recent parliaments have been less interesting because he had no replacement.

Geoffrey Dickens was a man of lesser ilk but bigger bulk. More a comedian, but funny peculiar rather than ha-ha. On arrival, he immediately told the whips to fuck off when they demanded that he stay and vote instead of going to his celebration party. He followed this by an amazing crusade when he discovered sex and satanic rituals as an issue. This culminated in a dangling 'will I, won't I?' suspense drama about revealing the name of an upper-class paedophile who'd left pornography on a bus. Geoffrey built up suspense about the name of this 'top person' (actually a minor diplomat), then went on to make fantastic claims about satanic witchcraft and paedophilia in Shetland (where he'd never been). Eventually he became so media-addicted that he called a press conference to announce that he was leaving his wife, shortly followed by another to announce that he was going back. Great fun. It came to a sad end when he died of cancer.

I've mentioned too many Tories, perhaps because their tribe was so strange to me. So I should add Walter Harrison, a character and parliamentary fixer. It was Walter as Deputy Chief Whip, rather than Michael Cocks, his boss, who kept the Labour government of the '70s going with no majority. Walter devised cunning stunts like getting MPs to break pairs or vote twice, and negotiated dirty deals. Joe Ashton claimed that he had a bog-trotter to run round the toilets in case anyone was asleep on the porcelain. He kept close to the wives of the two Irish Nationalist MPs to persuade their husbands to vote in extremis, a trick that worked right up until March 1979.

Walter also kept in close touch with the expenses department. My claims for travel between Grimsby, Halifax and London were so large that he warned me, 'They're keeping an eye on you. Watch it.' He knew all the fiddles and it may be because he'd retired and stopped warning fiddlers that the expenses scandal of 2008 exploded. He always refused to talk about how he'd kept Labour in power, but an ungrateful party never rewarded him with the seat in the Lords he so richly deserved.

Feminists will be furious if I only mention men, though in my early years there weren't many women and few of them were characters. But Gwyneth Dunwoody, the battling butterball, was a great lady in every way and my great favourite. She was one of Blair's bastards (I don't think he could stand her) and was prepared to take on anyone and any cause: Militant, ministers, the European Union, Blairite blandness and even the excesses of the feminist movement. This made her performance in party elections somewhat erratic, depending on whom she'd offended recently. When, in 1985, she lost her seat in the shadow Cabinet as the only female Member, she riposted, 'My colleagues in the PLP clearly felt that there were too many women in the shadow Cabinet.'

The daughter of Morgan Phillips, General Secretary of the party, she had an impeccable Old Labour pedigree, which was as strong as her Old Labour instincts. She also had the doughty temperament to fight for them. The rise of Blair pushed her off the front bench but set her free as a formidable critic. She began regular weekly briefing papers for Labour MPs, which we'd never had before. She emerged as the champion of transport when she became chair of the Transport Select Committee. She used that position to defend the railways and castigate the destruction of the workshops, the greed of the companies and the incompetence of the docks. She also put lead in my pencil (or, as Blairites saw it, led me astray) by helping and encouraging me to vote against the party's follies. A sad loss.

John Prescott loomed large in my life because the Hull MPs had regarded Grimsby as their backward colony, theirs to run while Crosland was away being a minister. John was easy to understand but difficult to like, a man of great ability who found problems in expressing it in coherent speech. Semi-literacy became his gimmick and it won him publicity because it pandered to the superiority of the clever-clogs hacks in the parliamentary commentariat. It also gave him a bond with fellow unionists, though in fact he was an autodidact who'd sought education at Ruskin and Hull and worked hard to master every subject he tackled.

He was instinctively suspicious of intellectuals. The heavy chips he carried on both shoulders neither balanced nor repressed him, though he was inhibited by an ill-concealed inferiority complex resulting from his lack of education. This made him defensive about smoothies, anyone who'd got a degree, and me.

John wore his working-class and union identity proudly. Once, flying to New Zealand, the British Airways steward, finding I was a colleague of John's, told me what a great bloke he'd been when they were stewards together and upgraded me to first class. The steward got off at Perth. The first-class cabin was totally empty apart from one new passenger, who had been allocated my seat. The new cabin crew ordered me back down to cattle class. I refused. They'd never heard of John Prescott. The plane was delayed. The argument rolled on. Eventually they took off with me and my fellow first-class passenger to New Zealand. He got a meal. I didn't. Not my favourite airline.

John was upset by the clever dicks (nearly his word) who made fun of his struggles with English, which he spoke as a foreign language. His brain moved faster than his mouth and by the time the mouth spoke, the brain had moved on to something else. He was blunt to the point of obtuseness but too deferential to Blair, who used him as his token leftie, just as he used Mo Mowlam and Clare Short to add feminist credibility to his government. A great user, Tony. John needed Tony to avoid the frustrations of being an internal opposition, and he defended his soft compromises. Tony, meanwhile, defended John's excesses. 'John is John' became the litany while John learned the new language of Blairspeak. When Tony began to talk about 'the rigour of the market', I asked John, 'Doesn't he really mean vigour?' 'I don't know what the hell he means, but rigour's what I'm going to say.'

Before I was elected, John had impressed me as the best and most hard-working of the Hull MPs. He made brave efforts to secure a compromise in the cod war and was very effective in trying to stop Imperial Typewriters closing their factory in Hull. He was helpful in my first election, teaching me to canvass, and when I began to agree with a constituent criticising the Labour government's proposal to widen the definition of dock work, he pulled me back, explained that the candidate had had a temporary brain fade, and defended the dockers. Later he brought down a Hull Corporation bus full of dockers to canvass, though the benefits were slightly diminished when the bus caused a traffic jam and some of the dockers got drunk.

I voted for him against Roy Hattersley in his unsuccessful bid for the deputy leadership, but after his defeat John made a deliberate decision to go positive. New Labour should have been more grateful. John was a bulldozer of a shadow spokesman on transport, but in power Blair preferred to use him as his working-class pet (well portrayed as a bemused bulldog by Steve Bell). He became Blair's link with the unions and a working-class world of which the Great Leader knew nothing. He ended up as New Labour's Vicar of Stiffkey.

It was like Big Daddy joining a ballet company, though John was brilliant as a conference performer. Labour audiences loved his incoherent tirades because they knew what he was trying to say even if he never quite managed it. But he was grievously misused, being given the low-priority departments on which New Labour wouldn't spend money – transport, housing, local government and the environment – where John's job was to disguise failure by bombast, particularly on housing policy. John did the job energetically but without charm, a skill he never quite mastered. New Labour's leaders treated him like the steward he'd once been and when he tried to bring Blair and Brown together he was ignored by both, and condemned to a curmudgeonly impotence, enlivened by croquet and other fun. He was forced to give up on the issue he'd pioneered, English devolution, when Blair castrated it.

Our relationship ended unhappily. Linda stupidly told a journalist in a casual conversation that John had touched her up the first time he'd met her. Fatal to tell journalists anything. John was angry and upset and demanded that I get Linda to withdraw. As if I could. I told him to forget it, but he responded in curmudgeonly fashion. I still viewed him as a friend but when I invited him to my great farewell dinner, he flatly refused, denounced Linda again and asked that his greetings be given only to Helen Clark, 'altogether a better class of woman'.

A nicer, and much smoother, character was my great friend (and a great man) Julian Critchley. I loved him. He was the best of MPs and a friend, but a political failure because, like me, he couldn't resist making jokes. He was out of place in Thatcher's army because he was a survivor of Tory paternalism and a friend of Michael Heseltine. He made too many jokes about Mrs Thatcher, 'the great she-elephant', and constantly warned that it would all end in tears, as it did. Yet he also wrote brilliant books on Parliament and the Tory Party, like a humorous Margaret Mead. He had a real feel for the hypocrisies and fake gentilities of Tory life, though less feeling for the rougher habits of the Labour tribe. Along with Charles Kennedy, he and I became a team of commentators (Critch, Mitch and Titch) much loved by our bank managers, who enlivened the 1983 election with our jokes. Julian loved to scandalise his party by dragging Charles and me to the Tory end of the Members' dining room, there to eat in shirtsleeves while the besuited Tories clucked their disapproval. He loved writing and produced a passable novel on a parliamentary detective and a book in which MPs wrote about their areas. Unfortunately, when he handed one to me, he thought in his upper-class insularity that Grimsby was in the north-east and gave me Newcastle.

As an undercover Heseltine supporter, Julian continued to give funny speeches and invent jokes about Mrs T, but as his health declined he became less active in his constituency of Aldershot. On one occasion he rang me to say he wasn't well enough to receive his constituency party on their annual visit to Parliament. Would I do the honours? I did, to their amazement. He moved to Ludlow to live with an old flame and began a feud with its Thatcherite MP. He was a great man, but too honest and too clever for politics, particularly the Thatcherite variety. Michael Heseltine and I were the only politicians at his funeral.

Tam Dalyell was a character, the kind of tenacious, awkward bugger every Parliament needs. We only had two: Chris Mullin, whose efforts won the release of the Birmingham Six to end a great British scandal, and Tam Dalyell. Chris was mild, almost apologetic, like a don in a brothel. Tam was angular and awkward, though it took time to appreciate him. At first I found his dogged persistence boring because I hadn't yet realised that in Parliament you've got to bang on and on to get anywhere. Even then, you usually don't. Tam did. He realised the importance of being awkward and had the social standing to sustain it as Laird of the Binns (yes, I did make the joke).

A switch-off on telly was a strength in Parliament. The establishment buries its misdeeds. It takes upper-class persistence, contacts and confidence to beat them. Tam had all three. At the first PLP meeting after the Falklands War, I was bored when Tam launched into a long speech about a meeting with the President of Chile during the conflict. I should have realised that Tam could bore to win. He was right on the *Belgrano* sinking and, though I thought him wrong on devolution, where he hung the West Lothian question around Scotland's neck and nearly strangled it, he was right to point to a major problem. Awkward buggers can't be right on everything.

Labour's eighteen-year misery was enlivened by Allan Roberts, an extravagant (and open) homosexual. He was fun; a wonderful poseur who was brilliant at organising parties in obscure East End theatre pubs, which provided a much better entertainment than the strippers Members had previously hired for parties. He died before he could win a morose PLP round to gay liberation.

A more interesting character was Frank Field from Birkenhead, where the left constantly tried to get rid of him. Frank was a secular saint and a voice of sanity in the militant takeover of Liverpool and of cool common sense on pensions, a subject he knew backwards. Blair reluctantly appointed him as Minister for Pensions to think the unthinkable. When Frank did, he was fired. Sad for the rest of us because Frank was one of the few Blair ministers prepared to consult with and listen to backbenchers. He retired, like a hermit guru, to his cave in Portcullis House, there to nurture his faith and his hostility to the EU. Later he got his reward as chair of the Pensions Select Committee, becoming the persecutor of Sir Philip Green, the man who sold BHS and its £571 million pension fund deficit for £1. A wonderful role for a saint.

Bob Marshall-Andrews, a barrister so wealthy that he needed

neither office nor Blair's approval, was another original. He insisted that he should be allowed to maintain his income as a barrister
and gaily disappeared from time to time to take the Filth (failed in
London, try Hong Kong) road to Asia, though he was far from failing
in London. In Parliament, he became Blair's tormentor on civil liberties and the Iraq War. He formed the Apostles to carry on the religious
mission the Great Leader had given his party. In this more feminist
age, the twelve would have to be six men and six women, but then we
had only Alice Mahon and Christine McCafferty. We presented the
bog brush awarded for the creep of the year and held several last (and
lost) suppers and boozy lunches to tell each other how brave and bold
we were.

Bob's speeches weren't as good as his jokes; a bit lawyerly for Parliament. His organisational skills were even less, though he did a good
job on some of Blair's assaults on civil liberties. He also provided
amusement for Simon Hoggart, the parliamentary sketchwriter, who
reported Bob telling a constituent who'd declined to vote for him, 'You
mustn't vote for me, I don't want votes from racists,' only to be told, 'I'll
vote for who I want.' Bob's seat was very marginal. He thought he'd
lost it in 2005, but survived until 2010. The House was sadder without him. So was the Labour Party. In 2017, he deserted to the Liberal
Democrats, whom he'd always found 'impossibly nice' over Europe.

Every orchestra needs its fiddlers. Two, one from each party, stand
out in the Commons symphonia: David Marshall and Derek Conway,
both the nicest of chaps, friendly, open and to all appearances honest,
by political standards. Both were high in the parliamentary travel
agencies, *aka* the Commonwealth Parliamentary Association (CPA),
the Inter-Parliamentary Union (IPU) and the British–American Parliamentary Group. Both did what everyone else was doing but on a

larger scale, lining their own pockets by employing sons, wives and other family members, buying houses and maximising claims. Marshall kept quiet. Conway was quite open about employing his family. Both fell victim to the new puritanism. Marshall saw it coming and got out, claiming health grounds before the *Daily Telegraph* hit the fan, departing for New Zealand's healthier climate, while Labour lost the seat. Conway hung on, only to be humiliated and expelled from his self-righteous party. He coughed with unrepentant charm, and retired. Both were luckier than the four MPs (all Labour, of course) who were sent to prison because they couldn't afford either to pay accountants or to cough up the large sums Tories repaid with ease.

I can't leave out two Labour friends, Alan Simpson and David Taylor. They stood out because they were exemplary characters rather than awkward individualists. Alan was a devoted and passionate environmentalist who could bore anyone for hours on the evils of GM foods or the dangers of nuclear power. Well to the left of the PLP, he was always better informed and more interesting to listen to than our leaders. He left far too early, to carry on his environmental missionary work with people who were more prepared to listen.

In Parliament, the good die young. David Taylor did too, but he'd been a genuine socialist, devoted to his principles. This made him a thorn in Blair's side, though his dissent was always expressed in rational, even moving, contributions. He never gave up his opposition to war, tax cuts for the wealthy and privatisation. On the rare occasions when I had to answer Public Accounts Committee questions as a commissioner, he always questioned me on public finance initiative contracts. I was delighted to stretch my brief to agree with him as much as I could. He was a lone voice on issues the party wanted to bury, but in the end he lost his seat – or rather, it lost him. He died soon after.

I include Bill Cash, not because he's a ball of fun (though his wife Biddy is) but because he bored for Britain. He could denounce the European Union and all its follies at a length that bored the House because few Members wanted to hear the truth about Europe and the consequences of its drive to an ever-closer federal union – but Bill was ever ready to tell them. He was impervious to yawns and criticism but independent-minded, and wealthy enough to have the staying power to keep an unfashionable cause alive. Eventually he reached his pulpit as chair of the European Scrutiny Committee, forcing it at long last to begin to do its job effectively by scrutinising the tsunami of EU regulations. The majority of his committee were against him but Bill soldiered on strongly.

This isn't a long list of characters. More of them were Members earlier in my tenure, perhaps because I was more sensitive then, or perhaps because career politics made us blander, more conformist and more politically correct. Both parties preferred processed peas to characters and, as central control over selections grew and party membership fell, they were successful in putting them in the parliamentary tin. Perhaps Britain no longer produces characters, and certainly those it does produce don't get into Parliament because the parties prefer blander, more malleable recruits. Plenty of fools, knaves, social climbers, pedants and pillocks, lots of aggressive loudmouths, but few larger-than-life characters. As Gloria Swanson might have put it, they make MPs smaller these days. Career politics requires conformist Members who are keen to get on and who rise without trace, rather than awkward eccentrics or delightful dilettantes. When the aim is to get on, fun gets lost on the way. Most of my gallery of characters failed in career terms, but all were better people than most of those who didn't. I admired them all the more because I am such a timid conformist myself.

CHAPTER SEVEN

FIGHT THE GOOD FIGHTS

Every Member should have a cause. Some have none. I had too many. Either approach leads to failure. MPs have influence, the power of publicity and a responsibility to use both for the benefit of constituents. The need for them to use their few remaining powers grows because bureaucracies can crush, regulations can be inadequate, public bodies are understaffed and governments are mean. Privatisation weakens the protective power of the state, and transfers power to markets, which are brutal and allow business to cheat and finance to gamble irresponsibly. All the intermediate institutions that once protected the people have been weakened or captured. Only the power of Parliament, wielded by MPs, remains.

That means that in this colder, harder world, MPs must be the defenders, advocates and protectors of the people. This requires them to take up issues, help the vulnerable and try to ensure fair treatment and fair play. As society and government become more complicated and the big become more powerful, MPs need to be local ombudsmen and public defenders. If they don't act, the people are vulnerable.

Their weapons are the authority of the job and the scourge of the publicity that Parliament provides. As a machinery for making a noise, the Commons provides debates to raise issues, petitions to protest policies, Ten Minute Rule Bills and Private Members' Bills to change the law, and Parliamentary Questions. All can draw the attention of the media.

A storm of questions can highlight a problem and force government into explanations, though getting the questions down is a game of chess played against clever minds in the table office. Very occasionally, questions can be asked about anything. In the brief periods of direct rule in the Falklands and Zimbabwe, it was possible to ask about chamber pots in Stanley hospital or bus services in Bulawayo. I duly did – but normally it's more tricky, as the joke about the refusal to answer questions about the Prime Minister's ironing board on security grounds indicates. The kernel of the problem is: does any minister have responsibility? When my TV partner, Norman Tebbit, and I agreed to ask how many of the signatories to the Maastricht Treaty were in prison or had been thrown out, my question was rejected with the response 'no ministerial responsibility'. In the Lords, Norman got the answer: four. It has grown since.

The effectiveness of the weapons depends on drawing the attention of the media. This process is messy and time-consuming. The odds are loaded in favour of inertia. The civil servants can always invent a dozen reasons for doing nothing, and Cornford's law tells them that the time is never ripe. Ministers don't like being inconvenienced. Their juniors are powerless and tend, or pretend, not to grasp the argument. The civil service is more adept at producing arguments against change than in promoting it, but they're particularly skilled at giving formulaic answers that dodge the issue, saying all's well when it isn't. Against all this, MPs have only their native wit, which doesn't always sparkle, and their sense of duty, which can be undermined by a desire not to rock the party boat. It takes a conscientious MP to battle on. Some don't bother. A few get tough when the going gets rough, though some are brilliant at making excuses for avoiding extra work.

I loved fighting causes. My first was proportional representation. It was fair and right. It would have stopped incoming governments junking the achievements of the outgoing. It would have prevented Thatcher's follies. But it wasn't in the interest of either of the big parties, both of whom preferred to wait their turn for power rather than promise to change the system and weaken their own power to do what they want when they won. So it got nowhere. In both parties, its fortunes rose and fell in inverse ratio to their prospects of power.

I joined the Labour Campaign for Electoral Reform (LCER), then a small group of right-wing MPs meeting in the Reform Club. Most PR supporters were Tories who wanted PR to keep out Tony Benn. My rise on the Labour side of the PR campaign was rocket-assisted. The officers and most of the members of the LCER left to join the SDP. So I became chairman. This made me responsible for touring the vast areas of the south, which were a foreign country for me. There were no Labour MPs and the PR supporters I spoke to were mainly Liberals, all nice but all bemused as to why a Labour MP was wearing their clothes. I wrote pamphlets and organised parliamentary meetings, and as Labour's prospects declined, it began to dawn on smarter Labour members, and even MPs, that without PR we faced a long period in opposition and decline in those vast areas of the south where we had no MPs.

Membership grew and reached the point where I could be deposed. First Jeff Rooker then Robin Cook took over the cross, as happens when issues become hot enough to attract the attention of the big beasts. That boosted the campaign, because both had more pull than I. They won a party commission and a proposal for a referendum. Then Blair came in, castrated the commission, junked the referendum and lost interest, just as the Tories had when they'd won in 1979.

I continued to support PR, but with only the Liberals to push it, the stone had rolled right back down the hill. In February 1974, Jeremy Thorpe had demanded it as one of the conditions for coalition. The party's more earnest leader by 2010, Nick Clegg, the bravest man in British politics according to Matthew Parris, was so eager for power that he sold out on PR and settled for only a referendum on the Alternative Vote, which wasn't proportional. My fellow PR enthusiasts, desperate for any reform, campaigned for it. I didn't think it worth voting for, and didn't. The Tories killed it.

Everything ended in anti-climax thanks to the weakness of PR's long-standing supporters. Yet the case remains strong and has become even stronger as the main parties split and divide. The messy results of the 2015 and 2017 elections and the divisions in both parties over Brexit prove the need for it. Not only could first past the post no longer do its job of providing strong government, but with parties irrevocably split, British politics has become so fissiparous that only PR can now make them work.

I also campaigned to get Parliament televised. Critics put this down to a desire to get back on telly, but I viewed it as essential to bring Parliament directly to the people and cut out the malign middlemen of the media. It's the people's Parliament. Why shouldn't they see it on the medium they rely on? I wrote articles and organised meetings to this effect but met with hostility, particularly from the old and the ugly. So I decided to bring in a motion for television and won it on the casting vote of the Deputy Speaker, Bernard Weatherill. This opened the door, though it took several years and a demonstration by the Lords that TV didn't turn them all into performing chimpanzees for the Commons to accept it when it was finally pushed through by a government motion. I seconded it.

TV was a gain, but not the great success I'd hoped for. In my naivety I'd assumed that people would watch it. They didn't, though occasionally constituents would say they'd seen it. Why wasn't I there? It didn't brighten the speeches, only the ties, and particularly mine. It didn't make us more serious but more exhibitionistic and rowdy. The public, for whom it was done, showed no great interest and the TV channels abandoned their duty to truth, choosing instead to pursue ratings. They began by screening regular summaries of debates and using extracts but stopped when this didn't bring in the viewers. Coverage was narrowed down to short extracts from Prime Minister's Questions, a noisy Punch and Judy show, which is the worst possible advertisement for Parliament, though popular in the USA, perhaps because they'd like to see their politicians in the stocks in the same way as ours.

In Parliament, TV boosted attendance in what had been an empty chamber, but the competition to get in and be seen on telly led to time limits on speeches, so tail-end Charlies (often me) got only a four-minute gabble. It also began the practice of doughnutting, clustering women MPs around the Prime Minister as he spoke. Not exactly eye candy, but brighter and better viewing than a lot of dark-suited miserable men, though I was surprised that feminists allowed themselves to be exploited in this way.

Women certainly brightened dull debates, but TV also brought in the nodding-dog syndrome, as ministers nodded sagely at every prime ministerial platitude as though it revealed fundamental new truths which hadn't occurred to them before. None of this was what

I'd expected, but all of it was better than rabbiting on to an empty chamber, so I was happy. Seeing Parliament was the nation's right. If they didn't want to watch, there's always *Coronation Street*.

Another early reform I backed, the campaign for legalisation of Citizens Band radio, was a folly. I led the campaign in Parliament with Patrick Wall, who was paid by the industry while I did it as an enthusiast. Endless meetings with nervous ministers and anxious regulators broke down the resistance. I addressed a mass meeting of enthusiasts from the plinth in Trafalgar Square, sensitive to the irony of using the same platform as Keir Hardie for a less noble purpose. We won. I installed a set in my car, only to have it stolen. Then another, also stolen. For a few weeks, 'Good Buddy' chat enlivened my journeys down the A1, but it didn't take long before the airwaves were filled with swearing and abuse. Constituents began to demand censorship and the fashion faded, having achieved nothing.

Some causes I lost only to be proved right afterwards. One was demutualisation of the Halifax Building Society. My parsimonious grandparents had made me a member, like most kids in Halifax. The management proposed to turn itself into a bank, with members bought off by shares but reduced to the impotence of shareholders. I campaigned against it. The chief executive told me I was a religious nut, opposing such a wonderful change (which benefited him so well), and I was heavily defeated when members were offered a bonus of shares to vote for demutualisation. Twenty years later, the Halifax went bust and had to be rescued by Lloyds because of greedy speculation by the whizz-kids and crooks who'd taken over from Yorkshire's great and good. They still haven't been prosecuted by the Fundamentally Compliant Authority, which has sat on the report detailing the folly for years to avoid doing its duty of punishing the perps.

Coal mines and the miners were more a way of life than a cause, but Yorkshire was central to both. So I did what I could – which wasn't much – to defend them. I was a friend of Arthur Scargill and had helped to make him a monster by giving him regular appearances on *Calendar* as that rare thing: an articulate miner ever ready to appear on television (if there wasn't a picket line of striking electricians to cross). The more he appeared, the higher he rose, eventually succeeding the cautious and canny Joe Gormley.

The miners had twice defeated the Heath government and Mrs Thatcher was determined to destroy them. She bided her time and built up coal stocks until she was ready to provoke a strike by the closure of pits. Arthur leapt at the challenge. In the ensuing strike, my heart was with the miners, but my head said that Arthur had walked into a trap by going out at the wrong time, in summer, and without a ballot. That produced a split. The Nottinghamshire miners largely stayed at work, as they had done in 1926. Having got the strike she wanted, Mrs Thatcher then used every instrument of the state to defeat 'the enemy within'.

It was as vicious as it was indefensible. The police were misused to wage a war on the mining areas. The security services spied on the strikers. Money was channelled to the Nottingham non-strikers. Humberside's chief constable, David Hall, organised transport and picketing blockades with a relish that was almost fascist.

It hit me right at the start. I was invited to speak at Cortonwood Colliery on proportional representation on the day the news came that the colliery was to close. Bugger PR. The hall filled with angry miners demanding to know what Labour was going to do about the closure. I flannelled about the importance of coal and the industry, though, like Neil Kinnock, I hadn't the foggiest idea.

In the steel strike I'd marched in protests, but the mines were a fight to the death. I gave money, supported the soup kitchens and did what I could to help in the mining areas, which were being treated like an occupied country by the police. It was appalling. A way of life, the mining communities and Yorkshire's industrial heart were wilfully destroyed. Coal, which had once plastered South Yorkshire with posters boasting 'Mining – a job for life', could and should have been run down more gradually, as it was in France and Germany. Instead, a profitable, well-organised industry was wilfully destroyed and the heart was knocked out of the mining areas. Mrs Thatcher was triumphant. She'd broken Labour's praetorian guard and opened the way to the decimation of an industry that had been Britain's industrial backbone. But at the end of it we were importing coal. The bunkers at Immingham previously used for the export of coal were turned round to import it.

I'd long backed home rule for God's Own County (*aka* Yorkshire). The Liberal MP Richard Wainwright and I started the *Northern Democrat* as a publication to campaign for it in 1975 and I'd led a protest march to York when the historic County of York was abolished. So I was enthusiastic about John Prescott's ground-breaking proposals for regional devolution. I wanted to take them as far as regional Parliaments holding powers like Scotland has now, but at least John had started something good, and I immediately launched into the Campaign for Yorkshire, speaking at meetings all over God's Own County, alongside too many quibbling Liberals and hostile Tories. With the Labour government unresponsive, the campaign petered out.

John got regional development agencies. Ours was called Yorkshire Forward, which it never quite lived down in Grimsby. Yet when John attempted to push the development further, into elected regional assemblies, Blair vetoed the extension and reduced the proposal to powerless bodies, incapable of running public lavatories. I urged John to stand up for better. He wearily replied that that was all he could get and we must make the best of it. Which was nowt.

The pathetic proposals weren't worth voting for and a referendum in the north-east duly didn't. Another of my enthusiasms bit the dust, taking a lot of hard work with it. So did the opportunity for decentralising power, leaving the job to the Tories with their pathetic Northern Powerhouses, which were really a way of decentralising the blame for austerity, so that weak and underfinanced regional authorities and mayors with inadequate powers could bear a burden of blame, which should have fallen exclusively on government. John is still trying to revive real devolution, though now it's via a Council of the North of the type Richard Wainwright and I proposed forty years ago. He's right: effective devolution requires big strong regions like Yorkshire, the East and West Midlands, London and the south-west if it's to provide effective centres of power with the ability to respond to regional needs rather than dance to London tunes.

Sid Shaw was a campaign on two legs. I came across him when he appeared on Capital Radio talking about a large statue of Elvis Presley which he'd had made but couldn't find a home for. Drink taken, I rang Capital and suggested that we should put the statue in Parliament. Why not? Elvis was better known and far more popular than some of the bronze presences there already. To my horror, they asked me to make arrangements. My assistant, Micky Chittenden, a public school chap who'd been Churchill's constituency secretary, was the only person who could pull class on the formidable Miss Frampton, head of the Serjeant at Arms' staff. She flatly refused. So I persuaded Ken Livingstone to accommodate Elvis in a London park. Sadly, before he could be parked, BBC television did an interview with me, Elvis and a Page 3 girl (so this clearly wasn't *Panorama*). Lifting Elvis out of the studio, they broke him.

I thought that was the end, but Elvis lived. Years later, I found him, repaired and painted brown, in a pawnbroker's on Victoria Street who told me Sid had pawned him for £15,000. It wasn't the end of Sid, either: he later asked for help to fight a claim from Priscilla Presley, who claimed copyright on the pictures and goods of Elvis he was selling at his shop, Elvisly Yours. I gave him advice and he won the case. That precipitated a stream of Elvis imitators coming to the Commons. First the Russian Elvis who danced on the tables in the canteen. Then four Elvises, plus, for no reason I could understand, a Diana Ross impersonator and a bonus Sven-Göran Eriksson (whom I took for the real thing). The Elvises (I'm not sure of the plural) performed outside the Norman Porch to promote Sid's idea of sending them round hospitals to entertain the sick. I took it to the Department of Health, who were unwilling to unleash Elvises on the ill, particularly when it emerged that they had to be paid for their services. But that wasn't the end of Sid. His landlord repossessed the shop. Last time I saw it, it was a Beatles boutique, though he never brought them to the Commons.

I had two brushes with the secret state, neither of them satisfactory. Harold Horsley, a Grimsby headmaster passionately interested in development, gave up his job to work for the International Development Department on education in Ghana. There he discovered a corrupt misuse of British aid. When he blew the whistle, his computer files were deleted and he was dismissed with neither pension nor compensation. I took up the case, saw every available authority and persuaded the National Audit Office to go out to Ghana, but they could only interview British officials complicit in the dirty deal, not the aid community, which knew what was going on. Nothing was found. Yet it was clear to me from the excuses made and the elaborate run-around I was given that something was being hidden. The veil of secrecy was impenetrable. Clare Short claimed not to remember, no successor would countenance an inquiry, Sir John Bourn told me they had no trace of the money and Howard Horsley was pushed into retirement without justice or pension.

The same frustration hit Tam Dalyell and me over the murder of Hilda Murrell, the aunt of Rob Green, the submarine commander who sank the *Belgrano*. Mysterious agents hanging around her house and the incredible way the body was dumped indicated either security involvement or activity from security contractors to the nuclear industry, which Hilda was opposing. It was clear that the man eventually found guilty couldn't have done it alone, and in an interview he told the indefatigable Green that he'd get £60,000 when he came out – though it won't be all that much when inflation has taken its toll. Again, nothing could be proved, but something smells. Individual MPs run into brick walls on security matters.

My longest-lasting and most difficult campaign was for a competitive exchange rate. The consequences of an overvalued exchange rate in pricing British production out of markets made it clear that the only way to get growth was by devaluation. I'd long thought this, but when I drifted into the inspiring company of Bryan Gould, Peter Shore, Shaun Stewart, Douglas Jay and John Mills, I was better able to prove it. All of them were members of the Labour Euro Safeguards Campaign. The two causes, both of which I supported, overlapped. We wrote pamphlets (to be honest, Shaun Stewart, a former Board of Trade official, largely wrote mine) and held meetings at party conferences and for any local Labour Party that would invite us. Few did.

John Mills wrote brilliant monthly bulletins for MPs and trade unions, and when the Monetary Policy Committee began I wrote monthly to the Governor of the Bank of England, urging lower interest rates and a competitive exchange rate. I might as well have been advocating high treason as a cure for the common cold.

In 1990, a young foreign exchange trader approached me. He'd been fired from American Express for blowing the whistle on point-skimming by foreign exchange dealers at the expense of clients. This was theft. I pulled every stop in the backbencher's repertoire to help him and to highlight the problem. I wrote to ministers, asked questions and took him to see Eddie George, then Deputy Governor of the Bank of England, a nice man who always seemed to get annoyed when I told him he was wrong. Eddie assured us that the bank had conducted extensive enquiries and found nothing wrong. This turned out not to be true. So I organised an adjournment debate in which the minister claimed I was wrong, but afterwards told me I was right but nothing could be proved because there was no paper trail.

The answer was to demand the time-stamping of all transactions. This too got nowhere. Both major parties would do anything to keep big finance happy. Twenty years later, American court cases against the Bank of New York Mellon and an FBI investigation (Operation Wooden Nickel) conducted by James Comey, later director of the FBI, revealed that millions of dollars were being skimmed off by banks and dealers in the enormous foreign exchange market. In the US, the markets worked in the same way as in Britain, so with this proof we went back into action. I organised further debates and wrote letters to the regulators and the Bank of England. To no avail, until my final debate produced a wonderful surprise. Andrea Leadsom replied for the Treasury. She became the first minister to reply to my adjournment debates who knew what she was talking about rather than just reading a departmental reply with some deterioration in the style. Better still, she actually did something about it by writing to the Bank of England asking them to consider reform. They were reluctant, but we persuaded the Deputy Governor to act, and the recommendation to use time stamps duly appeared in the report of the foreign exchange working group of the Bank for International Settlements. It's not yet compulsory, as it should be for both foreign exchange and gilts trades, because the body responsible for implementation, the Fundamentally Compliant Authority, is, as usual, dragging its feet, but we're on our way.

My major success was to break the solicitors' monopoly on conveyancing. I took this up when my former Liberal opponent from back in 1979 set himself up as a conveyancer but found his clients threatened by the Grimsby Law Society with dire warnings that their houses would be demolished, their children would get bubonic plague and they'd find their neighbours had rights of 'sheep walk' through their gardens if they didn't have their conveyancing done by a solicitor. Monstrous!

So when I came up in the ballot for Private Members' Bills and was offered a range of proposals, from Mary Whitehouse's bill for banning dirty videos to innocuous items taken from legislative pigeonholes, I was readily persuaded by Mr Private Bill, David Tench of the Consumers' Association, to end the solicitors' monopoly and make house buying easier by a House Buyers Bill.

Private Members' Bills are exciting. The Member introducing one has to be his own minister, steering the bill; his legislative draftsman, writing it; his pollster, demonstrating public support; his media manager, publicising it; and his own whip, to persuade Members to stay behind on a Friday when they usually bugger off, so as to get the hundred votes necessary to set the bill on its way. I even did the conveyancing on my own new house, to show how easy it was.

I couldn't have done any of this without the Consumers' Association.

On the day, the solicitors defeated themselves with pompous and incomprehensible arguments while the barristers let their brother solicitors down. Denis Healey left a lunch to vote for it, David Steel stayed down for it and I got the hundred votes for closure. Nobbut just. The bill lived. Norman Tebbit told me he'd accepted the Cabinet's decision to oppose it 'with gritted teeth', but once the Commons had accepted it, a free market government had to free up the market rather than defend a restrictive practice. It compromised, ended the monopoly and set up conveyancing as a new profession. Conveyancing charges fell. I was the hero of the *Daily Express*. Relations with the Grimsby Law Society became a little uneasy, though they'd never been too good anyway.

My success in ending that unjustifiable monopoly led on to a long failure to reform the legal profession. My friend Richard Lomax and I formed the Campaign for a National Legal Service to argue that the state should provide a paid public defender service, end the distinction between barristers and solicitors, and give people direct access to both. These arguments made little headway against the vested interests of the profession, though the chair of the Bar did take me out to lunch and an experimental defender service was set up in Scotland. Our campaign ended as a defence of the network of law centres financed by local government, but these were gradually closed down by spending cuts. To my horror, the Labour government failed to help them. Our new Lord Chancellor was keener on doing up his accommodation than on reform of the profession. Total failure. Though my efforts to protect solicitors from the impossibly tight restrictions on legal aid did get me back to the dinners of the Grimsby Law Society and a lot of work defending their interests, as legal aid finance was whittled away and they were moved on to production-line contracts.

Another success followed. Nirex, the body responsible for disposing of nuclear waste, wanted to dump some of it just outside Grimsby. The waste wouldn't have been particularly dangerous, though its half-life was longer than my whole one, but it was hardly the regional aid or the advertisement Grimsby needed. Meetings and protests had no effect. So we decided to picket the site and stop Nirex getting in. Environmentalists, greens, hippies and oddballs rolled up from all over the country to join the picket line and I spent much of the summer sitting sunbathing on it. Until 19 September, when a Nirex lorry broke through in the early hours of the morning. Tents and hippies disappeared, my tent and Primus along with them.

Further meetings and demonstrations failed to persuade a triumphant Nirex to get out, until my brave neighbour and friend Michael Brown, MP for Cleethorpes, launched the most potent weapon an MP can, by threatening to produce a by-election if the dump went ahead. It was abandoned. That was his triumph, not mine, but Eric Clements, a one-man Comintern and the self-appointed Grimsby representative of the Communist Party, graciously told me that I'd earned the respect of the comrades and, more importantly, Grimsby. My tan faded, though it wasn't replaced by a nuclear glow, and eventually the only place Nirex could persuade to accept the dump was Cumbria, where most of it was produced in the first place. The dream Nirex had held out of Britain making money by processing the world's dirty nuclear laundry was quietly shelved.

Some campaigns got nowhere. I campaigned against Freemasonry, the kind of perennial issue that comes up from time to time when the newspapers have nothing better to do. I supported Chief Inspector

Brian Woollard, who'd been dismissed for raising the issue in the Metropolitan Police. It fell on deaf ears, possibly because so many MPs and local bigwigs were members of that mafia for the mediocre. I gave up.

I did, however, have a partial success on the touchy subject of cannabis. I'd urged decriminalisation, but a friend's wife told me how it helped her with the multiple sclerosis of which she later died. So we decided to narrow the argument, drop legalisation and demand that cannabis be made available on prescription for pain relief so as to stop the senseless prosecutions of MS sufferers then going on. She took the name Clare Hodges for the campaign and we formed a committee with a couple of peers, a doctor who hoped to grow the cannabis for medical purposes and a couple of celebs. This met respectably in the Athenaeum. We gave evidence to a Lords inquiry and to departments, pestered ministers and finally got an agreement to allow it to be grown for medicinal purposes. The publicity ended the unforgivable hounding of the sick by police officers in different parts of the country. A victory of sorts because doctors and the police began to take a more lenient view, though legalisation has still not authorised medical cannabis as it should.

When toxic shock produced by sanitary tampons emerged as an issue, I leapt to the defence of the women – only to find that the stuffing for the tampons was manufactured in Grimsby. Ungallantly, I shut up and left the women to fight on alone. Reinforcements arrived later in the shape of Jess Phillips.

By this time, I had embarked on a fight that went on to the end of my career. When the Grimsby fishing fleet had been forced out of Icelandic waters, scores of vessels were laid up on Grimsby's North Wall. Thousands of fishermen were thrown out of work with neither compensation nor redundancy. Employment minister Harold Walker, other Labour ministers and lawyers, the civil servants and the trade union (which most fishermen hadn't belonged to) assured me that they couldn't pay redundancy because fishermen were casual workers. The owners got £180 million compensation but nothing was passed to the men. It was desperately unfair to men who'd given their lives to fishing, only to be told that they were casual workers entitled to nothing. As on so many other issues, Labour didn't dare break rules, however stupid.

However, in 1981, Grimsby fishermen, led by Dollie Hardie, the redoubtable wife of a skipper, formed the British Fishermen's Association (BFA) and formulated demands for £1,000 of compensation for every year of service. Hull crews joined in, SDP candidates in Grimsby and Hull leapt on the bandwagon and I resumed my efforts but got the usual brush-off, this time from Tory ministers. Deadlock Mark II. Then Humphrey Forrest of the Humberside Law Centre (later abolished because of government-imposed spending cuts) proved to a Hull industrial tribunal that the custom and practice on the docks tied fishermen to the industry almost as tightly as serfs. The tribunal ruled that they were not casual, and this forced the government's hand. The Department of Trade and Industry (DTI) had refused to countenance a proposal I'd developed to give back the contributions they'd made to the redundancy fund, and wouldn't accept the evidence I provided from the Fleetwood Fishermen's Disciplinary Register that the men were treated like slaves. Now they gave in. Ann Widdecombe gave way instantly, and with great charm agreed to an ex gratia redundancy payment – only ten years late.

It wasn't enough. Backed by the British Fishermen's Association in Hull and Fleetwood, we resumed the campaign but this time for compensation. Again, Tory ministers refused, but Labour's victory in 1997 produced a change of heart. Soon we had sympathetic ministers in Fisheries and the Department of Trade and Industry, and a new influence with the arrival of Alan Johnson, a Blair favourite parachuted in as MP for Hull West. (Stuart Randall, who'd supported our campaign, had been forced out by a row with the City Labour Party, which he claimed was corrupt, and transferred to the Lords because he knew where too many bodies were buried.) Suddenly there were renewed representations, new debates and bigger delegations from all three ports – and the door opened. Ian McCartney at the DTI agreed to settle on the basis of the BFA demands for £1,000 for each year of service in Icelandic waters.

DTI officials played a tricky game and proposed to pay the money on the basis of service on eligible vessels, but their list was incomplete. Meetings of the men in Grimsby and Hull extended it, and I added more when the Icelandic fisheries minister (who was more helpful and efficient than British counterparts) agreed to give me a list of vessels spotted in their waters by the Icelandic coastguard.

Then came a further snag. To save money, breaks in service, which could come for all sorts of reasons in fishing – vessel lay-ups, repairs, holidays, sick leave or disciplinary offences – were deemed to stop those suffering them from claiming for service before the break. So a fisherman with a lifetime of service could only get a few years' compensation if a short break cut him off from the major part of his service. We resumed pressure. New ministers like Nigel Griffiths were more sticky, their civil servants more tricky, but eventually we won an additional scheme to recognise claims before the break. Yet even this was more niggardly than it should have been, because it was based on days at sea as measured by the fisherman's port record. This produced more anomalies, because some books were lost, others inaccurate, and Lord Young of Norwood Green, the new, and stupid, DTI minister (how do they pick 'em?), refused to budge. I got the National Audit Office to report and, more successfully, Alan Johnson and I took the issue up with the ombudsman, who eventually agreed to a flat-rate sum for all who'd been deprived. After a quarter-century of inflation, the fishermen got less than they should have, but our long battering had worked.

End of story, though only in theory. I was dealing with a few particularly difficult cases right to the end of my career, and even after. Justice had almost been done, but thirty years late. The fishermen got their due, shrivelled by inflation. Say not the struggle naught availeth. But the moral was clear. In Britain, it's tough to right even manifest injustices.

On one issue, blackmail worked. When Blair was desperate to get a majority for his monstrous decision to charge students fees, to be paid through loans, I was strongly opposed to the end of the free education. I'd benefited from it and didn't want to push away the ladder I'd climbed. Gordon Brown rallied his troops against it, and I joined George Mudie's list of MPs ready to vote against, but then decided to roll the pork barrel. I offered to swallow my concerns if a bill of £20 million owed by the Grimsby Health Authority for the treatment of an asylum seeker who'd gone to Nottingham but stayed registered to a doctor in Grimsby was paid by government. Then I added a further demand: that Grimsby College be raised to the university status it should have had years ago. Governments in distress are amazingly responsive. I put my case to John Hutton and Charles Clarke, both enthusiastic Blairites determined that their hero shouldn't be humiliated. I got the money, though Charles Clarke couldn't give me college status because of requirements about numbers. So he elevated Grimsby to institute status, which at least made it eligible for more funding. I'd won and the lesson was obvious. Keep governments weak and MPs are stronger, though I felt bad about it afterwards. The government's eventual majority – five – was so small that with a couple of others I could have stopped a proposal that should never have been made. Blair should have realised that what he regarded as a clever settlement of the financial problems of tertiary education inevitably opened the way for the Tories to remove the cap on loans and impose a horrendous burden of debt on students generally, and my grandchildren in particular. To have done even a little to help him achieve that still makes me feel guilty.

In my last parliament I grappled with the problems caused by banks acting through their so-called recovery units, working with insolvency specialists from the big four accountancy firms, which pushed many businesses unnecessarily into liquidation or administration under the guise of 'helping' them. This scandal had gone on for years but it got much worse and stood revealed after the 2008 crash. Banks were desperate to repair their own balance sheets and weakened by the reckless behaviour of their own traders, who they'd failed to supervise effectively, or in some cases at all. Struggling companies, and even solvent ones, were suddenly told that the price of the bank's continued support, whether by way of overdraft or loan facilities, was to allow their 'experts' access to the companies' books and records. The 'experts' then decided that the business had to be shut down and the accountants and insolvency specialists collected substantial fees from selling the company's assets and paying themselves first and their clients, the banks, next. The banks were invariably secured lenders with charges over the saleable assets. Unsecured lenders lost out completely or ended up with a few pence in the pound while the fat cats licked the platter clean.

There was no right of appeal. Complaints to the Financial Services Authority or the regulatory bodies for the chartered accountants were useless, and dozens of small-business owners who'd seen their life's work sabotaged and their employees lose their jobs were in no position, either financially or emotionally, to take on these deep-pocketed behemoths or challenge them in the courts.

One who did was Keith Elliott, who owned and ran Premier Motor Auctions in Leeds. He was outraged by the actions of PwC and Lloyds Bank, which had pushed Premier into liquidation. I took up his case and raised the matter in the Commons. This got nowhere, because Parliament is better at ventilating complaints than remedying them. Equally fruitless were my efforts to get something done by the Fundamentally Compliant Authority or the Fundamentally Supine Authority or the accountancy regulator, which is dominated by the Big Four. Vince Cable, who was then the Secretary of State for Business, was sympathetic but felt he couldn't intervene, which was his position in most things under the coalition. PwC's 'General Counsel' condescendingly told me that it was a matter for the courts, not for Parliament, but when Elliott and the liquidator decided to sue both the bank and the accountants in the High Court, PwC and Lloyds did everything they could to stop it coming to court. They tried to get the case dismissed, arguing that the claimant liquidator couldn't afford to pay the very substantial costs if he lost. This is an old and time-honoured litigation trick, regularly used by defendants and their lawyers. First destroy a claimant financially, then argue that in English law a claimant has to pay the successful defendant's costs and must lodge appropriate security for those costs into court before the case can proceed. Thus the merits of the case are never heard, while the argument proceeds in an interlocutor process, which is itself very expensive.

The brave first instance judge rightly rejected the Lloyds/PwC argument, which was accompanied by the claim that relevant emails had been deleted and couldn't be recovered. Inevitably, the big boys then appealed. The court of appeal decided that the liquidator should put up £4 million as security to continue with the claim. He couldn't. The case was dropped without the damaging evidence prepared by Keith Elliott and the liquidator ever being heard.

It was monstrous, and the Tomlinson Report, commissioned by Vince Cable, showed that the Royal Bank of Scotland's 'Global Restructuring Group' had been treating many small corporate customers equally appallingly. The Fundamentally Compliant Authority, which acted as a PR agency for accountancy rather than the regulator of its excesses, had kept secret its report on these shocking activities, but Lawrence Tomlinson himself roundly condemned RBS for doing much the same as Lloyds and PwC had done. He said, 'The RBS files show the Royal Bank of Scotland and its executives took the opportunity to make profit from businesses in distress whilst telling them that they were there to "help".'

Like the behaviour of RBS, that of PwC and Lloyds in the Premier Motors case is a national disgrace, compounded by the unwillingness of the so-called regulators and the courts to do anything about it. 'Bastards,' John Major might have said. I won't. It must be difficult for PwC to uphold its commitment to build trust in society while adding yet another to it's accumulation of presentational difficulties arising from its audit of Tesco, its work at Carillion and BHS and the Lux leaks, though I would suggest in my mild fashion that the best way to stop complaints about a greedy and irresponsible culture is by effective regulation and by ensuring that the courts help David rather than being the last resort of Goliath, whose pockets are deeper than Kellingley Colliery. Self-regulation is useless if you can't trust the chaps.

My longest campaign produced a more pathetic result. The Tory government had run down investment in housing. The Blair government made things worse by building very few council houses (Mrs Thatcher had built more) and forcing councils to privatise their stocks to raise money from the private sector. This disastrous disinvestment in one of the basic requirements for a good society, which every previous Labour government had built on a big scale, led directly to rising rents, rocketing house prices and a housing crisis that hit low earners particularly hard, forcing them into high-rent unregulated lets in the burgeoning private sector. The massive reduction in public housing available for rent turned the remaining estates and the tower blocks from communities into ghettos by making them into dumping grounds for the poorest, rather than the mixed communities Bevan had sought to create. It was a social disaster.

The only effective protest came from Defend Council Housing, run by Eileen Short, sister of Clare, and Alan Walter of the Communications Union. As it was a Trotskyite organisation, few Labour MPs would touch it. But it was effective, had a strong tenant following and was brilliant at agitation. I backed them enthusiastically, along with such stalwarts as Frank Dobson (himself a council house tenant) and Kelvin Hopkins (a former chair of housing). I spoke at meetings, at conference and around the country in campaigns against local privatisations. I took delegations to a series of ministers, who were all clearly under instructions to do nowt, and we protested against the double whammy of selling public housing while refusing to introduce any rent controls. We managed to defeat up to a third of the privatisation ballots, though not in Grimsby, where the council cheated by bringing the ballot forward so that most people had voted by the time my pamphlet warning of the dangers reached them. I wasn't even called to speak at party conferences, which was flattering, though even without my oratory we defeated the government three times at successive conferences. Nothing happened. John Prescott, who'd failed to get his home city, Hull, to privatise its council stock, gloated at his victory in Grimsby. I suppose it was nice for him to have won a fight for once.

It was a bitter fight which divided Labour councils. Most Labour MPs kept their heads down. Yet it was well worth it. Eventually, after David Miliband and Yvette Cooper had stalled us, Gordon Brown did start building to counter the 2008 recession, only to have the Tories cancel it when they came in. Thirty years of sales and disinvestment produced the housing crisis that is now forcing both major parties to promise to build more, though even now the talk is still of 'affordable' houses, which really aren't. It should be about the public housing for rent provided particularly by councils to accommodate the high proportion who will never be able to afford to buy at our record house prices. We were proved right posthumously. That's probably the best a backbencher can get in politics, but the lesson still needs to be followed by a big council house-building programme of the type Labour once saw as an essential social security provision. Neither party has learned the lesson. Neither is keen to give power back to councils. Neither will allow councils to issue bonds to finance house building for their communities.

In Parliament, it's easy to go with the flow. Honours come to those who conform to prevailing trends. Troublemakers get shunned. Yet the good MP should be a nuisance to protect constituents and pursue causes against the monolithic machines, public and private, that grind over everything. The bigger the nuisance, the better the prospect, and, looking back, I wasn't obnoxious enough. So my career of cause-pushing produced only a mixed bag of results and no laurels. Yet it was more fun, and more valuable, than tramping through division lobbies to vote for policies I only half understood and sometimes didn't like. There's pleasure in tweaking the nose of power, though there's also a lot of frustration and hard work. I wouldn't have missed any of it. My only regret is that I wasn't better at it.

CHAPTER EIGHT

LOVING LABOUR: A STRANGE AFFAIR

Once upon a time, political parties were something to be deplored. Combinations that undermined democracy, cabals scrabbling for power, sordid conspiracies against general good, as Oliver Goldsmith suggested in his description of Edmund Burke:

> Who, born for the universe, narrowed his mind
> And to party gave up what was meant for mankind.

I had less to offer the universe or mankind. But I was ever ready to give whatever it was to the Labour Party because I saw it as the best instrument for the advance of both.

British politics work through a two-party system and there was only one I could ever choose. That was Labour. I came to it from outside rather than being bred to it. This made mine a less natural and more one-sided relationship than most. Yet it began well, was always affectionate and, despite all the ups and downs inevitable in affairs of the heart, still goes on now at the Darby-and-Joan end of politics.

The affair began as an intellectual enthusiasm rather than the love of Labour that my hero Hugh Gaitskell revealed to the 1961 party conference. I couldn't ever love a political party, great ungainly beasts that they are, but I could like one, and that was Labour. People support a party for all sorts of reasons: ambition, enthusiasm, eccentricity or conditioning. Most people inherit their political allegiance from their parents and go on to work and live in an environment that reinforces it, but the main influence for me was the social democratic ethos of the affluent post-war society emerging in the 1950s.

I wasn't conditioned to Labour. My dad was a dyeworks manager who became fed up with unions. He was a member of the Baildon Conservative Club, though probably because it was a cosy place for a pint. My paternal grandparents were stolid Yorkshire Tories of the most unthinking kind. My maternal grandmother had been a member of the Primrose League, which was organised to uphold God, Queen and country and the Conservative cause, and proudly presented me with her membership medal (which I lost). So I suppose they would all come under the description Disraeli once used of humble Tory voters: 'angels in marble' – though millstone grit was a more likely material for Yorkshire angels.

I was always in Labour but not of Labour, not having been by any stretch of Michael Meacher's imagination working class. I was lower-middle class, not born to the Labour tribe but coming to it through a dawning political understanding, developed from absorbing the social democratic mood of the times and a sympathy for the underdog. This was an intellectual conversion unbuttressed by the disciplines of work-place and union. It led to a political disability.

I started out as a Liberal and proudly wore a yellow rosette on my first job, a meat round, in 1950, to the surprise of the poorer customers (1/6d or less). A canvass return I made at Bingley Grammar School's

1950 mock elections shows that most of my fellow sixth-formers were Tory while I was one of a few Liberals. At university, I became Labour.

Which prompts a thought. In those days, young people absorbed the mood of the time: young Labour students at university educated each other through university Labour clubs and other organisations, senior politicians participated in the discussions, and a flourishing literature of books, pamphlets and papers interested the young and party members alike, so young people could come to Labour by an intellectual conversion as well as the normal processes of class conditioning.

Today, all those processes are weaker. Tory governments have, in part deliberately, undermined the conditioning process, breaking up council estates, closing factories, crippling the unions and shutting many of the pubs, clubs and institutions that nurtured communal feeling. Yet conservative socialisation through business, class and the print media is as vigorous as ever.

Labour's loss has been compounded by the dilution of the intellectual contribution. University Labour clubs are either dead or faction-ridden, while party meetings are endlessly boring rather than generating lively discussion. Few politicians attempt new thinking or write compelling theses on socialism, Labourism or any altruistic view on life. Like society, economic policy doesn't flourish in colder and harder times.

Worse still, no reliably Labour media remain. *Labour Weekly* became Labour Weakly and closed in the '80s. *Tribune* has dithered on the brink of bankruptcy and shrunk in circulation for years. The *Daily Herald* became *The Sun*. No reliably and consistently Labour newspaper survives, though the party can still rely on the *Daily Mirror* and, more intermittently and fussily, *The Guardian*. Only the pale pink *New Statesman* survives on the once flourishing socialist periodical scene, though millions of puff sheets are poured out by MPs, and even more by Euro MPs. These are vehicles for party debating points and Member achievements rather than persuasive argument.

There are a few websites that email you their thoughts every morning, like Labour List, but these are unlikely to inspire anyone. We no longer have party schools or Labour holiday camps and we don't try to educate our supporters in the way our European counterparts still do. There is no effective youth movement. Public relations have replaced party education.

I was lucky in my time, though my relationship with my party was neither a love affair nor a settled marriage. It was an affair of the head rather than the heart. An intellectual is less reliable, particularly a natural nit-picker like me, more querulous and questioning, less conforming than those who are conditioned to the party. I saw the reality of party: a clumsy bitch goddess who uses, hurts and dumps people with neither feeling nor sentiment. Love Labour. But have a prenup.

The two-party system has an implicit bias against understanding because the clash of ideas and argument which is meant to educate merely confuses. Being based on conflict rather than education, it requires an automatic rejection of the other side, a suspicion of their motives and an opposition to their policies. I wasn't incapable of any of this. I certainly saw some Tories as malevolent fools or as nasty pieces of work. Yet we had some of each on our side too. Total rejection was difficult.

On balance, I saw Labour as right, the Tories as wrong, but neither was either in every respect. I could be an enthusiastic custard-pie thrower. It was a necessary art in Parliament and the constituency parties loved it, but I couldn't totally abandon rationality or enthrone prejudice quite enough. I even discovered that some Tories were trustworthy and, though different, smarter than I. But fraternising with the enemy as I did, particularly on Europe, had got Eddie Griffiths thrown out in 1974 in Sheffield Brightside. His friendship with Ernle Money (as well as sitting in the Strangers' Gallery cuddling a blonde) was both a warning and a symptom of treason in the eyes of tribal loyalists.

Back to my *apologia pro vita sua*. At university I was enthused by Hugh Gaitskell and so excited by Tony Crosland's *The Future of Socialism* that I took to my bed for two days to read it, which worried my mum and annoyed my dad. The conversion was concreted by the Suez invasion, which produced my first demonstration, a rag-tag and bobtail procession of students which poured up Oxford Road in Manchester. When businessmen guffawed outside the Café Royal, the demonstrator next to me shouted, 'You'll laugh the other side of your face when you're hanging from a lamp-post.' Revolution in the air! It was deflated when we poured into Albert Square, unsure what to do, but demanding that the Mayor (who didn't seem to have any responsibilities in Suez) came out to be booed. He wouldn't. We dispersed.

This experience led me to the university Labour club, which amazed me by instantly producing hundreds of 'Hands Off Suez' posters (from the Communist Party, I later learned). I joined the party. I read Howard Spring's *Fame Is the Spur* and everything Shipley Library stocked on the Labour Party. I even contemplated doing my DPhil at Oxford on the party's history, but changed my mind when I found out that Henry Pelling, the doyen of Labour studies, was handing Labour's history out in two-year dollops. He offered me two years in the Great War, which I didn't fancy. So instead I wrote 'The Whigs in Opposition from 1815 to 1830', which turned out to be a good preparation for Labour's eighteen-year opposition. I relieved the boredom by joining the Oxford University Labour Club, and the Labour Party Group, which introduced me to discussions with Richard Crossman, Tony Crosland and Hugh Gaitskell. Exciting, all of them.

By the late '50s, Labour looked well on the way to power, but at this point I went to New Zealand, where Labour was already in power. Finding a Labour Party branch in New Zealand was more difficult than finding a Communist cell. A tired party was less exciting, but I joined and was treated as a breath of fresh (albeit Pommy) air, rising rapidly to become branch chairman, council candidate, press officer, even potential MP. Our Labour MP in Dunedin Central, Phil Connolly, called me in as chair of his only branch, to say he intended to retire. Was I interested in standing?

He prefaced it by the more important question: was I Catholic or Protestant? He didn't ask about my politics. That wasn't an issue in the New Zealand Labour Party. I thought I was too young to stand as an MP. I didn't fancy a future of rotund pomposity in the New Zealand Parliament, where the quality of the food is better than that of the debate. So I went back to Oxford to finish my PhD. God alone knows what a pompous pillock I'd have been if I'd become MP for Dunedin Central in 1963! Possibly like the man who did. He took to drink, was eventually deselected and went down as an independent.

I chose pedantry. On my return to New Zealand, politics took a back seat. Back home, Harold Wilson's government disappointed and with an overvalued exchange rate Britain was forced into another dose of the old stop-go, while Harold invoked the Dunkirk spirit rather than economic sense.

That failure looked clear to me in New Zealand, where I was rising in the media stakes. I became New Zealand's Robin Day (with touches of Tommy Cooper). Like all such plastic people, impartiality was essential, though when the New Zealand Broadcasting Corporation

(NZBC) began conference coverage, I was the only member of the team to be admitted into Wellington Town Hall. I was a delegate as well as an impartial pundit.

In 1967, I went back to Oxford to find the British Labour Party changed. The Labour Club was rent asunder by infighting, my friends had formed the Campaign for Democratic Socialism, and where earlier we'd gone on visits to comprehensive schools and car factories, now the excursions were to demonstrate outside Annette's, a racist hairdresser on Cowley Road who was turning away Asian customers. We picketed. Bodies came flying out of the shop, while I took photographs. A party that had swapped Harris tweed jackets and corduroy for denim had gone mad.

Earlier, social democracy had been the student norm and Oxford had churned out moderate socialists, the most active of whom went into politics. Many of the people I'd associated with, like Brian Walden, Stanley Henig, Bernard Donoughue and George Jones, had since become (or tried to become) MPs, or, like Maurice Wright, had gone into government. Now, in my second incarnation, Marxism was stronger, activism the norm. NUS playway politics eclipsed Oxford Union graces, and the polytechnics, coupled with Vietnam and student politics, were turning out a different breed of politician.

I had become a Rip Van Winkle throwback from the Gaitskell generation, talking a different language, lacking either a trade union programming or the new ideological preoccupations, and finding that party had become a picket line rather than a crusade.

Having rejected the idea of going into the New Zealand Parliament too early, I went into the British Parliament too late. I was middle-aged rather than young. I came in imbued with Tony Crosland's revisionism, but he'd passed away in 1977 and his ideology had already passed its sell-by date. I wasn't an offspring of the Labour tribe, more an awkward individualist in a party of union solidarity. I was also a right-winger in a party moving left in reaction to the compromises of the Wilson and Callaghan years.

My basic mistake was to assume that Labour is organised altruism dedicated to a few basic principles, among which the most basic is the greatest betterment of the greatest number. In practice, though, parties are shameless chameleons ever ready to stand on their heads at the whim of the polls. Tories change from conservative to radical, paternalist to gradgrinding, while Labour go from Methodism to Marxism to marketing. Both stood on their heads on matters European, changing from enthusiasm to scepticism and back.

I was on the right, but the party crept right behind me, leaving me on the extreme left just by standing still. Early on, I was jokingly describing myself as the last surviving Gaitskellite, a claim I dropped when Lady Jay angrily pointed out that Douglas was still alive. Very much so, as I found when I went to visit him to make amends and listen, enthralled. Sadly, my claim became true when Douglas Jay died in 1996.

I didn't realise it at the time, but Labour's loss of power in 1979 was the great turning point. In office, Labour had fought a rearguard action to prevent worse rather than advancing socialism. That produced a pent-up reaction which immediately exploded. The Tribunites opted for a sentimental return to good Old Labour by electing Michael Foot as leader. Bennites set out to radicalise the party to draw out what they saw, *de haut en bas*, as a socialist majority in the electorate. This quiet majority was to be roused by taking over the Labour machine, purging the MPs, then imposing a socialist programme. Meanwhile, Militant set out to build a party within the party by permeation.

Manchester University students protest against Suez; Austin Mitchell lagging behind

Paul Foot pickets *Accountancy Age* with striking journalists; another Austin Mitchell photo opportunity

© ANDREW WIARD

Austin and Linda at by-election victory, 1977

© *GRIMSBY TELEGRAPH*

Jumping for joy on Cleethorpes beach the morning after: Austin and Linda, 1977

© *GRIMSBY TELEGRAPH*

Les Gibbard cartoon from the 1977 by-election

© LES GIBBARD

BELOW LEFT A life on the ocean wave for the new fishing MP, 1978

BELOW RIGHT Austin Haddock with two of his mates on the *Alatna*, 1978

Politics at peace: Don Concannon (Labour) and William van Straubenzee (Conservative) working in the library

It will all end in tears: Julian Critchley MP

Harold Wilson reminisces in the Whips' Office with Michael Cocks and Ron Leighton

Sky News's *Target* presenters, Norman Tebbit and Austin Mitchell

LEFT Critch, Mitch and Titch, putting some fun into politics on the BBC: Julian Critchley (Con) in the centre, flanked by Charles Kennedy (Lib Dem) and Austin Mitchell (Lab)

LEFT Julius Nyerere, President of Tanzania, welcomes Austin Mitchell MP

BELOW LEFT The biggest fish finger in the world on the terrace of the House of Commons. Austin Mitchell and CEO Wynne Griffiths with team from Young's, 1987

BELOW RIGHT Staying Alive: the class of 1977 ten years on

"...THEN ONE DAY ON YOUR DRESSING-ROOM THEY HANG A STAR..."
(THERE'S NO BUSINESS LIKE SHOW BUSINESS)

FRI 3 FEB 1989

Sacked by Neil Kinnock: Garland cartoon from the *Telegraph*, 1989 © GARLAND

Mixed messages: canvassing in Grimsby, 1992

Fixed grins for the sales team: Mitchell and Blair

LEFT Blair and the boys: John Prescott, Gordon Brown and Jack Straw

At his happiest alone: Gordon Brown

ABOVE The story of the Apostles © MARTIN ROWSON

LEFT Apostles party: Paul Flynn, Kelvin Hopkins, Austin Mitchell, Bob Marshall-Andrews, Martin Rowson, Alice Mahon

LEFT Team Austin Haddock on Grimsby docks – a prawn in their game

1983, Michael Foot stands down – Bryan Gould calculates the odds

ABOVE LEFT Whip Tommy (now Lord) McAvoy applies some pressure

ABOVE RIGHT Miliband meets his lefties: Kelvin Hopkins, Lisa Nandy, Michael Meacher and John Cryer

LEFT Cameron and cronies: William Hague, Nick Clegg, George Osborne, Theresa May

ABOVE The Commons leavers, 2015

LEFT Leaving Grimsby, 2015: Austin says goodbye from the back of a trawler

BELOW Austin Mitchell, David Davis and guest squawker: the final push in Hull, two days before the Brexit vote

All three were real threats to Labour's broad appeal. They produced a panicked reaction. Major figures on the right and nervous nellies from the ranks decamped to form the SDP. Traditionalists formed Solidarity to fight back. I never thought of deserting to join the SDP's crew of egos and I played an energetic part in Solidarity under the leadership of Peter Shore and Roy Hattersley. With the narrow victory of Denis Healey over Tony Benn in the election for deputy leader, we won.

Healey's win checked the tide to what I saw as lunacy and opened the way for Neil Kinnock to edge the party back to sense by cautious gradualism, dropping the unsaleable and promoting the desirable. Both were slow processes, not fast enough either to win in 1992 or to satisfy the ambitious right, who took over after that election.

A new generation was taking over and I was beginning to feel out of date at the tail end of the great generation. The big figures I'd so much admired were retiring, going off the scene, dead, or part-way there in the House of Lords. Which left me, a relic, still hoping to change the world but watching it move the other way.

Labour lost confidence in itself, in the unions and in the possibility of advancing socialism in one country. Blair's answer was not a new programme for changing the world but to change the party, by diluting socialism, edging away from the trade unions, which were proving both unpopular and impotent, and looking to better public relations. Party political broadcasts, which I'd helped run, were taken over by Peter Mandelson. He dropped our laborious efforts to explain in favour of glossy image building. At much greater expense.

There was sense to all that. It was right to shift the party from the impossible imperatives of the radical shopping list of the 1983 suicide note manifesto back to the centre ground. I'd advocated such a shift at some length in my 1983 book, *Four Years in the Death of the Labour Party*. Now it came ten years late, by which time the centre ground had moved to the right. Effectively we were arguing for an accommodation with the neoliberalism with which Margaret Thatcher had replaced the social democratic consensus.

This was dangerous because it moved Labour away from all its traditional bases. Neoliberalism was about markets; Labour believed in management for social purposes. Neoliberalism was about individualism; Labour was about community. Neoliberalism boosted consumption and consumers; Labour was the party of production and producers. Neoliberalism preached incentives; Labour looked to progressive taxation. In economic policy, neoliberalism meant monetarism, not Keynes; discipline, not growth.

I could accept Tony's proposal to drop Clause Four. That was as relevant to reality as the thirty-nine articles to the Church of England and a leader should be allowed a few symbolic gestures. Clause Four was a relic of the past and had never been implemented, or even thought of. There was a strong case for modernising both our appeal and our party, as well as for making it more saleable, as New Daz had done with soap powder. What the leaders shouldn't do was to try to change Labour's essence and its role as well as its skin. Blair's accommodation with neoliberalism did exactly that. It wasn't a respray job on the old jalopy but a total re-engineering. The aim was to dilute socialism, privatise Labour's soul and embrace markets, whose brutality Labour had always fought against.

Tony made New Labour a very different party to the old Labour Party I'd joined and still thought I belonged to. I understood the transformation only slowly, not being as perceptive as the *pundittieri*, who are always quicker to see patterns where those tilling in the fields see only their furrow. It was not only a change in policy but a change in the essence of the Labour Party. We'd always been the party of the working class, aimed at advancing their cause and bringing their representatives to power. The party I'd joined was essentially a trade union party in which the trade union worker backbone had been strong enough to defeat Harold Wilson's 'In Place of Strife' proposals for union reform in the '60s and to weld an alliance for a trade union-enforced incomes policy in the '70s. Now, as society became more middle class, so did the party, dominated increasingly not by a trade union ethos but by a meritocracy, preaching not equality but education, which, of course, is both essential in its own terms and good for winning the middle-class support we were aiming at. What it isn't is an answer to poverty and exclusion. Only a direct attack on poverty can deal with that.

As Tony Crosland said, 'The purpose of socialism is quite simply to eradicate this sense of class and to create in its place a sense of common interest and equal status.' In becoming a meritocratic, middle-class party aiming to win middle-class votes, we were no longer trying to do that. The price of not doing it was to discount both the regions left behind by change and the people at the bottom of the heap: the unskilled, the uneducated and the deprived, who came to be regarded as a burden, as scroungers and a drain on everyone else just as the world was becoming colder and harder for them. Employment was becoming harder to get and increasingly casualised; social provision, particularly housing, was cut; benefits began to be means-tested not universal; and the trade unions, which had defended the working class, were weakened.

In the past, the deprived, the poor and the manual workers had benefited as the great army of labour moved forward. Now, as the aristocracy of labour became middle class, no one represented them in Parliament or voiced their needs. They were left behind, even ghettoised, their misery mocked in programmes like *Skint* and *Benefits Street*, their party too embarrassed to do much for them. They dropped out of politics and, after the poll tax, many even dropped off the electoral register and lost their right to vote. They were even losing their desire to do so, as their natural party gentrified itself into a middle-class party of professional politicians all out, the poor told themselves, for themselves.

I was naive. I saw advancing the people and creating an equal society based on public service and social unity as essential aims that could never change. I didn't object to the PR, the new colour schemes or even the title New Labour. Every little helps in a good cause and what had worked for New Daz might work for us, but what I hadn't foreseen was that a party desperate for power could change its essence. I assumed that Labour in power would do what Labour was supposed to do. In fact, New Labour was designed to do what Tony Blair and Gordon Brown wanted it to do: not what conference decided or party members and the trade unions wanted, but to achieve the Blair–Brown aim. This was essentially to win power, rather than to see power as the first stage of the more difficult job of changing the social balances of a conservative, class-ridden, selfish society.

The consequences of this change only emerged over Labour's thirteen years of government, as it became clear that the Blair revolution represented a public relations triumph rather than a substantial shift in power to the working class or a change in the commanding heights of the economy. Those I continued to regard as Labour's people were in fact largely excluded and ignored. The consequences came in the failure to build council or social houses, in the shift to means-tested benefits, in the gentrification of estates and cities and in the failure to increase taxes and make them more progressive in order to finance a general improvement.

At the time, it gave New Labour an impetus, undercut all the old fears and criticisms and, as the Tory government floundered, turned an inevitable victory into a 1997 landslide on a 1945 scale. The scale of the majority amplified the hopes, but in 1945 the party had come in with a plan and a programme. 1997's winning party came in with no plan, just a collection of happy hopes. It had a much less clear idea of what it wanted to do and a much softer agenda than its great predecessor. Power had been achieved at the cost of changing Labour's mission from equality to meritocracy. Doing so little, having won a majority to do anything, heightened not the achievement but the disappointment.

I was living in the past, though I only realised it slowly and it hardly troubled me. I plodded on in my own way, preaching my old basics of Keynesian growth, equality and state intervention to rebalance the economy to a diminishing audience and an unhearing government. Yet this made my relationship with a glossier and more heedless party more ambiguous. I still saw Labour as the class party of the non-possessors, the political instrument for furthering the cause of the people and advancing equality. But now a sprinkle of stardust and a lot of rubbish about triangulation had turned its attention elsewhere, and I couldn't put aside my increasing concern that this wasn't the path to the more equal society I wanted. I was too prone to shout my concerns from the rooftops, rather than working for change through endless committee persuasions. Again, the old belief that I was right and if others didn't listen it was their own fault took over. I also had an instinct for devilment, a handicap in politics. There, silence is a virtue, sobriety a mien, and intellectuals should be humble.

This created difficulties with those palace churls, the whips. For most of my early years I ignored them. I'd been appointed as a whip after the 1979 election but gradually dropped out of the whips' team, bored by the endless discussions of boarding houses in Bristol, where Militant was permeating (and eventually winning) the constituency of Michael Cocks, the Chief Whip. For months, no one seemed to notice my absence and, despite occasional grumbles from Derek Foster about how he'd like a little more loyalty (wouldn't we all?), the whips ignored me.

Blair's accession began a new relationship with the party machinery, which became clear when, having gone to Grimsby for some function during the parliamentary week, I was bawled out on the phone by a heavy Scottish accent. This was my introduction to Tommy McAvoy, the Deputy Chief Whip, an exponent of the new brutalism. I was as resentful and amazed as any self-respecting sheep bitten by a sheepdog.

My regional whip, an exponent of the Norman Vincent Peale approach, was detailed to do a psychological assessment on me. He offered me a drink as a preface to a 'serious chat' about the virtues of loyalty and its possible rewards. When I didn't respond, he must have passed the awkward case back to Tommy, who decided to set himself up as my father figure-cum-prison officer.

Before each crucial vote, I was called in for a little chat. I was even visited in my Portcullis eyrie to persuade me to vote with the government. I mostly did, but where I couldn't stomach things like invading Iraq or other enormities, Tommy's sugar-coated thuggery could persuade me to take the coward's way out and abstain, to help him keep a job he told me he might lose if Labour lost the vote. I'm nothing if not kind, though he never thanked me for my part in getting him to the House of Lords as his reward. Nor do I thank him for my drop in rank on the honour roll of mavericks as I abstained rather than voted against the party.

By this time, Labour had moved so far to the right that, as a newly christened dangerous leftie, I was becoming lonely. My hiding place of choice, the Fabian Society's home for battered right-wingers, which I'd joined in 1961 (with permission from the New Zealand Reserve Bank to pay the subscription), had always provided an interesting (and at times the only) forum for discussion and new ideas, both locally and nationally.

It had published our pamphlets against monetarism and about reforming corporate governance, but when Blairism triumphed, it was taken over by young aspirants on the make, some of whom moved on to work for Gordon Brown. It became his publishing house and declined to publish my pleas for council house building because its housing pamphlets were sponsored by the housing associations. It delayed another piece on regulating business by demanding endless rewrites to please Gordon. More importantly, it succumbed to the new Euro enthusiasm, which was, and is, particularly attractive to middle-class idealists like the Fabians.

After three decades of service, I lost my seat on the Fabian executive in 2014 and drifted away from the spacecraft like Major Tom. Where was I to go? Dennis Skinner was the Rockall of socialism, a one-man island, impregnable but alone. John Prescott, whom I admired, had become Tony's bulldog. Michael Meacher organised discussion groups but few attended. Those opposed to the Blairite flirtation with neo-liberalism were keeping their heads down. The Tribune group, which had become a flak-jacket camouflage for careerists, had wound up. The PLP was never a useful forum for discussion and was becoming impatient with left-wing voices, most of whom stayed away.

So I decided to abandon the loneliness of the long-distance Gaitskellite and join the Campaign Group. Not because I wanted to stand on every picket line Jeremy Corbyn organised or endorse every revolution he supported, or even because I'd become a covert Trotskyite (as Jack

Straw warned me would happen if I associated with John McDonnell), but because it was the only group in the PLP that had serious political discussions and took a firm line against soft neoliberalism. It was less a new home than a potential burial plot, but in my declining days it kept my brain alive and indicated that there was more to politics than sitting waiting for a pat on the head from Tony or Gordon.

During my long meander, the Labour Party had changed, even if I hadn't. The cult of personality, previously a Tory art form, took over. Campaigning was being reduced to sprinkling stardust and posing for endless photographs with Tony (or Gordon, who smiled less), holding big placards about whatever Peter Mandelson had decided was the issue of the week. Conference changed from a clumsy policy forum to a noisy sales conference for the brand, which was now in tasteful pastels rather than raw reds, a seaside rally not the party's parliament. Policy formulation was delegated to a forum where ministers told followers what they planned to do. The power of the branches, the unions and the members were all reduced, and party membership locally and nationally was falling as the old stalwarts who'd been the mainstays of earlier years died off, to be replaced by young cause-pushers, apparatchiks and -chaps.

Identity politics were taking over in a society becoming less proletarian, better educated and more complex. A party formerly tied to a few basic but broad objectives and kept in line by trade union domination became a coalition of a thousand causes. Feminism, ethnic-minority access, environmentalism, animal rights and LGBT rights eclipsed the old staples of class and growth. A party built for the betterment of the lot of those at the bottom of the heap began to neglect their growing needs to appeal to the educated and the middle class. The broad programme of betterment was replaced by a hundred calls and causes aimed at better headlines and smaller groups. So, as Labour's manual worker base shrank and the nation became more middle class, Labour became both more diverse and more divided. One person's cause is another's nutcase. Building an equal society and redressing the lot of the people at the bottom of the heap was more difficult than advancing women, cutting waste, getting more kids into university and saving the environment.

The resulting clamour drowned out the cry for betterment. Labour appealed less to the badly off and undereducated, who were in any case less politically interested. This produced a better response from a middle-class electorate which had become less concerned about equality even as those at the top of the tree enjoyed a bonanza of easy wealth, glamour and power, and as the extremes of inequality grew further apart. In my simpler vision, encouraging a thousand causes to blossom was not an adequate replacement for better support to alleviate the lot of the poor and the areas blighted by the death of industry. For the leadership, winning support in the south and among the middle classes was more important than delivering to those left behind.

I couldn't complain, having taken cause-pushing to an extreme. But there was a difference. My causes came to me as an MP. I pushed them because I saw it as my duty, but in the new dispensation, people were selected as candidates because they were cause-pushers rather than because they had anything more than a vague commitment to Labour's broader objective of a fairer, more equal society. In constituency parties, the smaller number of activists chose Members like themselves. MPs went into Parliament to push a cause. They were there not because of any broad altruism, any burning concern for equality or any desire to boost the economy to deliver betterment, but to further narrower objectives in what was becoming a war of each against all.

I lumbered on in my maverick way, preaching the faith, voting the votes, urging the need to expand the economy, and rebalance it to production and away from finance, as the only way to improve the lot of our people. But the world was changing around me, as well as the party. Altruism was out of fashion in a world growing more selfish and more slowly. The great army of Labour was dividing between the skilled and the better-off. Dependants became scroungers, viewed as leeches on the hard work of others. Politics was less interesting for a nation where other satisfactions multiplied. It became a minority sport played with increasing bitterness by smaller teams. Other causes became more clamorous than the simple job of building equality.

The old staples of equality, fairness and public service were certainly more difficult to sell in the zero-sum society. Yet no one was developing a new synthesis to replace Crosland's when he had adjusted old socialism to new affluence. More people were voting as consumers, making advertising and sales more important than policy and principles, and activism more important than thought.

Worst of all, the party had still not learned the art of balancing between left and right, exposing us to a pattern of alternate lurches. Broad coalitions are inevitably divided, though the Tories, with their common conditioning and better discipline, have managed their divisions more effectively, which has helped to keep them in power for longer. The Labour Party, on the other hand, is more a rag-tag and bobtail army than a regiment, and its divisions are matters of strong feeling, ideology, identity and class background, with the result that a more fractious party lurches left when it loses office then right to win power in a conservative country with a hostile media.

This struggle becomes a battle for control of the machine, leaving MPs feeling threatened by deselection and relegated to opposition, while the left feels resentful at the right's readiness to compromise for power. The left then sets out to control conference, the national executive and local selections to stop what is seen as a sell-out. A party obsessed with Ramsay MacDonald syndrome is always prone to see power as a sell-out of principle. There is some truth in this because being in government insulates leaders and shuffles ministers off the common coil, planting them into a world of billionaires, multinationals and the heavy self-interested lobbying that modern government is exposed to. Only strong principles, which Blair didn't have, could withstand that pull. Opposition, on the other hand, licenses irresponsibility and the politics of wish-fulfilment.

Unless it learns the art of balancing these pulls and begins to speak the language of priorities, the Labour Party will continue to lurch from left to right and back, the left gaining the upper hand in opposition, the right in government. The trade unions have ceased to be the ballast of the party and become its burden, while the parliamentary party is neither effective enough nor coherent enough to act as anchor or counterbalance to a boat continuously tilting to left or right. Indeed, under Corbyn, Labour politics have descended into yet another struggle for power, rather than building a united team pulling together for a few broad, common purposes that looks competent to deliver any of them.

In my last years in Parliament, leading up to the 2015 election, we were clearly moving back to yet another bout of the wearying and futile old struggle as the left advanced, the Blairites sulked and moved onto the defensive, and the Euro enthusiasts lost touch with constituents, who were much cooler about the EU and didn't see globalisation with the same approving eye. Been there, suffered that in the early '80s. Then, it had required a long period to recover.

It was clearly time for me to face the fact that I was not only old but out of date. A Gaitskellite in a Miliband party, a Eurosceptic in a Euro-enthusiastic party, a generalist in a specialised world, a softie in a bitter one, and a simple believer in equality adrift amid a clamour of causes, many of them second or third order, all of them a distraction from the goals I'd hoped to achieve through politics in the first place. Still socialist, or at least a social democrat. Still Labour and still instinctively egalitarian. But a geriatric on a children's crusade. The worst sin in politics is to be old, and to paraphrase the old Rolling Stones number, I not only didn't know what was going on, but boy was I out of time. Like the song, I was stuck in the '60s.

CHAPTER NINE

VOTE VOTE VOTE FOR AUSTIN MITCHELL

Elections are Britain's democratic moment. For a brief period, the people are in power and politicians must listen to what they want rather than tell them what they can't have. The political class becomes the servant of the unpolitical mass, and must beg to be given the thing they crave: power. They do this by deceiving their temporary masters in various ways: with bargain offers, a few bribes, promises of a new dawn and better behaviour, a mixture of half-truths and downright lies, deceit and reinterpretations of reality. All promises tend to dissolve or be discarded immediately when power is transferred back to the politicians. Then the dialogue reverts from poetry to prose, from generosity to meanness and from freedom to discipline.

Radicals have always wanted more frequent elections to keep power closer to the people. The Levellers in their Agreement of the People of England in 1649 demanded annual parliaments. So did the Chartists in their unavailing petitions to a parliament which then lasted for seven years. Tony Blair called elections when the mood, and the economic circumstances, suited him, which was usually at four-yearly intervals.

But the Conservative government in 2010 legislated for five-year parliaments, then fiddled a way of avoiding their own legislation by calling an election in 2017. I loved elections and wanted them as often as possible, but my amendments to require triennial elections like Australia and New Zealand received little support.

Supposedly about persuasion, elections are in practice a mobilisation of the have-mores against the have-lesses. Britain is a divided society conditioned by class, economic and social. The classes don't like each other much and have a different view of reality; those at the top and at the middle reaches thinking they've got on through their own efforts and virtues, those at the bottom looking to collective effort and the state.

Independents don't stand a chance and can affect the outcome only by taking votes from one of the majors. Which is sometimes the reason for standing. As a general rule, no man cometh to Parliament except by party. Raving loonies, whether designated by label or IQ, provide colour, though no one in Britain has had the initiative to do what seventy-two New Zealanders did in 1972 and change their names to R. D. Muldoon (and one to Jesus Christ) to stand against the hated Finance Minister. We didn't have any odds-and-sods candidates in Grimsby after the rush of oddballs such as the Malcolm Muggeridge Fan Club and the Sunshine Party, who stood there in 1977. From time to time critics argued that Grimsby was a natural home for the Monster Raving Loony Party, but they never came.

My views of the election process were formed by my background and confirmed by my academic work as a pollster. This showed that here, as in New Zealand, voting was class-based. Most people were conditioned to their political allegiance. They inherited it from their fathers and went out into a world that reinforced it. Few changed sides and elections were decided by floaters, who were usually less informed and less interested. As an MP, I always fought on that basis, but once elected I found that the old certainties were gradually fading. Party allegiances got weaker and more people were voting as consumers, changing sides under the influence of images, events and television rather than remaining conditioned to one side or the other. As in many other aspects of life, from marriage to TV channel loyalty, permanent allegiances were weakening, and more people were picking and choosing. These processes were slower in Grimsby than in the prosperous south, but everywhere the old adage 'I'd vote for a pig if my party put one up' was ceasing to operate. A few pigs still stood, though never in Grimsby.

Nationally, the core of each party's vote was still conditioned by class. So the basic job at elections was to get our people to the polls – a more difficult task for Labour because Tory voters, higher up the social ladder, are better educated, more involved and more interested, while those lower down are more likely to be apathetic and less likely to vote or follow their self-interest. Labour argues for the many not the few. But the many are more difficult to organise, less dutiful and less interested, while the few have more to defend and are better motivated to do so.

This process had a predictable regularity. Governments came in, declined over time (always longer for Tories than for Labour) and were eventually thrown out. Governments lose rather than oppositions winning. Over time, though, the weakening of social conditioning, the erosion of the class bases, the emergence of a more liberal middle class and the growth of the public sector meant that more people were up for grabs. This made the election task more difficult, and national factors and trends more important, so that the individual candidates became less important. The struggle was gradually transferred from the doorsteps, where I now fought it, to the media, which I'd left.

I'd been spoiled by winning a by-election. It was like a triumphal progress assisted by hundreds of party workers from all over the country and riding a golden coach (more accurately a red Chevette), smiling and waving at excited crowds and kissing babies – a practice which stopped after one proved to be the subject of a bitter paternity dispute.

My first general election on my own, two years later, showed me that real elections were very different and much harder work. They are an exhausting survival course, knocking on doors that aren't answered, fending off dogs that frighten but can't be kicked, holding meetings no one attends, and struggling to accost people who don't want to be bothered in the street while the brain dies from the endless repetition of mindless slogans. The real test is not winning votes but surviving without hysterics or insanity.

It was dismaying to find that after I'd tried to push politics down their throats for years on television, electors aren't much interested in them. Candidates try desperately to do so, but even reaching them is difficult. Fewer people are in the streets, more in cars, fewer stand in queues. Most voters have made their minds up months, even years back. Candidates struggle to change them in a few weeks. A party in the lead in the polls when the election begins usually wins. Results are determined by national trends, particularly the brand image of the leader, and the national campaign. Both are more important than the local. Yet candidates still think they can make a difference, that their seat is unique and that they can personally buck or boost the trend. Canvassing is the opium of party members, one of the few ways still open to them to make a difference, though for me it was like a door-to-door advice service. In practice, most electors don't get canvassed or phoned, though party workers still believe that their efforts are persuading them.

It's all self-deceit based on the activist's hopes that it's possible to stop predestination. Candidates certain to win nervously fear that they might lose. Others destined to lose begin to believe that some undefined miracle will carry them to power. Yet the reality is that most seats don't change. Some are so rock-solid that votes should be weighed, not counted: 225 seats haven't changed hands since 1950, Grimsby among them.

Candidates hope that their individual efforts and charms will succeed against all odds, though only around 40 per cent of the electors know who their MP is. The only incumbency benefit comes in the next election after their first victory, but peters out thereafter. Local effort has become less fruitful the more attention focuses on the leader and the national campaign. Moods become mercurial as doubt nags, even in the strongest psyche. If a Tory Party clearly on the way to victory can have wobbly Wednesdays in 1987, it's understandable that many candidates have wobbly weeks. I did. While my neighbour in East Lindsey, Peter Tapsell, wafted round in his Range Rover sampling local hostelries and waving at the peasantry, I jittered like a jelly.

Balfour's dictum that 'nothing matters very much and most things don't matter at all' doesn't apply to election candidates. For them, everything matters, trivia enormously so. Myths rule, reality is ignored and the political class is plunged into its traditional game while the public watches, bored and bemused. Candidates live in a fantasyland that dissolves in the cold and probably wet light of polling day. Then the electorate turns out and votes for whoever it was going to vote for in the first place. As Lynton Crosby put it, 'You can't fatten a pig on voting day.' But you can kill him, as Ted Heath did in 1974 and Theresa May in 2017.

Elections are a battle between change and stability: the opposition offering a new dawn; the government cultivating satisfaction. The differences are hyped up to Miltonian proportions, as if it's Satan versus the Angels. Most people would rather watch sport or pornography or do their gardens. They must be enthused to come out to vote. Policies are bound by economic realities, captured by vested interests or dictated by fashion, but must be sold as the new dawn, a revolution or the near arrival of heaven on earth. The reality is: 'Voter give an honest curse. Defend the bad against far worse.' No one can say it.

Mario Cuomo said that you campaign in poetry but you govern in prose. My elections were fought in doggerel, which I wrote myself, independent of the national theme songs. It had little bearing on the result. That's determined by the success or failure of the incumbent government and the economic circumstances of the time, whether they bring improvement or inflict pain. Even the effect of the national campaign is largely determined by national trends, though candidates and parties still campaign as if the nation's destiny and the state of local drains depended on them, and the particular circumstances of Slagsville or Poshton.

Alan Johnson said on his retirement that he wouldn't miss elections. I loved them. They were an exciting break in Parliament's artificialities and boring routines. No driving down to London and back for a few weeks, fresh air, exercise and a re-baptism in reality, though I was never an effective canvasser, always falling behind the team listening to people's problems and wondering what the hell I could do about them. Best of all, elections are a return to the roots of power and a chance to meet people in all their varieties of awkwardness, ignorance, alienation and anger to try to explain what is happening and why.

The people are the masters now, but it's a struggle to reach them.

American research indicates that people are more likely to vote for a party if they have some kind of contact with it, but in Britain fewer people are canvassed personally as party membership shrinks. MPs are regularly filmed going up to the doors of specially selected electors guaranteed to proclaim their joy and love, but in practice MPs canvass less and reach fewer people personally.

We should have more elections more frequently. Roots should be renewed every three years. Close Parliament down. Remove the title and the status. Send MPs naked out into the world as ordinary people, or at least as ordinary as anyone obsessed with politics can be, to renew the contract, refresh the mandate and restore contact with the real world. It's a marvellous exercise, a street-walking holiday getting physically fit and brain-dead pounding pavements, knocking on doors, pleading for votes. There are inconveniences. British letter boxes are small, stiff and too low down. Some trap fingers and tear up leaflets. Dogs aren't always welcoming. Some people go to enormous lengths to hide, act deaf or tear up your pamphlets in front of you. Others engage you in long conversations but turn out to be Liberals trying to hold you up. Some offer cups of tea so you end up sloshing. Many offer only ambiguities: 'We'll be there on the day' or 'We've always been Labour', with the 'but' silent. I've filled many dustbins and forgotten to close too many gates, but I loved meeting the people in all their perversities.

In 1977, the Grimsby Labour Party had felt itself side-lined by the professionals trundled in for the by-election. In the 1979 election, it took back control and showed itself to be a well-oiled, efficient machine. No gilded coach this time – it was foot slog all the way – but party members helped enthusiastically, people seemed to listen and Lil Bontoft (queen of the Co-op) organised the traditional 'carvalcade': a huge procession of cars with decorations, balloons and loudspeakers, all trundling behind me in my open car with Lil announcing, 'Grimsby is a Labour Town, keep Grimsby Labour,' over and over again. It demonstrated Labour's power and boosted morale. Our loudspeakers blasting out 'My Truly Truly Fair' (which Lil assured me Crosland had loved) may have annoyed the shift workers and kept babies awake, but the reception was exciting. Crowds came out and kids ran alongside.

The carvalcade was a Grimsby tradition which we used at every subsequent election. Sometimes it was chaotic, when the lead car led us into a cul-de-sac. Sometimes it was expensive, like when I buckled the roof of the car I was standing in. Sometimes it was a triumph, as when Seth Armstrong from *Emmerdale* came and proved more popular than me. Sometimes it was sad, when older cars broke down and had to be left behind steaming. We did it until 2010, when 'Truly Fair' was worn out.

1979 was a triumph for me, though not for Labour. My meetings were packed, and even attended by the Tory candidate, his wife and constituency chair. Ladies from Harrogate poured in, packed into Wallace Arnold coaches, to warn Grimsby that I was a Yorkshireman. The rumour that Linda was Arthur Scargill's sister (despite being a New Zealander) was circulated assiduously. Supporters came from New Zealand, Australia and South Africa. The latter told me that Nunsthorpe was worse than Soweto, but I kept quiet about that. I got the vote back up to Crosland levels but then had to sit in the town hall watching the roll call of my new friends in Parliament who were being thrown out. No Labour MP was left between Grimsby and London.

The next election, 1983, was awful. Michael Foot was leader, so I featured only Denis Healey on my leaflets. The Tory candidate was a nasty piece of work, the only one they ever picked. He called my wife 'a shit' but turned out to be one himself. The SDP split away, taking our party secretary, Paul Genney, with it. He went, assuring me that we'd always be friends and that he'd never stand against me, then stood as SDP candidate for Grimsby.

It was unusually bitter. Genney's posters appeared all over our areas. My publicity hit a high point when I went down early in the morning to lobby fishermen landing their vessels in the fish dock. There was a bigger Icelandic vessel in at the same time. Linda, bored with my harangues, strolled over to it, only to be hosed down by port security, who thought she was a lady of the night come to service the crew rather than the vessel. So much for their appreciation of London fashion. The story about the MP's wife accused of prostitution hit the front page of *The Sun*. It did me no end of good.

My friends came up to help. Micky went round the town awing people by telling them about how he'd been Churchill's constituency secretary, adding, 'Winston would have liked Austin Mitchell.' Shaun, who had an even posher accent, we sent round the Tory areas, where he explained the faults of the common market but came back every night utterly depressed about Labour's chances. As he sank into ever-deeper gloom, he persuaded me to write to Michael Foot suggesting that he should hand over to Denis Healey. I shouldn't have done it. It was pretty daft but I was anxious and at that time I didn't have any better judgement. I naively thought that Labour could make such a sensible change. I'd been appalled by film of Michael carried through Holmfirth by two aged MPs, pursued by baying hounds. So I wrote. I don't suppose Michael got the letter, though he stood down immediately after the election result. That was a bit late for me.

The end was painful. When Paul came third, he objected to our return on grounds of overspending. The main parties regularly over-spend, particularly at by-elections, but never protest at the other side because they know it would unleash a tit-for-tat contest. The SDP had no such inhibitions. Paul had been told he'd win by the local NOP pollster on her sample of twenty. Because no one had told the Co-op Bank that he was no longer Labour secretary, he was getting our bank statements. We had overspent, though by a trivial amount, but in those days an objection required the accused to prove everything to the court. Paul, a local genius who'd changed from dentist to barrister, deployed his newly acquired legal skills to the full. He didn't achieve his ambi-tion of getting me disqualified, but my agent, a Grimsby docker, was tried and fined £8,000. Nobody emerged well.

In 1987 and 1992, Grimsby politics reverted to pattern. The SDP surge petered out, as flashes in our two-party pan always will. The de-serters never came back, but their vote did. My majority returned to normal and I began to drive round shouting at people through powerful loudspeakers. Eric Clements, Grimsby's almost tame anti-European, decided he could destroy the common market with my loudspeakers and built a large silver fish which was mounted on the top of my car with huge boards promising to save Britain's fish. The silver fish later disappeared from the Labour Party offices, taken, Eric claimed, by Euro-vandals. Possibly by agents of the Commission.

Eric was my companion on speaker tours, though his repertoire was limited to stentorian calls to 'Get Britain out', assuming that everyone knew what we were to get out of. I decided to intersperse these with some songs, but Eric insisted on his favourite piece of folk music. This turned out to be a dirge about eighty dead fishermen, which had a somewhat depressing effect. So I replaced it with a bouncy piece of music from New Zealand Labour's successful 1984 election campaign.

Wonderful music and a good message, but every time the refrain of 'Labour for New Zealand' came up, I had to fade the sound down and shout, 'Labour for Grimsby'.

Elections began to change, even in Grimsby, where traditional practices and class divisions lingered longer than in the trendy south. Attendance at meetings fell and I grew tired of haranguing two or three bored party workers. There was less door-to-door canvassing, because the Tories particularly were doing more of it by phone. Church meetings continued and were as well attended as ever, but the national media lost interest as Grimsby became a safe seat. I got so little coverage, even in the *Grimsby Telegraph*, that I began to feel I'd have to drop dead in the street to get a mention. Even then they'd have kept the obituary back until after the election unless the other candidates had agreed to a group suicide.

Where the town had been one community, now social differentiation was hardening. The council estates were no longer solidly Labour, as the best homes were sold, many to be sold on to unscrupulous absentee landlords who bought houses at auctions and put in rougher tenants on housing benefit, increasing the costs and undermining the community. Areas in desperate need of repairs declined until they were almost no-go zones, with the result that bricks were thrown at my car on Yarborough estate and bottles were thrown in Guildford Street. My daughter, Hannah, was terrified. I was puzzled to understand why people should react in that fashion when I was trying to bring them a message of hope and improvement. The sullen mood was lightened in 1992 when I was canvassing a prostitute through her window as a client came in and started taking his trousers off. I'm still not sure whether I got a vote from either of them.

More dispiritingly, the Labour Party head office began to assert tighter central control. Where before I'd designed and written my own leaflets, now they were imposed by templates which left little space for personal views, though I managed to squeeze in withdrawal from the EU and an end to the Common Fisheries Policy. National figures, who hadn't come since 1979, continued not to come. Even the union leaders, who had come before, stopped visiting Grimsby, while their local officials took little part, the TGWU officer supporting the Lib Dems. We were less and less Grimsby Labour, more Blair's representatives on earth. I became his High Commissioner for Grimsby, a job as important as Governor of the Falklands is to the Crown.

Less fun. More hard work. Fewer cottage meetings. Soon no meetings at all, because no one came. No television excitement. Door-to-door activity declined as the party membership shrank, so fewer people got any personal contact with the party or the candidate. Once leader debates began, bringing people to the door to be canvassed in the evening was impossible. Canvassing interrupted the real campaign, which was coming over on TV. The old form of canvassing – 'You're going to vote Labour, aren't you?' – was replaced by a questionnaire, which almost ran to the extent of how their grandparents had voted and what they thought of Gladstone, to compile a 'voter ID'. Which we then didn't have the manpower to use on polling day. Later on, much of the campaigning went onto Facebook, which I didn't and couldn't use, though I did post long election blogs which no one read. Fortunately, the local Tories hadn't heard of Cambridge Analytica and, being Grimsby, couldn't afford them anyway.

I felt I was on my own. If only because I was. 2010 was the least happy election, as well as my last. Linda was being treated for breast cancer and took a smaller part. Bigger areas went uncanvassed. Brown and the Great Recession threw Labour on the defensive and the national debates on television took the steam out of local campaigns. I was slower, stiff and ponderous.

I canvassed less and even shouted less through the loudspeaker. Worst of all, the alienation from both major parties led to Cleggmania, which produced a surge in support for piggy in the middle, and the Lib Dems, at 22 per cent, took votes mainly from us. So did UKIP and the BNP, at a combined total of 10.8 per cent. Victoria Ayling, the Conservative, who later defected to UKIP, rented a property in the town, announced that she was going to send her kids to school there and joined the chamber of commerce. She fought the most energetic Tory campaign we'd ever seen. My vote fell back to the levels of 1983, when the SDP had surged. But then I had been younger and more resilient; now I couldn't help feeling it was all a consequence of age.

Instead of returning to Westminster from my four-week holiday in reality reinvigorated, I trudged back to work. The old warmth from the constituency seemed to be cooling. The excitement wasn't quite there. I didn't go back refreshed and confident as I'd always done before. MPs like to be loved and elections influence their confidence. Somehow, it wasn't fun any more. A disastrous symptom for any populist, and the prelude to my least happy parliament, struggling against the worst government of my time.

CHAPTER TEN

THE EU: MY PART IN ITS DOWNFALL

first stumbled across the common market, as the European Union then called itself, towards the end of 1962. The history department at the University of Otago in New Zealand organised a series of public lectures to demonstrate our skills. Mine was unmemorable, marred by the fact that the Bolshoi Ballet was performing the same night and the Governor General was giving his farewell reception. No one turned up to hear my words of wisdom. The next day, rather more did for my colleague Keith Jackson's lecture on the common market. To my horror, he endorsed it as 'a good thing'. Incredible. Almost blasphemy. Britain led the Commonwealth. New Zealand was its antipodean farm. Europe was there for us to defeat in war. How could an Englishman be so daft? No one brought up on the *Daily Express* could feel any different.

De Gaulle agreed with me and dismissed Macmillan's efforts to join a club he should never have applied for in the first place. I was further comforted when a succession of British politicians, some of whom I interviewed on television, came out to New Zealand to assure us that if Britain did join this alien institution then, scout's honour,

New Zealand's access to the British market would be protected. The old relationship would carry on.

They lied. Albion can be perfidious and was particularly so when it betrayed New Zealand. Back in Britain, I voted 'no' to the common market in the 1975 referendum just like Mary Wilson, who told me that she and Harold had gone into the booth together. She'd voted 'no'. He'd voted 'yes' and they came out smiling and waving. A united couple. My hostility increased when I was elected MP for Grimsby, whose fishing industry, ruined by the loss of Iceland, had not been allowed to rebuild within British waters because the Europeans had cunningly declared them common waters and given other members, even landlocked Luxembourg, equal access, just before we began negotiations to join. Fish were a common resource to be doled out by Brussels. They ensured that we got only a small proportion of our own fish.

There was more to my scepticism about Europe than a lingering desire to get back to the empire or to catch our own fish. I believed, and still do, that the nation state is not only the best but the only way of advancing the cause of the people while maintaining their democratic control of the process. There is nothing the EU can do for us that we can't do better for ourselves, because Europe, unless it becomes a genuine federal state like the USA, is not only too big but amorphous, divided and powerless. Like Viscount Castlereagh's view of the Holy Alliance, I saw it as a piece of sublime mysticism and nonsense. Not a democracy but a plutocracy with a powerless Parliament and a rootless bureaucracy always pursuing an ever-closer union the people didn't want, yet never able to reach it. The EU is a mirage, luring on but never delivering. It drained Britain but offered hope to those despairing of their own country and to politicians who found Britain's problems intractable. They couldn't succeed at home but could still win public relations victories on the bigger stage.

Europe is very attractive for those who don't like Britain, and for the liberal intellectuals and many of our elite, who saw themselves as cosmopolitan rather than nationalist, internationalists rather than insular unsophisticates, Europe was nicer than their brutal, xenophobic compatriots. Those suffering in Britain, the unions, local government and the Labour Party came to love the beguiling hopes Europe held out for them. They didn't see that it had no ability to help lame dogs over stiles and could only offer hopes that couldn't be fulfilled and gratitude for handouts that were really the nation's own money back with the EU's heavy costs taken out. Euro-hopes sprang eternal but never came, because the EU couldn't break away from its original purpose of protecting French agriculture and boosting German industry. These two states dominated Europe, which had embarked on a journey where few wanted to go, to an ever-closer union only the Brussels bureaucrats desired, imposing policies without democratic consent and ever prepared to overrule the people for their own good.

The fact that we'd gone in on bad terms and were condemned to constantly struggling uphill to get a better deal wasn't, however, my basic reason for opposing membership. That was economic. Europe is a drain on the British economy, not a boost. Before entry, enthusiasts had told us that there were strong political reasons for joining but the economic arguments were more finely balanced. Pure nonsense. The political gain was minor because the Franco-German axis continued to dominate and they were unlikely to allow change to suit us, but the economic consequences of joining an organisation that is weighted against us and isn't designed to give a sucker an even break were damaging. The European Union drained Britain of jobs, money, demand and growth. It became a brake on our economy, not an accelerator.

Being a deal between the interests of Germany, which needed a bigger market for its manufacturing, and France, which wanted agricultural protection for its food, it didn't suit Britain, a net agricultural importer with a less modern and less well-invested industry. Ted Heath was so eager to get in that he had joined on less than favourable terms, meaning that we were asking to be clobbered and duly were.

Contrary to the optimistic forecasts of captains of industry like Donald Stokes, our goods didn't conquer Europe, but European and particularly German production swamped our market. No one had understood that it's easier to penetrate a small market from a large one than vice versa. The basis of British trade had been buying cheap food, particularly from Commonwealth countries, and sending them our manufactured goods in return. That stopped after entry to the common market. The Common Agricultural Policy (CAP) required us to buy France's more expensive food. Costs went up and every family of four lost £20 a week.

Labour's effective regional policy, the Regional Employment Premium, had to be scrapped because it was against the rules. What had been a surplus in our trade with Europe before we went in became a steadily growing deficit. Our membership contributions, our payments for being damaged, went up year by year, draining money to Europe, particularly to the powerful German economy, which generated ever-bigger surpluses at the expense of everyone else and particularly us. To cap all this, Europe's fast growth, which enthusiasts had claimed Britain would hitch up to, slowed substantially.

All this ensured that the attack on the common market played a large part in my 1977 by-election campaign and an even bigger one in the 1979 election, when my friend David Lange, the future premier of New Zealand, joined me on a soapbox outside the Bird's Eye factory to denounce Brussels. Attack is always better than defence in politics. Given the economic difficulties of Labour's years, there wasn't much else to attack on.

I could sum up my attitude to the European Union in four words, three of which were 'the European Union'. In Parliament, I joined the Labour common market safeguards campaign, which then had the support of a majority of Labour MPs. I was enthusiastic about the commitment to withdraw in our 1983 manifesto. I formed Save Britain's Fish, which attracted support from all over the country, particularly Scotland, and from many MPs, though Edwina Currie wrote back to tell us, 'You don't want to save Britain's fish. You just want to eat them.' Which of course was true, but far better for us to process and eat them than have them gobbled by undeserving Europeans who took the jobs and the processing industry with them. I went to Iceland and Norway to urge them not to join and to Denmark to warn them not to join the euro, and was modestly happy to see that all three adopted my view. Britain, for some incomprehensible reason, didn't.

My views remained unchanged as the common market grandiosed into the European Community, then the European Union, much more impressive and friendlier-sounding titles than a mere market. The EU also began the most effective and powerful advertising and public relations campaign since the launch of fabulous pink Camay in the 1950s. Then, every household had been given a free bar of soap. Now, the EU doled out soft soap, setting out to transform its image from the capitalist plot and agricultural protection society which Labour had once seen it as, into a benign social union dedicated to protecting British trade unions wearied by the struggle against cuts and neoliberalism imposed by right-wing governments.

Labour, losing confidence in itself and its mission of building socialism in one country, was very susceptible to this treatment. Major figures from Roy Jenkins to Peter Mandelson and leading trade union officials went to Brussels, prospered and came back to proclaim Europe's benefits. The social compact seemed to offer better prospects than another social contract of the type that had failed in the '70s. The party's Euro MPs, mostly Eurosceptics led by Barbara Castle, were purged and replaced by enthusiasts who used their propaganda allowances to propagate the faith. Busloads of Labour Party members were carted off to Brussels to see its wonders, and Labour's leaders found a bigger and better stage to strut on, where people actually listened to them rather than dismissing them out of hand, which was Margaret Thatcher's approach.

The trade unions, tied down by Tory laws, battered by government hostility and losing both members and influence, were won over by the EU President, Jacques Delors, and his promises of legislation on workers' rights and all sorts of other improvements beyond the frigid hostility Margaret Thatcher offered. Trade union leaders went on pilgrimage and some, starting with Jack Peel of the Dyers and Bleachers, then senior figures like John Monks of the TUC, took jobs in Brussels, becoming advocates of what their movement had once opposed.

Local authorities, starved of funds and powers by Tory cuts and centralisation, were invited to send delegations to Brussels to plead their case and were given promises and grants, neither of which was available from Westminster. Twinning with clean, wholesome European cities became a more accessible alternative to relationships with poverty-stricken dumps in the Commonwealth. Special assistance like the Coal Fields Community funding poured money into areas depressed by the home government. Projects carried hoardings announcing that they were funded by the EU, without saying that the money came out of British taxpayers' pockets.

Bingo! It worked. Mrs Thatcher claimed that her greatest success was to have converted Labour to neoliberalism. Europe's was to have converted Labour to Euro enthusiasm, in the biggest conversion since St Augustine. Neil Kinnock sent his family to work in Europe and began the process of rapprochement. His successors, Smith, Blair and Brown, were enthusiasts, while middle-class party members began to view it with an almost religious enthusiasm. So much nicer than the frustrating, uphill teaching job of changing Britain. Europe came near to eclipsing social democracy as a system of belief. Vested interests established themselves; those suffering, like manufacturing, declined. It was all built on hope rather than delivery, prospects rather than performance, but then so is the European Union. A party of progress is about hope. It brightened Labour lives in the misery of impotent opposition, and a party of internationalism saw the opportunity to pursue at least some of its objectives through Europe as it became weaker. When losing in Britain, it's always nice to have friends in Brussels.

Our safeguards campaign continued to criticise the flow of regulations from Brussels and to argue that we could do better for ourselves than we could get in Europe, but MPs began to withdraw support. The long list of names on our letterhead shrank to a handful as the ambitious conformed to the new religion. Strong supporters like Peter Shore, Douglas Jay and Lord Bruce died and Lord Stoddart was expelled from the party. The flow of union subscriptions and donations shrank. We struggled on, becoming a sect rather than the broad church we had been.

Soon, the issue was whether Britain should join the Exchange Rate Mechanism (ERM). Here, I was able to make a valuable contribution by chairing a subcommittee of the Treasury Select Committee to inquire into membership. I appointed Shaun Stewart, a brilliant retired official of the Board of Trade, as adviser. With him, I steered the committee to a report recommending against joining.

In vain. Gordon Brown was purging the Treasury Committee of troublemakers like Diane Abbott and Brian Sedgemore. He refused to let me back on after I'd stood down to take the frontbench job (where he hadn't wanted me either). My replacement, Giles Radice, a more enthusiastic Euro-creep, chaired another inquiry. This endorsed membership.

Gordon Brown, who had supported the Eurosceptics when our cause was fashionable and spoken at Labour Common Market Safeguards conference meetings, changed his mind, decided to ignore all our warnings and commit Labour to joining the Exchange Rate Mechanism. He told the PLP that it would give him the exchange rate stability he needed to build socialism. It was difficult to see how anyone who had seen the follies of 'stop-go' produced by defending a fixed exchange rate could make such a claim, but Gordon ignored all the lessons of the old exchange rate regime, which had forced Britain into stop-go by its periodic requirements to defend the pound by putting up interest rates. Nor did he seem to understand that Britain would inevitably be crippled by going in at anything like the existing rate, which was overvalued but which the government, the Bank of England and the Europeans would insist on maintaining.

Gordon's conversion to the ERM cause made it easier for John Major to join the mechanism, but the decision to go in was a disaster. Fortunately, the collapse of the whole system destroyed faith in Tory economic competence as well as giving a clear warning of the dangers of fixed exchange rates and servile compliance to Europe. Britain was forced out humiliatingly, George Soros made billions, Gordon fell silent and the Liberals, who'd been demanding a move to even narrower bands, looked more than usually silly. We sceptics heaved a sigh of relief, forgetting the propensity of dogs to return to their own vomit, which now led the EU to turn to an even stronger monetary union by creating the common currency, the euro.

Unable to get electoral support for ever-closer union, the EU bureaucracy used the euro as a way of smuggling union in through the back door. A common currency, they hoped, would lead to convergence and develop the central institutions necessary to manage it. Tony Blair, daft as a Liberal and a sucker for anything that would demonstrate his Euro-enthusiasm, was passionately in favour. Not understanding economics, he didn't realise that Britain would be shackled by a fixed, and inevitably overvalued, exchange rate, with consequences ruinous for our weaker economy. Fortunately, Gordon, advised now by Ed Balls, had learned the lesson of his ERM mistake. This time he saw the dangers and managed to think up five tests, failure in any of which would deny entry until the time was ripe. Which, in my view, it never would be. So, Britain remained committed to go in maybe, sometime, never, but this was only a pretence. We stayed out, which made us peripheral to the EU's great adventure into the clouds. All action in the EU now concentrated on the Eurozone, from which we were excluded. This turned out to be an inestimable benefit. A single currency without a single government is unworkable. It forces deflation on weaker and less competitive partners, one of whom would have been us, but has no machinery for redistribution. It punishes those like Greece who can't keep up to German levels of competitiveness and inflation. They're forced to cut costs and deflate in the hope of getting down to German levels of inflation instead of devaluing as the French and Italians had done in the past to maintain growth. It starts by showering the weaker economies with money, because lenders assume that the euro guarantees repayment. Then it cripples them with unsustainable and unrepayable debt, as they find that it doesn't because the Germans won't allow it, and any grudging help that is forthcoming goes to save the banks, not the nation, as the EU refuses to write national debts down. The Germans won't allow such irresponsibility.

Staying out was a victory for sense, but not for our dwindling crew of Eurosceptics. We tried to recover with a demand for a referendum. We'd campaigned for one on the Maastricht Treaty. Now we began to argue for one on the EU's new constitution. When the constitution was vetoed by votes in France and Sweden, the Commission switched tactics and imposed the same document under a new name, calling it the Lisbon Treaty. Blair and Miliband promptly argued that this was a new document, and a treaty didn't require a public vote, a devious dodge which took us back to the deadlock. So our demand was now for a referendum on membership itself. Clegg, who thought he was turning off the heat under the Lisbon Treaty by demanding an in/out referendum, stumbled into joining us.

As the EU became more fashionable in the Labour Party, the costs of membership were becoming excessive. Blair gave away some of Mrs Thatcher's hard-won rebate, and membership costs reached £11 billion by 2016 – the second highest payment in exchange for the fewest benefits. The trade deficit rose to £80 billion in 2016 because the single market is designed to serve the agricultural purposes of France and the industrial dominance of Germany, not Britain's comparative advantage in services, the only one of the 'four freedoms' (movement of capital, people, trade and services) which hadn't been fully implemented. The costs of the CAP added another £15 billion, totalling a loss of around £100 billion, all paid across the exchanges by a nation which, by that stage, was borrowing and selling assets to pay it.

The euro mired the EU economy in deflation. All over Europe, unemployment was high, with a quarter of the EU's young people out of work. Germany's insistence on building up huge surpluses, which it didn't spend or recycle to the less successful economies, was leading to balance of payment problems in deficit countries like Britain and debt crises for euro members, most strikingly in Bailoutistan – Greece – which was harshly punished because Germany refused to write off its massive debts, which could never be repaid.

The EU was losing its shine and becoming deadlocked, unable to move forward, unwilling to go back. It could only move forward by greater federalism to create 'ever-closer union' as a straitjacket, but the members didn't want that. It needed the economic institutions of the nation state to manage the euro, but the Germans couldn't accept that. It was hit by the refugee crisis and couldn't agree on what to do about it. The euro could only work if there was redistribution, but Germany wouldn't accept that. It could possibly have conciliated British public opinion by delivering benefits to Britain. But it wouldn't and didn't. It was deadlocked, rudderless and dominated by Mrs Merkel, the most cautious politician in Europe.

Britain was still clinging to the edge of the rickety raft, but interest there focused on the Eurozone. We had little influence. The polls showed that the public was unhappy. Our contributions were rising while everything within Britain was being cut. To compound all this, the economy was doing badly. Our trade deficit (most of it with the EU) was one of the highest in the advanced world at 5 per cent of

GDP and rising. The pound was kept up by the steady sale of assets, companies, utilities and property, and the borrowing necessary to finance the deficit. We were exporting demand, bearing higher interest rates to pay for it, and financing the German surplus, thus creating a vicious circle in which we had to sell everything to pay our way but the sales pushed the pound up further, crippling exports and boosting imports. This was compounded by the membership costs of the organisation doing much of the damage.

Yet the public were told to be happy with this developing disaster, and a Euro-enthusiastic government did nothing about it. That is, until an overconfident David Cameron buckled to pressure in his own party and announced that he would solve his party problems by replaying the trick Labour had perfected in 1975: holding a renegotiation followed by a referendum to endorse an improved EU membership. He reminded the EU that he was a winner and asked for changes to make the EU more acceptable in Britain. He got nothing worth having but still embarked on what he confidently assumed would be an easy victory. To his amazement and that of all Britain's elite, he lost. The British electorate, two thirds of whom had voted for entry in 1975, had changed its mind after four decades of austerity, neoliberalism and deindustrialisation.

The referendum provided the opportunity to achieve what elections couldn't. Parties turn to referendums only as a last resort, when they're too divided to take a decision. The question of EU membership had been central to the way the country had been run for forty years of comparative failure, and part of the medicinal cocktail of EU requirements, neoliberalism, globalisation and austerity which had been prescribed for Britain and administered in lavish doses. The educated and the liberal middle classes who had suffered less and didn't particularly like their own people had come to identify with Europe as part of their privileged way of life, and supported a union they saw as the symbol of enlightened internationalism and civilised (i.e. their own) values. The less well-off, the less educated and the people who'd been left behind felt different.

In our non-existent constitution, Parliament, not the people, is the home of sovereignty. This works well as long as the politicians stay in tune with the people and the government takes care to consider and represent them. After decades of cuts, austerity, stagnant living standards and economic failure, people and Parliament were out of kilter. Inevitably, then, when a deadlocked government asked the nation to endorse the wisdom of its leaders, the people took the opportunity to express their unhappiness by blowing a raspberry at Europe, the politicians, Parliament, globalisation and the whole caboodle.

Consternation. Britain's elite were shocked by the nation's rejection of their wisdom and advice. Orwell remarked that 'England is perhaps the only great country whose intellectuals are ashamed of their own nationality'. That remained true of the liberal intellectuals, who'd given up on Britain and saw Europe as the future. For the people to reject the EU just showed how irredeemable the British were. It was, as they saw it, a surrender to racism, xenophobia, insularity and everything liberal intellectuals dislike in their own people.

On the other hand, Eurosceptics like me saw the vote as the result of a forty-year learning experience. The people had voted for membership in 1975 because then they were fairly contented, and referendums are weighted to the status quo. Since then, they'd not been happy with the harder, meaner society neoliberalism had built. So, in another referendum, which also favoured the status quo, they rejected the policies that had governed them since.

This made it a vote about Britain and what kind of society the two sides wanted to see, something not to be settled quickly or easily, because it required the rejection of four decades of failed policy. Having opposed the first referendum, the Remainers began to demand another to allow the electorate to stand on its head. They denounced the vote as the result of fear, ignorance, Russian deceit and Cambridge Analytica's manipulation, and unleashed another, even bigger tide of fear about the consequences. They did everything they could to discredit the British case for withdrawal, to shackle, soften and weaken the government's negotiating position and to collude with the EU to resist it, in the hope that eventually the people would give up their foolishness and stay, unhappily or not, in the promised land. Those with a divine right to rule don't give up easily.

The Brexiteers, in contrast, could only wait and see, hoping for a good outcome which can't emerge until negotiations end. The British government has been weakened by its second election and Remain's long rearguard action. The EU is unyielding because twenty-seven nations find it easier to just say 'no' and to pursue grievances, such as Spain's on Gibraltar or Ireland's on Ulster, though, surprisingly, not Greece's on the Elgin Marbles. The Commission, struggling to keep its rickety show on the road to the mirage of ever-closer union, and facing unmanageable difficulties in Eastern Europe and Italy, wants to punish Britain *pour décourager les autres*. These are the symptoms of an impossible negotiation. Yanis Varoufakis's account of the way the EU crushed Greece's aspirations by intransigence, delay and simple bloody-mindedness is a telling tale of what's to come, but now I can only heckle from the sidelines.

CHAPTER ELEVEN

THE LITTLE TOWN THAT SANTA CLAUS FORGOT

Grimsby is the best of constituencies and the worst of constituencies. The best because it's still a genuine community, not a slice of somewhere bigger; a borough in its boundaries, not a job lot of villages rammed together to make up the numbers. Isolation gives it pride, an identity and a sense of community, but a beleaguered one. New fashions come late to Grimsby. Old verities and attitudes linger. It's neither metropolitan smart nor trendy, but it's comfortable, a good place to live and less expensive. My predecessor, Tony Crosland, had always taken it as his measure of the real world. So did I. But given the rise of the big cities, metropolitan London and the more prosperous south, it was a real version of an older country.

Yet Grimsby can also be the worst. It's underprivileged educationally and socially and below most national averages. Those who'd made big money there had taken it away rather than endowing their hometown with facilities as the wealthy woolmen did in the West Riding. It had been deeply damaged by the loss of its basic industry, distant water fishing, just before I arrived, a disaster greater and more cataclysmic than any of those later to come as Britain deindustrialised. It has neither recovered fully nor got its fair share of help, support and investment to rebuild. Its people die younger and smoke more. Unemployment, particularly for young people, is worse. Too many move to where the jobs are, and others work away, coming home at weekends. Grimsby has more underprivileged wards and people than most parts of the UK. Definitely not Waitrose country.

For the MP, there's the additional complication that it's 200 miles from London, with inadequate road and rail connections. Only late in my career did I learn that more than two hours' driving a day damages both heart and brain. But I already knew that it wastes a lot of an MP's life, the only consolation being that because people die earlier in the north, I may have extended my lifespan by going south four days a week.

Grimsby's first MPs were elected in the 1290s. Parliament then met in Lincoln so Grimsby didn't have to pay travelling costs to Westminster. Since then it has provided an electoral base for local merchants, resident bigwigs, anyone who could afford big enough bribes and whoever the Earl of Yarborough cared to put into his pocket borough. It expected, and got, little from its MPs (except bribes, for it was a notoriously corrupt borough), but it preferred them local. The last two Tory MPs, a merchant and a jam manufacturer, were both local businessmen.

After 1945, they were followed by two distinguished Labour MPs from the political elite, both of whom lived in London. By the time I was elected, the job was changing as the MP's role became more mundane and Members were required to be social workers and local ombudsmen. The constituency became less of a stepping stone to power, more demanding, expecting its MP to listen, serve, succour, dance attendance on and defend it in the competitive battle for jobs, support, investment and development as growth turned into a zero-sum competition. Schizophrenia became a lifestyle for MPs, straddling two sets of demands, miles apart. Westminster with its parliamentary role, whips and responsibilities, is the mistress. The constituency, with its demands for time and attention, is the wife, served, loved and occasionally hated, but never satisfied.

Some MPs, particularly the perpetually insecure Liberals, are especially assiduous in devoting time and effort to the constituency and pounding pavements rather than Parliament. At the opposite extreme, others huddle and hunker in Westminster, where the political action is and where ambitions are realised. Some even seem so afraid to go out into the world that they hover round the building even when Parliament isn't meeting in the long summer recess. I rarely went there then, but when I did I always found a few troglodytes using the facilities.

London MPs can manage the two roles easily because of their proximity. The rest must travel miles to be present at constituency functions, serve local groups, and open fêtes. It was said of US President Herbert Hoover that he would attend the opening of a drawer. Some British MPs would attend the opening of a whole chest, each drawer pictured on Twitter. Collectively, MPs are now the opener, speaker, ribbon-cutter and visitor of last resort.

For most MPs, the constituency is to be treasured like a Patek Philippe watch: not theirs to own, but something to hand on to the next generation, preferably to another member of the same party. It's their base, their roots in the real world and their contact with reality. The days when an MP could neglect their constituency to live in Crete or represent Oldham from Scotland, as Jim Lamond did, are over. Even ministers facing heavy demands in London must make time to do surgeries and attend functions to remind people that they're still alive. Don Concannon found his ministerial security guard particularly useful in the constituency, where they were often the only audience at his election meetings. Which may be why Roy Mason hung on to his bodyguard long after everyone else had given theirs up.

An early part of my acclimatisation process was to be taught how to behave on royal visits. Bow, don't touch the Queen's bottom (you're not in Australia), address her as 'ma'am' and don't try to sell her anything – all useful things to know in the rich tapestry of Grimsby life. The town loves royalty, though this had its practical side, as I found out on a later visit by the Prince of Wales. A Cleethorpes restaurant owner put a ribbon across the door, handed the passing prince a pair of scissors to cut it, and put up a plaque saying his joint had been opened by HRH Prince Charles – an accolade even Le Gavroche doesn't have. Royal visits were fewer after the royal yacht was decommissioned, when it could no longer sail up the river to Grimsby. When I expressed my sadness at this, the Duke of Edinburgh tersely replied, 'Who scrapped the bloody thing?' Labour, of course. However, Princess Anne and the Duchess of Cambridge have been assiduous in coming by car and doing their duty by Grimsby. I hope they enjoyed it.

The balance between constituency and Westminster has swung to the constituency. Parties began to turn to local sons and daughters rather than picking Members from among a national elite, preferring local roots to IQ. The days when MPs could be greeted by the station master on their rare visits to their constituency have gone. Most MPs now live locally and have offices and staff there.

My start in Grimsby was auspicious. I was welcomed by a party desperate to win. The *Political Register* forecast that it was mine for life. But Grimbarians aren't demonstrative.

I lived there, sent my kids to school there and performed regularly at Grimsby's functions, but I never felt quite accepted. Like my colleagues, I proclaimed my love for the town. It was genuine, though never quite reciprocated. Grimsby's too phlegmatic for warm affection, prefers its own to incomers and doesn't, for some reason I could never quite fathom, like Yorkshiremen. Probably this is because of the old fishing rivalry with Hull, though it may also have something to do with the charm of Leeds United supporters on their rare visits to the town. I felt it best to keep quiet about my Yorkshire origins and my output of Yorkshire jokebooks, but they were always held against me, and long after the graffiti promising 'death to all Icelandic bastards' had faded, others appeared warning Yorkies to prepare their coffins. Indeed, forty years later, when the anniversary of my first election came around, my Liberal opponent of 1977, a councillor born in Guyana, lamented that I was really an itinerant Yorkshireman who 'never really used to live in Grimsby'. By that time I was vainly trying to sell the lovely Grimsby house in which I never used to live. No one has bought it. Before that, my occasional jokes about me being Grimsby's immigrant problem always produced a sullen silence in a town that didn't seem to want any at all.

Few votes are won by devotion to the constituency or its people, but many can be lost by criticising or discounting it. Early on, Iris Critten cheered me up by bawling her thanks across the road for getting her a catheter bag, though my hopes that she'd shout it everytime I saw her were disappointed. Many wrote thank-you letters, though I don't think the assistance I gave won me any votes. Most of those who are helped have forgotten it by polling day. When they say they'll vote for you if you help them, they're probably lying. I'd once done a day's surgery with the leader of the New Zealand Labour Party. At the end of the day, he checked his customers in the marked-up register. Most of those who'd avowed their loyalty to Labour hadn't even voted. The result would be the same here. Most people coming to surgery are in the group that most needs help but is least likely to vote.

MPs regularly claim to have achieved this, that and a lot of the other for their constituency. From the leaflets they pour out, you'd assume the MP had brought in (or in Labour's case saved) hundreds of jobs and millions of pounds' worth of investment and made it a heaven on earth, though they paint a different picture when begging for help from ministers. Politics is the art of exaggeration, but to be described as a good constituency MP is considered a sign of failure, carrying the implication of being unpromotable and therefore out of the big game. I found it the most satisfying part of the job. It was my responsibility to help people. That was more important than ranting on about the iniquities of the Tory government, which were the cause of their misery.

The constituency is the MP's roots. It tells them what the people feel, though there's no way of knowing the balance of opinion in the constituency, so MPs tend to be like cushions, bearing the impress of whoever last sat on them. MPs are there to be sat on and the constituency tells them about the moods of real people. But most MPs still follow the party line wherever it leads, hoping for one of the knighthoods awarded for years of betraying their constituency to their party. Some are occasionally allowed to vote against their party on major closures, flood relief or other government vandalism, though not all do so. Craig Whittaker voted against more flood relief after his constituency had been flooded, which made him popular with the whips but less so in his constituency. With Elizabeth Peacock, it was the other way round. When she bravely supported the miners in their strike, she was roundly and publicly abused by the whips and removed from her post as a PPS, but admired in her constituency.

The local party is the key. Grimsby's was one of the best: loyal, moderate, trade union-dominated and pro-European. Its senior figures – Matt Quinn, a retired docker; Ivor Hanson, a union official; Alec Bovill and Muriel Barker, both later council leaders; and Margaret Darley, a former mayor – taught me the MP's craft, protected and helped me and showed me how to handle constituents and understand the constituency. They, and the party, saw their role as to support their MP, not to undermine him in the way some parties did, or to issue instructions in the way that became a problem later. My friend John Sever told horrifying tales about the way he was treated in Ladywood.

In Grimsby, lefties were few and discounted. When the Militants arrived, they didn't last long. Their leader was a friendly social worker who occasionally asked me to hide him in my car boot when I went over to Hull on the ferry. His supporters got themselves laughed at when they demanded that I live in a council house like the people. Rebuffed by common sense, they gave up in Grimsby and drifted off to Cleethorpes, always a more fertile ground for the left and a more erratic one than the solid and serious Grimsby party.

My general management committee included trade union officials, teachers, health workers, housewives and councillors. It became my tutor and guide, making a naive academic more realistic. The benefits were brought home early when I supported the continuation of Labour's incomes policy, only to be told by trade unionists that it wouldn't hold. Their members just wouldn't wear it. They were right. After that, I listened almost as much as I lectured, and the GMC was my guide to the problems and feelings of the town, the strains of the health service, the problems of the schools and the council, and the views of the workers. Its large and sensible membership were firmly rooted in the town and its people, and the local Labour council was focused on serving the local community. Local Labour parties, and Grimsby's in particular, then had a kind of collective wisdom and political nous that was an invaluable support to MPs.

Grimsby didn't have the deep, ingrained Labour traditions of the mining areas. Fishing had been barely unionised, workers in food processing were mainly women, and the Labour Party was more middle class and more docile than in Yorkshire. It wasn't a militant area and apart from the TGWU with the dockers and drivers, the unions were neither militant nor strong. Indeed, when I joined the GMB, as my predecessor had, the secretary lost the cheque for two years before they realised I was a member. Yet it did have an effective Labour council and a Labour Party used to power, battle-hardened and well run by men and women of great experience, many of them councillors. It was moderate in politics and had a big membership and a full-time agent – a retired docker, Matt Quinn, who was paid a whole £10 a week to run the office. Labour had served the town well in education and in development, bringing chemicals, oil, Dunlop and Courtaulds to the Humber Bank.

Like the Labour Party nationally, the Grimsby Labour Party changed. Mostly, not for the better. The experienced figures who'd selected me and taught me my craft passed on. The next generation of members were less wise and less experienced. The influence of the unions was broken as the dockers and the drivers were casualised, the graving dock and engineering services closed and full-time union officials lost interest. The councillors were weakened by the steady erosion of their powers and even more by the constant local government reorganisations facing an authority that didn't quite fit in anywhere and was constantly reshuffled by the creation and then abolition of Humberside, the closure of the Borough, amalgamation with Cleethorpes and a later straddle between two local enterprise partnerships. A Cleethorpes clique took over the successor council of North East Lincolnshire, purged the moderate leaders, turfed out sensible council officers and opted for defiance of government cuts, which landed them in a financial mess.

A row over whether to keep sixth forms lost us some of the teachers. The SDP revolt took away some of the moderate middle-class figures, including the party secretary. Trade unions, particularly the TGWU and the GMB, battled for control, but then lost interest and ceased to play a part. Councillors deserted – two to the Tories, two to the Liberals in a game of musical chairs usually caused by disputes over council selections. When the SDP and the Lib Dems surged, they drew deserters from Labour, though some came back as their bubble burst. Grimsby politics don't mean lifelong brand loyalty, and the loss of local government powers meant that the flow of mute inglorious Miltons into local politics dried up.

I failed in my responsibilities. Believing that I should avoid taking sides in local party arguments and personalities, I kept my hands off. I published regular newsletters and attended every meeting. I bailed them out financially and tried to boost membership by offering prizes for recruitment and support for those joining, all to no avail. Membership shrank from around 700 when I came in to 449 in 1990, 361 in 2000 and 170 by 2013. That decline was paralleled by local Labour parties all over the north. The older members who'd gone door to door to collect subscriptions died, and the national party began to demand payment by invoice for ever larger membership dues. This policy lost several members. As the party shrank, my office and I had to take on more responsibilities because the party was becoming a small group of activists and council seat seekers, not the efficient machine it had been.

My assumption that I had my job, the party had theirs and we should each get on with it became less relevant as the council lost power, government funding, functions and the ability to help their citizens. The party's vigour declined. Members aged and became less active. Experienced figures were replaced by cause-pushers, people who'd joined to become councillors, and transients who didn't attend. Some, who'd failed to get selected, left, while others were driven out by petty squabbles. Our strongest member, Alec Bovill, Mr Grimsby, mayor and council leader, was undermined by the Cleethorpes clique, lost his seat because of a silly squabble over allotments and died. Which left us like a tent without a pole. The party I handed over in 2015 was a shadow of its former strength. Weaker, less vigorous and more amenable to management by both the regional and the national organisation.

As membership fell, the local party became less useful in telling me about the community, keener to put the demands of identity politics first and peddle causes. Fortunately, long experience meant that I needed the party less and was better able to relate to Grimsby directly. People stopped me in the street to give me their views, or came to surgery to air their complaints, and organisations invited me to their functions to discuss their problems, needs and hang-ups. In the neoliberal years, hope became weaker and everything turned more negative as grumbling replaced enthusiasm. The town was a whirl of activity, but less of it was political.

Perhaps it's a result of isolation, but Grimsby produced more characters per acre than Hollywood. They gave the town life, interest and tales to tell. There was Dr Haddock, who streaked naked round the park, or monocle-wearing Eric Clements, a party member who claimed that he'd been instructed by the Communist Party to keep an eye on me. A former building worker, Eric had done up his house as a medieval castle, converting the dining room into a debating chamber. His wife, a statuesque blonde, was regularly paraded dressed as Britannia (or maybe Boudicca) in his anti-common market demonstrations. He was also a source of odd and interesting information, mostly about the iniquities of Europe but also about the new SA80 rifle, which he claimed was useless. I checked with Jonathan Aitken at the defence department and he assured me it was OK, but when I visited army units in Cyprus, they told me it jammed in desert conditions. Eric was right. The Grimsby party saw him as a bloody nuisance.

Another member, Mo Mendel, was an old rogue who tried to recruit me as his nocturnal witness to expose doping and bribery in horse-racing, which he claimed was going on in Tory Lincolnshire. His idea was that he would make a rendezvous with the cheats; I would provide enough £10 notes to wrap around sheets of newspaper, to create a wad that would deceive the dopers while I surreptitiously took their photographs (in the dark!). Mo pioneered the techniques of entrapment that later became common on television, but I declined, and lost what could have been a great opportunity as the Fake Sheikh of Parliament. Mo came regularly to Grimsby's civic functions to steal sandwiches. In 1983, he smashed the windscreen of the SDP's speaker van, though it didn't seem to stop the surge in their vote.

A Chinese student at the college came back month after month to tell me how to turn water into wine – or was it the other way round? Former fishermen took to painting and came to surgeries to sell me their productions. One, Mr Murray, painted on fibreboard, bringing ever bigger paintings as he demolished his garage and used the panels to paint on. I still have them, though they haven't increased in value.

Skipper's wife Dolly Hardie came almost every week to put the case for compensation for the fishermen and brought a series of complaints about Hull, immigrants and social security grants of cars, money, houses and travel costs to Muslims. There weren't many in Grimsby but she was sure they were all being provided with transport to a mosque in Skegness every week. She claimed that she had it all 'on good authority', which turned out to be the *Daily Mail*, but she always demanded that I investigate each alleged abuse personally.

Vasos Vasiliou was more fun, as he vainly struggled to right the wrong of bankruptcy that an incompetent lawyer had inflicted on him in the '60s. He also fought, more successfully, with HMRC over VAT, and with the banks. Vasos always provided an entertaining commentary when we started using his Greek restaurant as our work's canteen.

The most entertaining was Steve Hill, a flawed genius at social work. He ran a brilliant bingo hall in Nunsthorpe and gradually extended his activities into a Respect Centre, which took over a church, huddling the congregation into one end. At the other, Steve built a jungle gym and fun house to provide games, entertainment and fun for the deprived kids on the Nunsthorpe estate. This was far better than anything the youth service could do. He was supported by the police, won a series of grants, appeals and TV competitions and branched out into a dance troupe and go-kart racing. Crime fell, and the kids came in off the streets.

Steve took a busload of constituents to London to be addressed by his heroine, Louise Casey. Dame Louise Casey was at that time the government's head of the Respect Task Force and the Anti-Social Behaviour Unit. The morning after the talk, there was a hold-up. The bus had to be searched to recover all the sheets and towels stolen from the hotel. The church, which had initially supported him, lost faith and forced him to give up the centre. The bingo hall was closed. The church now stands empty. Nunsthorpe and God both lost out.

Eccentrics, a dying breed in the outside world, continued to flourish in Grimsby. They provided more fun and more work than Parliament ever could, and all of them helped to humanise this particular political prig by teaching a crash course in the problems of the real world. Yet that world too changed as Grimsby suffered. The town was deflated by depression. When I came, it had been cosmopolitan, with Jews whose families had arrived on their way to America and decided to stay, fishermen who'd worked in Greenland, wives who'd been to Iceland and Norway, Danes who'd come over in the war, bringing their boats, and the Ukrainians who'd come after it. Their New Year celebrations always left anyone who was no one in Grimsby in an alcoholic haze, until the community died out.

In the decline as fishing was run down, the young left for jobs elsewhere. All but one of my daughter's sixth form went south. Local businesses and pubs closed and the chains moved in, transferring managers and senior staff in and out of town. Freeman Street, once Grimsby's bustling Main Street, became a desert as every effort at regeneration failed. Shops closed. Ministers came, saw and did nothing. The last one caused me huge expense when, in driving him down the streets of closed shops, I drove into a Tory councillor's car, causing hundreds of pounds worth of damage.

Grimsby was hard hit by the decline of the one-industry towns that went on all over the north, but the blow it suffered had been both harder and more sudden than, say, wool in Bradford, because, hard as the life was, fishing had brought good money into the town and sustained not only a large number of jobs but a huge market and distribution system. The town needed a boost and new alternatives only government could provide. It didn't, leading to a wind-down of ancillary jobs in engineering, the decline of what had been the main shopping street, and lower levels of commercial development as local spending power declined. The town suffered with a stoic fatalism and government failed to do its duty. I invited the Monetary Policy Committee to come and look at our problems, and one of its members, DeAnne Julius, came. I brought the Agriculture Committee to look at fishing and asked ministers, both Labour and Tory, to come. None did. Both parties failed us – the Tories by doing nothing, Labour by lavishing its available resources, trams and goodies on the big cities, where the votes are.

To help win the by-election in 1977, the Labour government had given Grimsby development area status. Before it could attract industry, the incoming Thatcher government cancelled it. We were robbed of the Nissan plant that wanted to come to Humberside by a dirty trick by Norman Tebbit's department. As the civil service was cut back, functions were privatised, services were hit and instead of civil servants being transported out of London to places like Grimsby, local offices for tax, valuation and customs were transferred to Hull or Lincoln. New estates were built and the block council house vote was fragmented by right-to-buy. Privatisation shrank the unionised workforce. The old Labour bases of the dock labour scheme, the graving dock (which closed after trying for ages to sell a submarine it had reconditioned and moored in the harbour) and the power of the lorry drivers in a transport hub were either broken or eroded. Then, as a final blow, came the decline of retail, which closed Woolworths, Marks & Spencer, BHS and others, hitting the Freshney retail centre hard.

My work increased almost exponentially. My staff used my authority as MP to right wrongs and take issues up with departments, agencies, the council and businesses that produced problems for constituents. My view was that the constituent was always right. It wasn't always possible to prove that to recalcitrant departments, but it was usually possible to get an explanation and, in up to a third of cases, a change, a benefit or an accommodation. When private agencies took over services, there were more mistakes but more successes in reversing the original decision on appeal. Which meant a lot more work.

This was a new and growing role for MPs. I once came across the constituency file of a London MP in the '40s. It mainly consisted of efforts to get people telephones. In my time, the caseload covered everything except telephones. The end of full employment produced social security and benefit problems. Benefit suspensions and cuts produced debt problems. Unemployed building workers needed passports and retraining to get onto sites. Putting services out to private companies meant that they were badly run. Most of the new providers were grossly inefficient, being more concerned with profit than with protection. They all provided priority lines for MPs to complain, but few then rectified the complaints, which had to go to a long and slow process of appeal to the courts and official regulators. Changes in disability provision meant a lot more work and many more appeals. More complaints came from the health service, and getting people dental treatment under the NHS became desperate. All this was tackled by my skilled office team, who knew the rules much better than I.

The local party could no longer afford a paid secretary-agent. Joe Ashton told me this was for the best, as too many of his agents had worked harder to replace him than to help him. National pressure groups encouraged supporters to write to their MPs, often with pro forma letters (which some posted unaltered) to demand my views or support under threat of withdrawing their votes. It looked to me as though other parties were supplying critics with information about my every vote, and after every appearance on Russian or Iranian TV, local critics wrote in to ask how much Russian gold I'd been paid – though it could just be that Grimsby has some of the best-informed grumblers in the land.

As Thatcher's cuts became harsher, more work fell on MPs, but their powers were restricted. Privatisation of council housing meant that I could no longer get houses for the homeless, or even caravans in Cleethorpes. Social security reforms meant that I was no longer able to get furniture, loans or even emergency cash for the needy. Council officials were no longer there to deal with noise pollution, boundary disputes or trading standards, and a cash-strapped council couldn't clear slums or control landlords. The tightening up of immigration meant that I could no longer get the departmental duty officer to let people out of Heathrow or detention centres, hold up deportations or stop the scandalous dawn raids on immigrant families or the grabbing of asylum seekers from takeaways and restaurants at tea-time. Prison overcrowding made it impossible to get prisoners transferred to some-where nearer home for their families to visit. The transfer of schools to academy chains meant that I could no longer deal with education issues, exclusions and admissions locally. In areas where I'd once had power, I was reduced to pleading with unheeding departments or un-caring contractors.

The Department for Work and Pensions was keen to use MPs to sponsor job fairs, but unresponsive to pleas for travel grants or pass-ports to work. They wouldn't restore benefit suspensions for trivial offences and had clearly been set suspension targets, though they all blandly denied it. Loans were provided only by lottery, then stopped altogether. My staff, my workload and my correspondence grew as my powers diminished.

Grimsby's heart had been knocked out by the collapse of fishing after the loss of Iceland and the opening up of British waters to EU vessels. The big distant-water vessels were scrapped or sold off. The middle-water fleet fished in British waters for a few years but was then transferred to Hull and scrapped. Hundreds of vessels in the port dwindled down to around a score, most of them the old Danish seine-netters. Processing and engineering jobs disappeared. The tough man's world 'down dock' dwindled, its businesses closed down and its two poles of power, the offices of the owners and the exchange for the merchants, were shut. The fish dock gradually emptied and the fishing vessels were replaced by yachts and other craft looking for a cheap mooring.

Mining areas got coal field community support. Development areas got greater pulling power. Fishing ports got only a one-off EU grant, which had to be devoted to areas other than fishing. We put it into a fishing heritage museum, which the council then had financial difficulties in sustaining and refreshing, particularly after an expensive effort to get it national museum status was rebuffed. As for our poor bloody infantry, the struggle to win compensation for the fishermen took twenty years.

All this hit a community already below national levels in education, employment, poverty, health and life expectancy, making Grimsby the little town that Santa Claus forgot. Austerity produced intense competition to attract jobs and development. We were weak compared to development areas and big cities with bigger development departments. We were fiddled out of Nissan and beaten for Toyota. Siemens went to Hull because that suited Associated British Ports (ABP) better. Abel UK decided to build a factory site for wind-power engineering but ABP opposed it so bitterly and for so long that it missed the opportunity to attract new business and is now used as parking for imported cars. I took on a new role as Grimsby's booster, urging firms to come (or stay, in the case of Marks & Spencer, Findus and Bird's Eye).

I changed my name to Austin Haddock to promote fish. It got me lots of free fish and chips up and down the country, and ridicule from Tories who would have changed their names to Champagne Charlie for a large fee. It was a memorable wheeze, though after some weeks, when Hansard proposed to report me as Austin Haddock, I decided it was time to change it back. I did, though tearing up the deed poll turned out to be illegal, so I may still be Haddock. I also promoted a fish market in Westminster Hall, which the Serjeant at Arms' department threatened to stop as a commercial activity, until Betty Boothroyd arrived and started buying quantities of our good Grimsby fish.

I promoted, and ate, Grimsby products, campaigning for Bird's Eye fish fingers until Unilever closed the factory and transferred production to Germany. I then transferred my affections and diet to Young's, embarking on a memorable stunt with its chief executive. Along with two Page 3 girls dressed as mermaids, he and I stood in the rain opposite Parliament with the biggest fish finger in the world, giving away free fish fingers. As the rain poured, the six-foot fish finger and the CEO had to be protected by umbrellas. The mascara of the mermaids ran and Peter Luff MP went past and sneered contemptuously that there was nothing I wouldn't do for Grimsby. He was right. We transferred our show to Waterloo Station. Southern Trains can't be providing refreshments on their cattle transport, judging by the speed with which fish fingers were guzzled by hungry commuters.

Promoting Grimsby brought me into a close relationship with Iceland. My first job in Grimsby's international relations was to meet the Icelandic Foreign Minister to plead for the restoration of fishing rights. No chance. Icelanders are adamantine. Every time I went there, the spectacular development in Iceland and the depressing rate in Grimsby made it very clear who'd won and who'd lost the cod wars, and brought out the benefits of taking control of our own fishing waters, which the EU had denied us. Iceland was transformed, prosperous, with the highest standard of living in the world. It was taking the fish we used to catch and exporting it back to us. In Grimsby it took time to eliminate both the graffiti urging 'Death to all Icelandic bastards' and the hostility. One of my first jobs was to address a mass meeting of the 250 lumpers who landed the fish, and persuade them to lift their ban on the Icelandic landings, which were now essential to keep the fish market and its distribution system going. They agreed, but it wasn't long before I was defending them against decasualisation, which reduced the lumper force from 250 to a handful of casual workers paid in cash. Neoliberalism doesn't do gratitude.

Gradually, we built a better relationship. I went to Iceland to warn them not to enter the European Community because the Common Fisheries Policy would do to them what it had done to us. I tried to persuade them to admit British vessels. They did, but only to catch red fish. When the vessels didn't catch much, I protested to the Icelandic Fishing Minister that they'd been allocated to areas where there were no red fish to catch. He replied with Icelandic frankness, 'That's the whole idea.' Tough cookies, these Icelandics.

I became chair of the Parliamentary Icelandic Group and responsible for receiving the stream of Icelandic officials and ministers coming to London. In 2008, Gordon Brown seized all Icelandic assets to stop them being transferred when the banks went bust. This was a severe blow because the Icelanders had been buying everything that moved and some things that didn't, such as West Ham Football Club. Stupidly, Gordon did it under anti-terrorist legislation, claiming that was the only method available. This produced an explosion of anger in Iceland and a large deputation came over and formed a chain over Westminster Bridge, all in traditional dress with placards saying, 'I'm a poet [artist, fisherman, office worker, you name it], not a terrorist'. They then converged on the Commons demanding to see a Treasury minister. As chair of the Icelandic Group, I organised a meeting of as many MPs as I could gather and tried to get a minister. None would come, as is usual when departments are asked to defend their sillier schemes. So, I gave the visitors my support and accepted their massive petition carrying the names and email addresses of three quarters of Iceland's population. The Treasury refused to receive it.

The row grew. The Icelandic fisheries minister rang me to say that they were stopping fish supplies to Grimsby because the British banks wouldn't transfer money. This was clearly an insane overextension of the ban, so I rang the Chancellor. No response. I rang Mervyn King, the Governor of the Bank of England, who was much more helpful. He instructed his cashier to bang some sense into the banks in Hull and Leeds. Payments resumed. The fish began to flow. The fish-and-chip shops, vital to the north, were saved. Triumph. The Icelandic President later assured me, 'The name of Gordon Brown will live on in infamy in Iceland, long after he's been forgotten in England.' I was made a Member of the Order of the Falcon in the Icelandic honours system for my achievements on behalf of Iceland.

I had more success at home by helping to bring Euro-park, a development which provided new factories and jobs, to Grimsby. I supported the creation of a new landing company to take the fish dock out of the inert hands of ABP and create the best fish market in Britain. I'll always remember the part played by local businessman Frank Flear in this development and the look of amazement on the faces of the struggling fishermen I took him to meet when he told them, 'Money isn't a problem.' For them it was an overwhelming problem given their reduced catches and the unwillingness of the banks to lend to fishing. Hull got the Siemens plant for building wind turbines, but we got DONG Energy and the maintenance and supply vessels in the fish dock, with 300 jobs. I helped in the struggle to get planning permission for the new development by Able UK to build a dock and site for the ancillary developments.

Every little helps. Yet none of my efforts, speeches, representations or pleas could get the full and fair treatment Grimsby needed and deserved. Under Labour, it all went to the big cities, and under the Tories to the south and Toryland. Under both, London got more than its fair share: a much bigger spend per head, as well as all the big developments, like the Olympics and Crossrail. The efforts to disperse government departments never sent anyone to Grimsby, though cuts took several away. The train operators never provided the direct service to London we need, despite all the lunches and dinners I gave them.

I soldiered on. Grimsby became inured to a bum deal. Still proud, still trying to pull itself up by its own bootstraps, but falling slowly behind as the local economy stuttered, shops closed and pride gave way to bitterness. Nothing happened. A fishing community is good at suffering. The neoliberal years gave Grimsby every opportunity to practise that skill.

But it made my job more negative. I did my best to promote Grimsby, to improve communications and transport links and to attract development and jobs, fight closures and defend fishing and food processing, but comparative decline brings resentment rather than gratitude. I could neither join the chorus of Tories congratulating themselves on the prospects of their southern constituencies, nor whinge with the plaintive skills of the Scots, who had the political punch of the SNP. It's a hard life, though towards the end we got more from the coalition government than from Labour, which took Grimsby for granted.

Grimbarians don't do gratitude, and have had little occasion to practise it. Failure produced a stoical kind of resentment where rioting and throwing rocks might have done more to attract attention to our problems. Then the expenses scandal brought a collapse of respect for MPs and a flood of abuse in email, letters and phone calls. Some of it was organised by the Tory Party or UKIP. Most was just local grumble-guts, of whom there are plenty, exercising their talent. Either way, they had a field day.

This collapse of respect made the job more difficult and less pleasant. MPs began to fulfil a similar role to the rubber dummies of the boss on which Japanese workers vent their anger. As the exposed part of the system, MPs act as its whipping boys and girls, if that's not too sexual an image. As government failed to fulfil the expectations of the people for growth, jobs and rising living standards, the consequences fell on MPs. Twitter, a form of mental health treatment by keyboard, compounded the problem and amplified the abuse. A survey indicates that 5 per cent of the emails MPs receive are abusive. For some, and certainly for me, the volume of abuse that came in by email was far greater than the number of unsigned letters in green ink that used to come through the post, but in any case the main volume of abuse came not through my own emails but through the website of the *Grimsby Telegraph*, which provided a playground for the political curmudgeons bred by decline. The internet is a wonderful world of opportunity for the grudge-bearers, the misanthropes, the haters and the mentally unbalanced. It's nice for the rest of us to see them happy and it keeps them off the streets.

That website, supposedly a forum for the people, turned into a festival of abuse, illustrating the inadequacies and problems of Grimsby by providing an opportunity for the disgruntled (who appeared to breed in Grimsby) to stoke each other's misanthropy and compound each other's anger. They abused the council, the paper and me. I hope it kept them as happy as such miserable sods are ever going to be. Only a masochist could enjoy reading it. MPs just have to put up with it. Parliamentary selections should measure how thick a candidate's skin is.

Women Members receive more threats, some of them sexual, and often feel more vulnerable. (Threats of sexual violence tended not to come my way.) I don't see any solution to what's become part of the job. I've no idea how to stop it, though I would require users to give their name and address on all communications, whether tweeted, written to editors or merely shoved through letter boxes. Gladstone and Disraeli never had to face the same manure showers. But then they didn't represent Grimsby. Yet this negative side of the job was both heart-breaking and depressing. Grimsby deserved better than it got from history, from governments and from economic forces draining so much away to London, and its people deserve a better and fuller life.

At times, the fortunes of the football club seemed to symbolise those of the town. I'm not a football fan and therefore didn't go much, though it was always interesting, given the situation of the ground, to watch the shipping traffic on the river whenever the game got boring. In my time, Grimsby Town managed to reach the second division but then went downhill remorselessly, eventually falling out of the league and unsuccessfully struggling to get back. The fans remained loyal. Local businessmen, particularly Councillor John Fenty, continued to finance it, but every effort to break out, move to a new stadium, or get back to the big time failed. And there wasn't much that I or anyone else could do about it. For an MP, the failure of the constituency that Grimsby Town symbolised is heart-breaking.

Like every MP, I regularly and inevitably got the question 'What have you ever done for us?' I should have replied, as most Members do, with a long, prepared list, beginning with Iris Critten's catheter bag and going on through every development, abortive or successful, with which I'd ever had any association, however vague. I didn't. I always answered the question about what I'd done for them, the town or fishing by saying, 'My best. And if you don't like it, chuck me out next time.'

In 1734, Anthony Henley is reputed to have written to three constituents of his rotten borough of Southampton:

> Gentlemen, I received yours and am surprised by your insolence in troubling me about the Excise. You know, what I very well know, that I bought you. And I know, what perhaps you think I don't know, that you are now selling yourselves to Somebody Else; and I know, what you do not know, that I am buying another borough. May God's curse light upon you all: may your houses be as open and common to all Excise Officers as your wives and daughters were to me, when I stood for your scoundrel corporation.
>
> Yours, etc.,
>
> Anthony Henley

Joke or not, no MP would dare write or even think that today. I always proclaimed my love for Grimsby and genuinely felt it. It struggled through proudly despite the lack of government help, despite the losses of power, money and facilities due to centralisation, and despite its inability to attract the full range of business facilities and opportunities lavished on bigger centres. If Calais was engraved on the heart of Queen Mary, Grimsby was on mine. Though I'm not sure I was on Grimsby's.

CHAPTER TWELVE

SCHIZOPHRENIA AS A CAREER

I suffered from career schizophrenia, which made my parliamentary role one of two lives. Television is an addiction. I had it. I loved the excitement of the studio, partly because of my exhibitionist streak, but basically because there's nothing more thrilling than working in a live studio, where anything can go wrong (and, in my day, did), and reaching out to a huge audience. Yet the academic idealist in me also loved being a participant observer of politics, discussing policies, bringing out personalities and pursuing goals while pretending to understand what was going on in this most unpredictable of arts. This dual enthusiasm was a disadvantage in pursuing either career. Our age demands more specialisation. I loved being a jack of two trades. Each enlivened and enlightened the other and, if I'm honest, I couldn't have managed without both. If you can combine them, as I was able to do and enjoyed doing, why not?

My television addiction had begun in New Zealand when current affairs television was developed in 1964. The NZBC thought television was 'sound radio with pictures' and wanted people to paint them who were disposable and could be dropped without the complications of staff rights and explanations. Tried out as a guest commentator (which I already was on radio), I could learn my scripts (no autocue then) and gabble them off in a Yorkshire accent, which must have made them incomprehensible to Kiwis, though they were kind enough to give me the benefit of the doubt and assume I was talking sense. I was deemed to be acceptable and gradually did more and more TV, ending up with a programme of my own and as presenter of the major current affairs programme *Compass*, both of which I combined with my academic duties at Canterbury University.

It was exciting. I flew up to Wellington two days a week and recorded the programmes, which were then copied and flown to the four main centres (no national link then – so fog meant no politics). Our small and, I thought, talented current affairs team was left to do what it wanted, since no one in the hierarchy had much idea of how TV worked. We invited whomever we wanted, from the Prime Minister to the head of the security service. We made our own rules, promising the French ambassador that there would be no grilling on French nuclear tests, then attacking him about them for half an hour. I even did a programme on NZ women, with Miss New Zealand behind me in a bikini digging the garden for some reason I can't now remember. All this was compulsory viewing for Kiwis, who had only one channel, though I found from Christchurch water consumption charts that more was consumed filling baths and flushing toilets when I was on than during *Coronation Street*.

When I came back to Britain to an official fellowship at Nuffield College, David Butler organised one of his regular conferences, bringing the great and the dud (Whitelaw, Burnett, Bernstein, Day et al.) together to discuss TV coverage for the 1970 election. I chatted with Geoffrey Cox, a New Zealander and creator of ITN, who'd become deputy chairman of Yorkshire Television to make a bob or two. Two days after he'd left, I got a letter from Donald Baverstock, YTV's director of programmes, saying that if I was ever in Leeds I should drop in. I was on the train the next day. The studio was silent because they'd all gone on strike, but he offered me a summer job for the magnificent sum of £12 a day. I took it, loved it and never went back to Oxford.

The jewel in the Yorkshire TV crown was *Calendar*, its regional current affairs programme. This soon had an audience of two million or more. Developing a new programme and a new company is the most exciting thing it's possible to do and *Calendar* was a nursery of TV talent, many of whom went on to national programmes and bigger things. Start-up was something I enjoyed twice: once at YTV; the second time in founding Pennine Radio in Bradford in 1975, where I was programme director until I crippled myself in a parachuting accident. Both were joyous efforts, providing the excitement of learning a new job in a new industry. At YTV, that process was supervised and stimulated by Donald Baverstock, a wayward TV genius.

Two aspects particularly enthused me: go-go girls and politics. I never managed to combine the two. My colleagues complained more about the girls than the pols, though the audience's reactions were the other way. I put it down to a late second childhood as I discovered discos, dancing and music, which hadn't existed in sober, serious New Zealand. Complaints mounted when I brought Hull docks to a standstill by putting a go-go girl on a mounting platform and raising it high. The dockers' leader, Walter Cunningham, was particularly angry. Stopping dockers working was his job, not mine.

There was even a retrospective kick from the go-go girls when, as chair of the All Party Media Group, I chaired a Media Committee meeting in Parliament addressed by Charles Allen. He'd become MD of YTV when Granada took it over and brought with him a videotape of me watching a big-breasted stripper (billed as the great tassel-twirler), my eyes rolling as she twirled. Charles reminded me of what was on the video (as if I didn't know, given the row it had caused at the time) and quietly intimated that he'd show it to the assembled peers and MPs if I was critical of the Granada merger (which I certainly was). He got an enthralled hearing from his chairman. Now I thank God the feminists haven't got hold of it.

Politics were slightly less exciting, and probably less interesting to the Yorkshire audience, but I did lots of interviews with Cabinet ministers, since the Labour Party was then (rightly) dominated by Yorkshiremen and women. I was even allowed to interview Margaret Thatcher after being suitably vetted and the studio was painted blue. Our weekly political programme, *Calendar Sunday*, allowed us to interview every regional MP who could string three words together. We staged confrontations, discussed issues and presented fascinating debates, including one between surviving miners from the 1926 strike and police and volunteers who'd tried to beat them. Old hatreds still survived. All politics is local, as the Speaker of the American House of Representatives once said, but in overcentralised Britain we tend to ignore this and concentrate on political chatter about who's up, who's down and who's out in London, as if it were more interesting than the closure of pits, the death of fishing or the deprivation in the north. On *Calendar*, we reversed this perspective to concentrate on that which was important to real people rather than political groupies.

I transferred to the BBC for a year but didn't like it. The current affairs department was like All Souls in exile, filled with public school chaps and run by a nervous bureaucracy who never gave straight answers and were far too cautious to discuss their performance with interviewers. Not as much fun as working on a commercial pirate ship where the crew are left to do their own thing. So I upped sticks and went back to Yorkshire, where the fun continued as if I'd never been away and no one seemed to notice that I had. Four years later, I was elected for Grimsby to turn my enthusiasm for politics on television into the practicals.

That changed my status. People like TV personalities, seeing them as the nearest thing they can get to glamour, show-biz and royalty, but they're suspicious of politicians, probably wondering, like Paxman, 'Why is this lying bastard lying to me?', though without his insouciant insolence. The professional politicians, who are in that game because they're not good-looking enough for telly, don't particularly like their more glamorous rivals on the box, and long for revenge for being humiliated on television. In the competition for public attention, TV has won hands down, and the politicians resent it. So I was greeted with a certain amount of suspicion and treated as an alien and a media nark. This was compounded by the fact that I continued to do programmes for Yorkshire and anyone else who'd hire me.

My dual career produced the suspicion that I wasn't a dedicated politician (if only because I wasn't) and some jealousy because I wasn't as miserable (or as badly paid) as the rest – a suspicion boosted when I joined with Jonathan Aitken to put in a workers' bid for the Yorkshire contract in 1981. Now I was a greedy capitalist too. Jonathan was brilliant at raising the money, and we persuaded Harold Wilson to chair it and Donald Baverstock to become programme controller. The ITA rejected us, but granted one of our objectives by breaking up Trident Television, Yorkshire's effort to weld the three eastern franchises into Britain's first TV monster. I don't think I was forgiven by Paul Fox, programme director of Yorkshire Television.

Double whammy. The bid damaged my relationship with YTV as well as boosting mistrust in the Labour Party by making me look like a budding television mogul as well as an addict. That ambiguity continued right up to 1987, when my two lives came to a parting of the ways. Bryan Gould had promoted me to his Trade and Industry shadow team and I'd begun to speak from the front bench – though not always to the approval of the leadership, as when Bryan asked me to wind up on the debate on the privatisation of Rover but declined to tell me what to say. I warned that if Rover failed in the private sector, Labour would take it back into public ownership, a proposal that brought shudders from the modernisers and convulsions from Denis Howell, so unfashionable had nationalisation become.

The second break was even better. Rupert Murdoch was starting Sky, his new satellite service, which ran rings around the officially endorsed British Satellite Broadcasting, a kind of BBC in the Sky. Rupert created a mean machine broadcasting on Astra and immediately leapt ahead of the top-heavy official project, which quickly collapsed. His CEO, Andrew Neil, asked Norman Tebbit and me to front a new political programme called *Target*, copied from *Crossfire* in the US. It was a brilliantly simple programme: a two-sided interview grilling political guests, which was later copied, less successfully, by the BBC and by Icelandic TV. I accepted immediately but asked Norman, as a former trade union negotiator, to negotiate our contracts. He got me £50 more per programme than I'd have asked, and off we set to share the excitement of helping Rupert Murdoch in his new venture and his greatest risk.

The result was an explosion of anger in the Labour Party, where Rupert was regarded as the devil incarnate, if not worse. Hostility shrilled as I went round with Rupert and an enormous dummy of

Homer Simpson to promote Sky. The left loves belting bogeymen. It's a solace for political impotence, and Rupert was the super-bogey, a threat to Labour, women and civilisation. He'd broken the powerful print unions by the move to Wapping, defeated the left's siege of the plant, exposed breasts in *The Sun*, shifted his papers to the right and backed Margaret Thatcher. No Labour politician should have anything to do with him. Bob Cryer, nothing if not a purist, demanded in the PLP that I be fired, and when I attempted to reply, Max Madden moved next business and I was shut up. Neil Kinnock, unwilling to face the storm, called me in. 'Make him fire you. Don't resign,' Dick Caborn said. To no avail. Neil was more sympathetic than condemnatory, and more interested in how much I was to be paid than in the principle of the thing. But he still announced the next day that I'd resigned. Having taken a day to think up a reason for my resignation, he dredged up the excuse that it would be wrong for a Labour MP to interrogate shadow ministers. Just working for the devil incarnate wouldn't do, because Tony Blair was writing regularly for *The Times*.

This invented reason was total balls and quickly shown to be so as leading Labour figures flocked to come on board and eagerly took Rupert's shilling. The leadership had to find some reason for a wholly unnecessary sacking but couldn't come up with a good one. Bryan Gould felt his position was too precarious to defend me. After a bitter meeting to discuss my treason, the Grimsby party decided that it was easier to indulge my insanity than get rid of an MP they quite liked. The only beneficiary from all this hypocritical folly was Rupert Murdoch, who got publicity for his great new venture, Sky. The party only realised how daft it all was when Blair began to cosy up to Rupert and *The Sun*, but that was too late to save me.

It was all a waste of bile and time. *Target*'s initial audience was small, leading me to overuse my joke 'What's the difference between Sky and the Loch Ness Monster?' 'Some people have seen the monster.' But the viewing figures grew steadily, particularly, it seemed, among taxi drivers and the black community, and despite the council's efforts to stop it, houses in Grimsby and all over the country were soon festooned with Sky dishes. Our interrogations were interesting and educational, though I did more research than Norman, who could vamp it on his greater knowledge and his prejudices. Working together in this way made me realise that far from being the 'semi-house-trained polecat' of Michael Foot's description, Norman Tebbit was a highly skilled operator – pointed, pithy and witty. Before each programme, our producer Martin Levene would bike round his proposed questions and clippings. I'd arrive with mine read, scribbled over and rewritten. Norman would arrive, open the envelope in makeup and say, 'Who've we got today, then?' – quite the opposite of Norman Fowler when he occasionally stood in for Tebbit. Norman Fowler had always read it all and usually stuck rigidly to the script.

Norman Tebbit's ability to play it by ear did, however, cause some problems with books, such as *The Zero-Sum Society* by an American economist I admired, Lester Thurow. Norman, plainly, hadn't read the book. What should have been a fascinating debate got bogged down into a scrap about unemployment figures, with Norman claiming Thurow's were wrong. On the other hand, when we interviewed Norman Vincent Peale, the author of *The Power of Positive Thinking*, Norman was all charm, even though that wasn't exactly his approach to political discourse.

Labour's hostility to *Target* gradually abated. Gavyn Davies accused me of being disloyal to the Labour Party. Peter Mandelson complained continuously about our bias against Europe. Both of us were

Eurosceptics, which suited Rupert fine, but not Blair or Mandy. But Labour and Tory leaders all streamed on and the results were seriously good telly. Our producer, Martin Levene, was an enthusiast who constantly devised good interviews and approaches. We had some exciting adventures going to Davos for the World Economic Forum, and to Berlin when the wall fell. Norman strode through the Brandenburg Gate shouting a triumphant, 'We won!' I also learned a new joke about the Stasi, who'd all taken new jobs as taxi drivers. This provided a brilliant service because customers had only to give their name, and the drivers knew the address.

Murdoch proved to be more human, and much better to work for, than the right-wing monster the left feared. He never interfered but came to the studio a lot, and was always encouraging. He was open and approachable, his technique being to employ good people (usually Australians), pay them well and let them get on with it. As we did for eight exciting years, eventually presenting the tapes of all the programmes to Essex University for their political library. I can't say that doing it interfered with my parliamentary duties in any way. In fact, it helped by educating me about the issues and the people.

Target led to two other media adventures. LBC asked Norman and I to do their morning phone-in, which I was delighted to do (Norman less so) because I'd done phone-ins on Pennine Radio in Bradford and loved them, though Yorkshire folk are more taciturn than Londoners. When Norman dropped out, I carried on single-handed and it became an education in populist politics and the opinions of taxi drivers. I was on air the day the IRA shelled Downing Street, taking calls from taxi drivers, eyewitnesses and the police as it happened.

LBC wasn't heard in Grimsby, so it did me no harm there, but when Kelvin MacKenzie asked me to do a national phone-in on Talk

Sport, it resulted in complaints that I wasn't doing my duty in Parliament – even though the House wasn't then sitting in the mornings. That phone-in was even more exciting. The 9/11 attack occurred in the middle of it, which made everything dead easy. All I had to do was listen to a flood of complaints, fears and news updates. Critics in Grimsby then complained that I wasn't in Parliament for the memorial service. True, but I wouldn't have attended anyway, for such occasions are Parliament at its most pompous. However, I did listen to it on the radio!

After that, media opportunities became more intermittent. I remained a regular on local radio but I wasn't fresh and new any more, and I appeared less often nationally. Unlike the US media, ours don't like the old unless they're Dimblebys. Perhaps it was this media starvation that led me to accept the worst media job I've ever had.

Love Productions proposed a film about life in tower blocks. I was keen to do it because of my interest in council housing and my concern at the fate of the tower blocks, which were being turned into a dumping ground for the poorest of the poor. My interest was well known, but, for some reason I didn't quite understand, Love approached several other Labour MPs before reluctantly turning to me. I soon found out why. I knew too much and was on the tenants' side. Love's aim wasn't to show the sad realities of life in the flats, but to make fun of MPs.

Journalists had gone north in the '30s to highlight the plight of the people and build sympathy. In our more commercial age, they came to make money from misery. Programmes like *Skint* and *Benefits Street* caricatured the working class and unemployed as scroungers, fiddlers and pathetic. Too many of this type came to Grimsby doing good for themselves but nothing for us. It was totally unlike the noble Jarrow Marchers of yesteryear. Love's plan was that I should live a few days each with a gambler, a recovering alcoholic and a prostitute who was a recovering addict, only one of whom lived in a tower block. My plan was to move into a tower block as a family, live the life and mix with the people to show the world how awful it is.

I won the first stage of the argument. They found us a particularly grotty flat (with free turds in the lav) and Linda and I moved in. Linda made it almost habitable with furniture borrowed from friends and the YMCA, and we gave a party for the neighbours, few of whom came, because, as I quickly discovered, tower blocks aren't a community but a collection of isolation cells in which the old hate the young, the young escape supervision and the kids have to be protected. But the weak director felt forced to adhere to the original plan and kept telling me she had a mortgage to pay. She stuck to the programme, which was designed to humiliate the Member rather than illustrate the misery of the tenants. She filmed me visiting friends to borrow furniture as if I were escaping the flat to live it up. She edited out all moments of emotion and concern. She failed to film the strains of living in a block that had no concierge, where needles littered the balconies, kids rode motorbikes round the corridors and up and down in the lift, and the bells rang all night as people tried to get in for drugs, sex or a little warmth. Instead, she shot endless footage of the prostitute denouncing me for not wearing 'trackie bottoms' like others on the estate (but not the other pensioners) and filmed me being initiated into betting shops or fitting condoms onto wooden phalluses in the youth club. My efforts to get the inhabitants of the tower blocks to describe their own plight, which was appalling because of Hull Council's inefficiency and inability to spend money on renovation and staffing, were ignored. If tower blocks don't have a concierge living in, they quickly become hellholes. Hull's had.

It was an eye-opener, but mainly for me. Grimsby's tower blocks were better run and better served. Hull's were appalling, but there was little I could do about it. The local MP, with whom I felt obliged to take up the problems because of the parliamentary rule against interfering in other constituencies, was a lovely lady but more interested in her career in Parliament than the miseries of her constituencies, so she either did nothing or referred problems to the council, who'd caused them in the first place. As a result, what came over was a caricature of a callous MP who wouldn't mix with the people and did nothing to help them. The only consolation was that this was better treatment than they gave the poor Liberal Democrat MP, who was filmed lying on the grass sobbing as a result of his experience. Yet it bemused Grimsby, where people asked why the hell I'd gone to live in that dump across the estuary. Our Grimsby tower blocks were much better.

I don't know if the locals were paid by the greedy production company. I fear they weren't, and it proposed not to pay the MPs either, until the Tory MP organised a protest. That was some revenge, but a great opportunity for showing the disastrous consequences of relegating tower blocks to social dumping grounds had been lost. Fortunately, Love Productions, which would have been better named Greed Productions, found an easier way of making money, by baking cakes rather than exploiting misery.

In the end, my media career gave up on me rather than I on it. It had enlivened my years as an MP, making them less boring and far more enjoyable and productive than the futilities of eighteen years of opposition. Why do one job when you can do two?

Having said that, I have to admit that I'm opposed to MPs taking more demanding jobs, such as dentists, lawyers, financiers, company directors and every source of easy money that demands more time and effort outside Parliament. If second jobs are done to make money, the Member taking them can't do their job as MP as effectively as they should. That's a disservice to constituents. Working in television and the media is different. Politicians need television and TV needs them. The one fertilises the other and working in both extends the MP's reach and illuminates his job. That's my excuse and I'm sticking to it now that I'm too old and ugly to do either. Indeed, Britain should have full-time channels for the political class, with debates, lectures, conferences and education programmes of the type C-SPAN provides in the USA and Parliament gives in Canada. How are we to reach the people if we only speak in a Parliament few listen to or watch?

CHAPTER THIRTEEN

SEEING THE WORLD
AT PUBLIC EXPENSE

MPs like to pretend that they devote all their time to their parliamentary duties of shouting at each other. They give the impression that they work day and night to do their duty and serve their constituents. In fact, at any given time up to a fifth of our Members of Parliament aren't there. Many of them are overseas, some as far away from their constituents as it's possible to get. More of an MP's time is spent travelling round the world in pursuit of an ever-expanding supply of facts than they care to admit.

The joke is that several parliamentary noses would burst if they came below 30,000 feet, and certainly many MPs are sent on parliamentary package tours – some as a reward for devotion, others to get them out of the way – though my suggestion that they should all be required to donate their air miles to a parliamentary travel fund received even less support than my other proposal that they should also donate the wine glasses which used to be given with every ten gallons of petrol to the dining room.

Dennis Skinner is the only MP that I can recall who refuses all travel overseas, seeing it as a form of corruption. Like Michael Heseltine, he prefers to tour Britain, though in Dennis's case he likes to spend his trips preaching socialism, collecting votes for the NEC. Douglas Jay disliked going overseas and took British sandwiches with him to avoid foreign food. Both were rare birds in Parliament's travelfest.

Travel is supposed to train MPs for the job and help them to understand the world. It's handled by the three parliamentary package tour operators: the Commonwealth Parliamentary Association, the Inter-Parliamentary Union – both well-staffed – and the British–American Parliamentary Group, which is more specific and more educational in its role. Most Members join all three in their efforts to create international understanding, particularly between countries with good hotels and beaches.

There are, however, several competitors to these official travel agents in the parliamentary tour business. Businesses are anxious to sell their wares and show how effectively they can kill or cure people in other countries. Foreign regimes, particularly dodgy ones, are keen to demonstrate their virtues – South Africa was long a Mecca for Tories, many of whom came back to justify apartheid. Pressure groups and aid charities want to show their achievements in saving children, elephants or wildlife and highlight the coenobitical virtue with which they do it. The armed forces love to show off their hardware and the value for money they get by sending ships and troops to exotic locations.

On top of all this, foreign producers want to show how much their workforces like low wages and the educative value of child labour. The Department for International Development takes MPs to see the bottomless pits into which they've thrown British aid. Select committees came late to the act, but soon all had travel allowances which need to be spent within the financial year, leading to an explosion of interest in New Zealand, South America, the Maldives (global warming, of course) and even Afghanistan.

There is, in short, no lack of sirens luring reluctant MPs to desert their constituency duties and fly (premium economy, these days) abroad. In terms of miles per brain cell, Britain must have the best-informed MPs in the world. It can even be claimed that travel has a therapeutic value for our overworked legislators and helps to keep them sane. An older generation of working men took allotments to escape household pressures and worries. MPs, exhausted by the pressure-cooker world of parliamentary politics and the hard grind of constituency work, seek the same solace in escape overseas. The paradox is that those who do less work on either treadmill seem to get away more than the conscientious ones. As we know, a change is as good as a rest. Hard-working parliamentarians deserve a bit.

I took full advantage of the travel opportunities offered. I'd been bitten by the travel bug by working in television, but was happy to face the difficulties of studying poverty, development, exploitation, trade and aid from the swimming pools of luxurious hotels I'd never have been able to afford in real life.

I became a Thomas Cook socialist, though mainly in my early years in Parliament, when I seized every opportunity to see the world as a necessary learning process. The opportunity came up quickly. I was rewarded for winning the by-election by being sent to Rhodesia, and was later rewarded for my work as a talking whip on the first Tory finance bill by being sent to take parliamentary presents to the Parliaments of Fiji and Vanuatu. Unfortunately, the table I presented to Fiji was subsequently badly damaged in a military coup which turned out the parliamentarians who'd received it. The visit to Vanuatu also turned funny when I tried to show off by addressing their Parliament in pidgin, a fascinating language which describes God as 'big feller belong heli-copter'. My speech turned out to be a mixture of pidgin, French and English, all delivered in a Yorkshire accent. The five interpreters gave up. The parliamentarians smiled in baffled incomprehension.

The dodgy regime circuit took me to Korea and Uzbekistan (which Tony Blair later took more profitably). It was interspersed with as many CPA and IPU trips as I could get. Which was several, because the whips use trips as a form of patronage and in my early years I was impeccably dutiful. Official visits were always accompanied by parliamentary officials, making it like travels with my aunt. Their job was to dole out the dosh, negotiate airline upgrades and ensure that MPs coughed up for any late-night pornography or booze. They also hushed up any scandals, such as Lord Taylor's inappropriate breast grabbing in some country where they'd never heard of the aristocracy's *jus primae noctis*.

I spoke at university seminars in the Virgin Islands (scuba diving included) and conferences in Guernsey. I represented New Zealand universities in Malaysia. As a devout Eurosceptic, I kept out of the gourmet wine and food travel of the European assembly, and invites to Germany dropped off after I objected, at a conference in Bad Go-desberg, to a press release announcing our wholehearted agreement with an EU decision that had been drawn up before the conference had even started. I was never picked again for the Königswinter circuit after heckling Helmut Kohl about why the EEC benefited Germany so much and Britain so little. A great shame. I admired Germany and loved France, but neither invited me to any further functions, to avoid infection.

The travels of Marco Polo Mitchell began when I was made an Industry and Parliament fellow with Tarmac. They took me round

quarries and housing projects in England but also to the Arab Emir-
ates to see their construction work. There, they took the opportunity
to take me and my fellow Tory Member to try to impress the Emir of
Sharjah into paying the bill for Tarmac's construction of an international airport which no one seemed to be using. He didn't cough up,
but it was a happy trip, rounded off by being taken into the flight deck
of the departing plane to hear Jim Callaghan's announcement that he
was postponing the election. I breathed a sigh of relief. Too young to
die in some corner of an Arab field.

My next trip, also privately sponsored, was to Korea, where I was
impressed by the growing power of their manufacturing, particularly the huge steel and car plants and shipyards designed for them by
British advisers. These demonstrated the competitive advantage of
government-boosted development and capturing world markets by a
competitive exchange rate. Having seen the sad failure of Lame Swan's
dockyard on the Clyde to break into the supertanker market, it was a
depressing lesson.

I learned the virtue of the closed mouth. Driving back from Pan-
munjom in the Korean demilitarised zone, where I'd been taking
photographs of a North Korean border guard taking photographs of
me, I launched into a critique of the massive military effort on the
border, wondering why my travelling companion, Bruce George, was
frantically making silent throat-cutting and mouth-gagging signs. He
later told me, *sotto voce*, that it was to shut me up in front of the Korean
official listening eagerly in the front seat.

It was on this trip that I first glimpsed the sexual opportunities
of overseas visits. Having heard about the lubricious delights of
geisha girls, I was amazed when the party was taken to Korea's 'Best
Geisha House' to find it plastered with photographs of American

Vice-Presidents and generals, as some restaurants are with famous pa-trons. A pleasant evening seemed to be sliding towards an affectionate ending, when the madam suddenly clapped her hands and the geisha girls fled from the room twittering.

A Geordie Member told me in the car on the way back that I should have booked my geisha girl to come back to the hotel afterwards. I hadn't. But it may not have been necessary. At the hotel, a nubile lady made her desire for closer Korean–British relations clear by grasping my testicles in the lift. It could have been a cancer check, I suppose, but I got out a floor early anyway, and later discovered that this was not an uncommon form of welcome for visitors. A teacher at the Ranch School in Rhodesia asked me if I wanted tea or fucky-fucky (one hump or two). In Cuba, sex and opening restaurants in private houses appeared to be the only form of private enterprise allowed, though I was never sure whether all the young women thumbing lifts in the streets were soliciting or students trying to get home from school.

My first CPA trip was to Uganda and Tanzania, two contrasting experiences. In Tanzania, I was impressed by the saintly Julius Nyerere, whose assistant, recruited from the Labour Party, later retired to an old people's home in Keighley. Uganda was a more brutal experience. We were accompanied by a heavily armed military escort (who threatened me when I attempted to photograph them) and greeted everywhere by dancers singing what appeared to be the party song. They demanded that I take their photographs.

President Obote (restored to power after the fall of 'General' Amin, self-proclaimed King of Scotland) was more impressive than his Vice-President, who was a thug, but his suasions were put into perspective when I saw the piles of empty vin rosé bottles in the back-yard. It was a brutal regime but the brutes were clearly living off the fat of the land, and for a week we swilled in the same trough, which at least stopped us seeing how the people were faring in what had once been the jewel of Africa. At my request, we were allowed to visit prisons, where I talked through the bars to Bob Astles, Amin's Mr Fixit, though shouting at someone in a dead and dark dungeon, surrounded by warders and officials, was hardly the most enlightening political *conversazione*.

I took several photographs of him and the crowds of prisoners, which Ugandan exiles later inspected in an effort to identify victims, but a cunning scheme we developed to help the prisoners was frustrated. On school visits we'd been presented with a miscellaneous collection of ugly, heavy furniture made by students. My gift was a three-legged stool which fell over whenever sat on (perhaps symbolically?). We didn't want to cart this bulky collection home and had the brilliant idea of presenting it to the prison service as a gift from the British delegation. When we departed, we found it on the runway at Entebbe being loaded onto our plane.

I went out to the Falklands shortly after the war on a delegation redolent of the old days of empire, which was entirely appropriate since the Falklands are one of the last bits left. It was led by Julian Amery, a Churchillian figure who much impressed the islanders and was kept Churchillian by supplies of brandy from Tony Beaumont-Dark, who appointed himself Amery's batman. Matthew Parris (who described me as 'extending the flipper of friendship to the penguins') also thought he was Amery's adjutant, which doubled the brandy supply but produced a brilliant outpouring of Churchillian oratory at a mass meeting of islanders. They were rapt as he invoked a new imperial mission to develop the riches of South Georgia. Though I don't think it's yet happened.

I tried to build contact with the man in the Falkland street (there was only one) but years of isolation and inbreeding had made Falklanders somewhat inarticulate, unlike the recent post-war arrivals, some of whom had brought mobile fish-and-chip shops to recreate the joys of home, only to find that it was impossible to secure regular supplies of fish. A family from Barnsley told me they secured much of their fish supply by driving their Land Rover at speed over streams, killing fish. How different from Grimsby! It was gratifying to find that a few islanders recognised me from television, though it turned out it was from New Zealand TV not Yorkshire's, and certainly not from the stocks of dirty videos, which seemed to fill every mantelpiece except that of the Governor.

I shouldn't sneer. The islanders are sincere, people who were more British than the British and wanted to stay that way. It was moving to see the locations of the battles that reduction of British protection had made necessary and the impressive work of our military and the effort at recovery in health and education. The most spectacular development was the new airport, which featured a huge mural of Grimsby to greet arriving tourists. It had been painted by a Grimsby artist, John Hopkinson, who'd left the philistine British art market to come and work on the construction site. It was magnificent, though it seemed unlikely to attract any huge influx of tourists from Grimsby. I hope it's still there to remind visitors of home, because tourism looks to be the only way to develop the Falklands. They're a bit far away to provide the same tax haven and financial services that other British dependencies have used to allow the wealthy to dodge tax.

The airport promised to be a great asset that would end the inflight fuelling of the heavy aircraft on which we came out and went back. It also promised to protect the bottoms of the female flight attendants, one of whom told me that when the plane carried troops her buttocks ended up black and bruised from their inappropriate attentions. She didn't face the same problem with us, but then our flight was both empty and luxurious by military standards. Two Portaloos had been installed for the convenience of the parliamentarians.

The best overseas visits were to small nations such as Iceland and Norway, to both of which I went to warn against joining the EEC; Denmark, where I spoke against joining the euro; and New Zealand, where I warned them against privatisation and urged proportional representation. In the Nordic states, my warnings were successful. In New Zealand, the record was more mixed. It adopted PR, which now works very successfully, but the privatised utilities were all flogged off in a fire sale to pay down debt. Everywhere I was impressed by the advantages of small nations, which sustain a more active and intimate democracy than is possible in Britain's mass society.

Visiting large chunks of the known world was the most enjoyable part of parliamentary life, though it yielded fewer benefits to my constituents. I saw both the joy at the fall of the Smith regime in Rhodesia and the sad decline of Zimbabwe as Mugabe's tyranny destroyed their rich agriculture and turned the country sour. My next-door neighbour in Nuffield College, Bernard Chidzero, had been made Finance Minister but gave every appearance of being a broken man, and the friends I'd made earlier at the university had all fled. I enjoyed the friendly hospitality of Canada, which stimulated all sorts of ideas, from their people's jury on proportional representation to parliamentary television and affirmative justice. I was impressed by German efficiency, and their insistence on requiring every visiting MP to include Berlin in their itinerary introduced me to the joys of opera. We don't see much of that in Grimsby.

Two visits leading Fabian schools to China brought out the importance of the state in stimulating development. I saw the benefit in the huge contrast between two visits. In the first, we saw the old China of heavy industry and antiquated factories such as the Shanghai No. 2 toothpaste factory. On the second, we saw a huge flowering of hotels, housing, consumer electronics and infrastructure. The most moving sight of the first, pensioners stood by the roadside waving cars on, had now gone. Our hosts' desire to learn had been replaced by a desire to show off their achievements.

Visits to Sweden, Norway and Austria with Fabian schools and to Denmark and Spain with the Environment Committee provided even better learning opportunities about politics, social democracy and waste disposal, though hours of touring Danish waste dumps (more like leisure centres with libraries than tips) began to pall after a time. Yet everywhere facilities for the old and the young and the social security systems were ahead of Britain's meaner social provision.

The most enjoyable overseas visit was to south-east Asia, Singapore, Hong Kong and Papua New Guinea with the CPA. Unusually, wives were allowed on this, at Members' own expense, and Linda was able to wangle a deal with Qantas which allowed us both to go for the price of the CPA ticket. The disadvantage was that instead of going on from one destination to another, we were required to fly to Brisbane and then back to each new country from there as part of the deal. Still, Queensland's a lovely state.

The visit was wonderful. Bill Cash's wife graced every destination with a new outfit. Singapore's social discipline and lust for growth and education impressed. Papua was simply amazing. Naked dancers wearing masks and woad didn't seem to have much tourist potential for Grimsby, though it allowed the public school chaps to see naked breasts. Hong Kong was wonderful in Patten's last days as the colony's last Governor. Harry Ramsden's had established a Yorkshire High Commission in a fish-and-chip shop there, though when I asked if the fryers were sent to Guiseley to learn the trade, I was told that they all came from Nepal. All the while, Peter Hain, preparing for the greatness that was shortly to come to him, plied our leader with questions such as 'What's it like to be a minister?' and 'How do you handle civil servants?'

For our leader, Tim Yeo, it was more a tour of golf courses than an effort to build international understanding, but the rest of us swam, gorged and learned. On our return to London, Linda wrote up our travels for the *Sunday Times* in a jokey article, 'Five Go Mad in Papua New Guinea'. It so angered the CPA executive, particularly Speaker Betty Boothroyd, that I was banned from future CPA travel.

The most informative visits were the ones to the USA, where we met fellow politicians and top people such as Paul Volcker, Martin Feldstein and senators like John McCain, Bernie Sanders, Joe Lieberman and Patrick Leahy. Elsewhere we met Prime Ministers, most memorably Olof Palme, the Swedish Prime Minister, assassinated in 1986, who was the most exciting statesman I'd met since Hugh Gaitskell. The Canadians were the friendliest, the New Zealanders and the Americans the most open. Fabian visits to schools, factories and social care centres gave me a feel for society and industry which was more relevant than CPA or IPU visits, when host governments and British embassies provided too much tourist sight-seeing rather than the nitty gritty of life. The lavish hospitality and thrills (such as being carted around the US in the presidential plane Air Force One) made me feel guilty about the grudging welcome and the complacent concentration on our imperial and aristocratic past given to returning delegations in Britain.

I enjoyed it all enormously. Learning about other countries is exciting and I began to understand other regimes, such as Deng Xiaoping's revolution in China and Castro's in Cuba, an island struggling gamely to raise standards and develop in the face of the pointless American embargo. I learned a great deal. I'm gibberingly grateful and I don't feel guilty. Indeed, I probably travelled less than those inveterate palace bludgers Tony Blair and David Cameron, and they had a country to run as well.

I saw the effectiveness of British naval invigilation in checking drug running in the Caribbean (though they refused to allow me to publish my photographs of a spectacular arrest). I witnessed the effectiveness of army jungle training in Belize, though I wasn't too happy at being turned loose in a mock jungle battle with live ammunition on the day government announced a freeze on army pay. Just a coincidence, I'm sure.

Being escorted into towns and factories by a motorcycle escort swerving in front of us and waving other vehicles out of the way (something I never got in Grimsby) made us feel important. When, as *presidente* (leader) of our delegation to Cuba, I got a limo all to myself, the others begged and pleaded to ride with me. Patronage at last!

The only time the escorts seemed excessive was in Bangladesh, where I went to teach about public expenditure control. It provided one of a number of tests I learned to apply in political tourism: the bigger the bodyguard, the less stable the regime – though I always discounted the danger of kidnapping, not seeing a posse of British MPs as having a high retail value. Second test was the gold Rolex index: the more I saw on the wrists of politicians, the more corrupt the regime. This applied in Africa, though it began to worry me when I glimpsed them on the wrists of New Zealand Labour politicians after their 1984 victory. Most countries set out to hide unpleasant realities like corruption. The incidence of Rolexes is a better test than the search of foreign bank accounts or property purchases.

The third test was the discovery that the posher the hotel, the more the country had to hide. Segregation of foreign visitors and business-men was a form of protection which gave little idea of the lives of the people. However, this wasn't the case in Cuba, where we were accom-modated in what looked like an abandoned Butlin's, with ancient cha-lets and a swimming pool filled with bricks. My last test was that the better the health services and education, the better the regime. Cuba's good public medical facilities, which were being widely marketed as the health centre for South America, put Cuba ahead of the USA, where accountants are more numerous than nurses at hospital bedsides.

Everywhere there were lessons to be learned about growth, industri-al development, Parliaments, party management and social provision. Everywhere, too, I saw the value of the British Council, not so much in exporting national culture or parading poets, something the French are better at, but in educating, encouraging the English language and providing insight into the British way of life.

I saw less value in the Foreign Office. Our High Commissioners and ambassadors went to considerable trouble to help MP delegations and committees, I suppose because we would report back. They were well informed about the countries, their economies and prospects, but less sound on British national interests and economic and commercial realities back home, which looked like a class failure to me. Norman Tebbit joked that the Foreign Office is there to represent foreigners. Almost true, but it has certainly absorbed Euro-think and takes a European rather than a British view, particularly in France and

Belgium. I kept pointing out that Britain has different interests. They smiled indulgently.

There was too much tourism and not enough nitty gritty in all this parliamentary peregrinating. In the unlikely event that a constituent came to my surgery to ask which Intercontinental hotel had the best swimming pool, my knowledge might have been useful, but most was of real value mainly to me. It made me a better-informed MP. It took the edges off the insularity with which we British are born. And as rampant Remainers are now fond of pointing out, we don't want insular MPs who know only the nasty north, do we?

Grimsby got a more knowledgeable MP, though I wasn't much use as a roving High Commissioner for our town. I met constituents doing fisheries training, serving in the forces in the Falklands, and touring in China (where my wife overheard them saying I must be there to receive my instructions). I dutifully visited the graves of Grimbarians killed in action in Hong Kong, Korea, Belgium and the Falklands and took photos of the graves back. I even met the chairman of the Fleetwood Fishing Vessel Owners' Association in Spain, though he spoke no English and I no Spanish, a weakness demonstrated when I went looking for the little fish the Spaniards were accused of catching illegally in British waters. I finished up at a pilchard sale, which wasn't quite what I'd wanted.

Most visits were back in the days when newspapers published contributions from Members of Parliament. So I reported my travels in the Grimsby papers, but the reaction was angry letters asking why the hell I hadn't been in Grimsby. When I tried to get jobs in New Zealand's nascent fishing industry for redundant Grimsby fishermen, the CEO of Sealord told me, 'I'm not employing any of those drunken bums again.' Disappointing.

Overseas visits produced great moments and happy memories. Waking up in a safari hotel in Tanzania to find an elephant looking at me through the bedroom window (fortunately, I had my pyjamas on). Flying in a two-man military helicopter over the Belize jungle from one Mayan temple to another. Snorkelling among the other exotic fish in the Maldives and on St Croix. Being shown round Soweto by one of the Black Sash ladies. Flying over Doris Lessing's farm in Rhodesia, and climbing the Lion's Rock in Sri Lanka. All live in both my memory and my fading colour slide collection.

There were also sadder moments, such the burnt-out cars and fortified farms in Ian Smith's Rhodesia; the school devastated by terrorists in Uganda, with schoolbooks, love letters and sad diaries of the vanished pupils scattered round the room; the jails in Uganda and the Maldives; and the furtive talks with opposition leaders in Uganda, Sri Lanka and apartheid South Africa.

Travel broadens the mind as well as parliamentary behinds. It certainly improved my understanding of other countries, though in some countries governments changed more quickly than I could travel. Overseas regime change regularly outdated everything I'd learned. Milton Obote was overthrown by a military coup in Uganda, Olof Palme was shot soon after talking to us, the Liberals lost power to the Conservatives in Canada, apartheid collapsed, Hong Kong was reunited with China (but continued to sell fake Rolexes for ten quid), and Lula took power in Brazil, then lost it. In the Maldives, President Abdul Gayoom, who'd lectured us at length on his desire for democracy (eventually) and presented each of us with his book on the glowing future, was put in jail by a new President, his half-brother.

In most countries, politicians as a class were a self-constituted elite who'd done more to further their own interests, feather their own nests and entrench themselves as a political caste than our British political elite. They also had to be better protected. Threats were greater and change was more likely to come from violence than from the boredom that brings it in Britain.

Some contrasts were striking. In Tanzania, MPs had Land Rovers (courtesy of British aid) to take them back to constituencies. New Zealand MPs got better travel and computer support. German MPs were financed to bring busloads of constituents to Bonn and Berlin. Canadians had better media facilities to communicate with constituents, and Americans bigger staffs, boosted by penumbras of students from their home states on work experience.

This particularly struck me when I visited the offices of Senator Gary Hart, who later became a candidate for the presidency. He had a staff of seventy in Washington, and others back home in Colorado, plus an elaborate computer system programmed with answers to every possible question. His computer could assemble a coherent letter about his views which was rounded off by an automatic signature machine without touching a human brain. Perfect, and providing more free time for Hart's *Monkey Business*.

The European Community was less inspiring. It sucked in visitors and delegations, took them round the magnificent buildings they were paying for, and sold the virtues of the EC, rounded off with a few glowing promises to take home. This was a public relations machine rather than a Parliament or a government, but very good at it and even better at providing well for the bureaucrats and MPs who keep Brussels going. I was particularly surprised at the lavish second homes of Euro-MPs and officials in Tuscany and the Dordogne. All were living better than they ever could at home, but my envy was coupled with annoyance when I reflected that Grimsby was financing them.

In one field, Britain was ahead of the world. That was posthumous control of public spending. The Public Accounts Committee and the 800 staff of the National Audit Office who served them were viewed with envy everywhere. Everywhere we went, the Controller and Auditor General Sir John Bourn was greeted like the Pope on a papal visit, with the Public Accounts Committee as his twelve apostles. Even I got an adulation I was totally unused to when I went to Bangladesh and Australia to tell them about the workings of our British system.

This was appropriate and Bourn's enormous travel expenses were well justified because others have much to learn from our public spending controls. Britain leads the world in closing stable doors after horses have bolted, though sadly we're also better than most at burying the bodies of the dead horses. Only in America, in the Government Accountability Office, did I see any system that was anywhere near as good as ours. The EU system, run by a bloke called OLAF, is particularly pathetic.

I wasn't the Paul Theroux of parliamentary travel. I travelled a lot because I was an MP for a long time. On a yearly basis, I travelled no more than the average MP. Yet it would be hypocritical to conceal the gallivanting. It helped to make me a better MP. It strengthened my arguments for change at home. We're too inclined to think we lead the world, but my travels showed me that we've got much to learn from others. They gave me a better understanding of the dynamics of development and industrialisation, demonstrated by successful competitors, and of Britain's strengths and glaring weaknesses. It was a necessary part of the job and should be – unless we want to be represented by ignorant insular xenophobes.

At least Grimsby was spared my permanent presence on local radio and TV for a short period, though sadly I never dared to show any of the thousands of brilliant photographs I'd taken of foreign parts. They might have made constituents feel that I'd been having too good a time while they struggled for a living. Who wants an MP telling them how much nicer it is to live in the Maldives, New Zealand, Canada or, indeed, almost anywhere in the sun, when they have neither the time nor the money to go there?

CHAPTER FOURTEEN

A PARLIAMENT FIT FOR PURPOSE

Parliament is its own worst enemy. Treated with awe, respect and more reverence than common sense, it is better viewed as an antiquated legislative factory which should be subjected to a time and motion study, modernised and made fit for the purposes of the twenty-first century rather than the nineteenth. A chamber which once echoed to the oratory of Charles James Fox and the duels of Gladstone and Disraeli is less relevant to the needs of a mass democracy in a complex, pluralistic, modern society. It served the days of empire and war well but is less efficient at fulfilling such basic roles as auditing the performance of government, providing the forum for the national debate, and putting out the information, the facts and the ideas the people need to make their judgements on policy and party. The media does all three better, and has the audience Parliament has lost. We can't return to the good old days of parliamentary primacy or make the old grey mare what she used to be. Yet we can, and should, make it relevant, representative and effective.

The magnificent 1986 painting of the Commons in session painted by June Mendoza illustrates the problem. I featured in it as a small speck on the canvas (though 200 other Members were excluded on what may have been photogenic grounds), but it does provide an idea of what's wrong with our much-venerated sacerdotal institution. In the painting, one brave, lonely woman, Margaret Thatcher, commands the attention of 400 overweight, sober-suited men, while in the gallery a collection of the giants of the past, including Charles James Fox, William Pitt, William Ewart Gladstone and Benjamin Disraeli, look down in benign approval on their heirs and successors.

This veneration of the chamber and of the importance of tradition typify a palace stuffed with statues of the giants of its own past and encased in a beautiful gothic building, elaborately designed to inculcate awe in all who enter and to require the nation to conduct its politics in a cathedral.

This gives rise to what may be the only funny parliamentary joke but one which exemplifies the attitude. When Speaker King was leading his daily procession through the huge crowds gathered to witness it, in a state of happy inebriation he spotted an old friend in the crowd and called his name: 'Neil!' The entire crowd knelt. Awe in action. More seriously, it also makes Parliament a national shrine rather than an effective institution relevant either to the workaday lives of the people or to the needs of a modern society.

What this reveals is a Potemkin Parliament, a debating chamber which few hear but which can be swept into damaging wars, political follies and counterproductive policies by a herd instinct whipped up by a febrile media and clever oratory. The cathedral setting is a respectable disguise for sordid politicking and the leaden fist of the elective dictatorship. In it, an unrepresentative set of national representatives chunter away in their political backwater, largely irrelevant to the problems of a society under strain which is dominated by powerful monoliths and beset with grumbles, abrasions and iniquities against which there is little redress.

Perhaps nations need their myths and perhaps Britons are happier living in a past that was certainly more glorious than their present. But the people must live in the present, and for Parliament there is no going back. A nineteenth-century institution for an aristocratic debating society needs to be updated and made efficient by focusing it on the problems and needs of a complex, pluralistic society which has lost both its old deference and its respect for politics, politicians and pretenders to power. Parliament should protect the people, redress their grievances, make power in all its forms accountable and provide a popular representation which is both genuinely representative and better able to lead an educative, informed national debate than to throw custard pies at each other and play Punch and Judy politics.

One basic role of Parliament, that of a squawk box, will remain. Parliament is an amplifier giving problems, complaints, grievances and issues a much wider audience. The parties use it to fight their never-ending battles; the Members use it to air their egos and put the needs of their constituencies; pressure groups use it to put their cases. All this is done on the assumption that someone is listening and that it will produce action, and too many MPs like to create the belief that having raised an issue or a problem in Parliament is enough. It isn't. It's a plea for action which will probably be ignored or go unheard. The only time I found that a speech produced an action from the powers that be was when I announced in a Finance Bill Committee that I'd once bought a premium bond but had lost it. Ten days later, a replacement bond arrived. Plus a cheque for £14, which the old one had won over the years. For the rest, the most a noise in Parliament can do is get something in the local papers, because it no longer reaches the wider audience it is meant to educate and the powers that be have their fingers in their ears to avoid embarrassment.

A new age demands a more serious and a more efficient Parliament that can take on the other roles required in a more complex, sophisticated society. It may be more mundane, more routine and less impressive than today's pretentious irrelevance. It may be manned not by MPs recruited from the elite but by lesser mortals more representative of the society and the localities they spring from. Both will make Parliament more relevant than pursuing roles appropriate to a dead empire and a world role that has gone.

Parliament is always in transition, though the process is so slow that it is always behind the times. In my time in the Commons, I saw the changes in the composition of membership, the nature of the work and the relationship of Parliament with the world outside. I also watched its slow decline as it became less relevant, less respected and less interesting, processes typified by the loss of the full-length press reports and the replacement of commentary by comedy. The respectful seriousness of Harry Boardman was replaced by the comic abuse of Bernard Levin, followed in my time by the humour of Simon Hoggart, Matthew Parris and Frank Johnson as well as the vitriol of Peter Oborne. All wrote as if reviewing a play in the theatre or a game of chance played by self-obsessed fools rather than summarising serious debate on serious issues. Behind the humour was the belief that neither Parliament nor the politicians were up to the job.

In 1982, I published a book, *Westminster Man* (feminists protested at the title but there were then only nineteen women MPs – a number which had risen to 191 by the time I left), describing the composition, the work and the lives of the Members of the Parliament I sat in. It was one Parliament, two tribes (later joined by SDP and Lib Dem gypsies).

Its membership, though solidly middle class, had moved a couple of rungs down the ladder since the elite politics of the nineteenth century. It was no longer the mine owners, manufacturers, land owners and wealthy elite on the one side versus the trade union officials, manual workers and middle-class socialists on the other, which had caused Stanley Baldwin to reflect that he'd never met anyone as stupid as the miner MPs until he met the mine owners.

By 1982, it had become a battle of class surrogates. The Labour ranks had moved up a notch: fewer workers and union leaders, but many sons and daughters of the working class, their offspring now working as teachers, journalists, public servants and the YAP professions. Against them were the lawyers, professionals, farmers and financiers (who'd replaced the industrialists). Still two class armies, the have-mores versus the have-lesses, facing each other in mutual incomprehension and hostility, with the Tories down a notch and Labour a notch up.

That's still true. Tory MPs are better off and their average is raised by the presence of a few people of serious money. Indeed, Cameron's was a government of millionaires for millionaires by millionaires, and the green benches now have more millionaires on both sides if house prices are counted, while the Tories still bring in a few with personal fortunes, like Jacob Rees-Mogg, the MP for the nineteenth century, whose annual income is over a million. Labour has only one, Geoffrey Robinson. The difference shows in the suits, the education and the accents. I was always surprised on overseas trips with Tories to find how much money and how many class contacts they had all around the world. For Labour, trips were posh package tours. For Tories, they were renewals of friendships and business contacts, even an opportunity to visit their money – or at least that part of it that isn't hidden behind brass plates in the Cayman Islands.

By the time I reached my rendezvous with P45, the major change was that career politics had driven out the amateurs and processed peas had replaced the characters. A career in politics offered better prospects to those down the ladder keen to climb than to the elite who'd once monopolised it, which meant more barrack room lawyers and fewer fine minds of the Bryan Magee, John Mackintosh, David Marquand and Phillip Whitehead variety. The fine minds were less attracted to the more mundane role. More MPs were there to get on, a change seen in Labour's two civil wars. In 1981, several MPs were driven to leave the party for fear of being deselected. In 2016, many more revolted against Jeremy Corbyn but mainly, now, because they saw him as a drag on their prospects of office. The party struggle in Parliament was still between the privileged and the less privileged but now it was fought by surrogates, not genuine representatives of anything much except themselves. They were fighting for jobs more than policies, and party policies were being geared to prospects rather than national needs.

Labour was less a class army than a coalition of the less well-off middle class, many of them second generation from the working class and the council estate who still defined themselves as workers (a claim Michael Meacher was so proud of that he took to defending it in the law courts at considerable cost when a journalist branded him middle class). Noblesse oblige socialists like Attlee are now as rare as genuine proletarians in the People's Party. The basic reality on both sides is that MPs are now professional politicians, people on the make rather than class warriors.

Parliament became more representative and in doing so it moved down market. The most dramatic change was the increase in the numbers and proportion of women Members. There were twenty-seven female MPs when I came in, reduced to nineteen after the 1979 election. After that, the numbers rose steadily: forty-one in 1987, sixty in 1992, 120 in 1997, 143 in 2010. Labour showed the way by using compulsion, with all-women shortlists taking away one of the last remaining powers of local parties in order to ensure a house-trained party in Parliament. This weakened local democracy but boosted the number of women. Other parties followed suit more cautiously, using persuasion rather than compulsion. This meant that they didn't do as well. The total numbers of women are now coming to a level which will soon be natural and self-sustaining without discriminatory inducements – though feminist demands for them probably won't stop unless the demand to go on shortlists by self-designating as a woman brings the whole process into ridicule.

The big improvement in the position and the proportion of women has not produced the benefits feminists looked for, though it has civilised the Commons, getting rid of the laddism of public school games, the bum-wrestling for seats and the rugby scrums in the voting lobbies. It has focused attention on issues more relevant to the lives of the people and made the place more colourful, more normal and more human. All to the good.

Yet the changes have reduced the quality of debates. Parliament's strength should be to test both arguments and ministers, sometimes to destruction. Brilliant speakers such as John Smith and Robin Cook could apply a withering forensic analysis to government policies, and clever ministers could defend them with eloquence. More recently, debates have deteriorated into a ritual exchange of prepared speeches, many written for the Members by civil servants or party researchers, which follow no thread of argument but allow backbenchers to push their policy barrows all over the landscape in no particular sequence.

Too many speeches are read like sixth-form essays to be got through as quickly as possible. There is little development or argument and too many interventions are designed to trip up rather than question the points being made. Some Members, particularly those with a business background, would be happier if they could use Powerpoint. Fortunately, the use of illustrative boards (which is allowed in America) or objects to shock the audience (like the Members attempting to bring aborted foetuses into a New Zealand abortion debate) are banned. The present Speaker has been much fairer than many predecessors in giving the opposition more opportunities to raise issues and giving backbenchers a better deal, though he hasn't been able to stop the deplorable habit of applause, which turns debate into party rallies, and questionable policies, often damaging, are too easily smuggled through. TV coverage has heightened the numbers attending debates but broken the thread of argument. The main channels used to focus on giving a fair summary of the debate which followed the argument, but they did so only for a short period. When it didn't bring in the ratings, they opted instead to use gobbets and parliamentary sound bites rather than allowing an argument to be developed. Coverage now concentrates on Question Time, particularly the Prime Minister's, which has become a noisy clamour of exhibitionists throwing prepared debating points at each other. PMQs fascinates American audiences but leaves me cold as an awful advert for Parliament, comparable more to the public bar of a noisy pub at happy hour than Britain's senate.

There have been no proposals to advance other groups with all-ethnic minority, all-LGBT or even all-Scottish or, better still, all-Yorkshire shortlists, but the Commons have become more representative, more real and more like the society that elects them than the old Parliament, dominated as it was by middle-aged men playing middle-class games. Selections have changed from picking quality representatives from the elite to preferring local people, local councillors, local heroes and local cause-pushers. Local issues and constituency ties have become more important, with the result that a third of Tory candidates and two thirds of Labour candidates have local roots, and MPs are more likely to live in their constituencies than ever before.

The social range has been compressed. The moneyed and the intellectual elite have less desire to play the game now that it is no longer the Great Game of Power it was in nineteenth-century politics. They've seized better, and less painful, opportunities for making money. The real working class have also gradually dropped out. Labour's working men would fill a phone booth now that the mining areas have been taken over by women, and the proletarian north-east by ministrable smoothies.

This has created a vacancy increasingly filled by picking from the political kindergarten of interns, spads, apparatchicks and -chaps and the myriad cause-pushers of identity politics. Burke wouldn't stand much chance of a political career today, but neither would Balfour, Baldwin or Gaitskell. Parliament is more middle management than an assembly of CEOs; less clever, more polytechnic and comprehensive schooled and more ordinary. More representative but less respected.

The MP's work has also changed. It's more detailed and mundane and constituencies are more demanding, making the job a form of social service. Constituencies need active defenders, promoters and ombudsmen, and MPs have a responsibility to provide all that. So they need a substantial local staff to act on their behalf, rather than a party agent to shoulder the load for them.

Self-appointed experts still debate the affairs of other countries, but Parliament has less to say about empire, war and world affairs, and more about the problems of the people, health, jobs, education, welfare, kids and women. The media has replaced Parliament as the forum for the national debate and MPs now dance to media tunes, rather than vice versa. Parliament's role is to provide more rationality and variety in public discourse and to question and criticise the holders of power rather than pretend that it is the great forum of national debate.

Traditionalists may hanker after a return to dignified rule by the elite. It won't and shouldn't come back. Parliament is only one of a widening range of career choices available to people of ability. Most others are better paid and easier. So why should the able devote themselves to what they see as hack work and be abused for not solving problems which are insoluble? In any case, the MP's job is no longer one for fine first-class minds dissecting major issues. It's the more mundane task of voicing the plaints of the people, educating and informing the nation, exposing and analysing problems and abuses of power and helping those who can't help themselves but have no other resort in an age of big corporations and public relations. Only the Commons can take up the problems of the people, question power and offer leads to better. That requires hard work, not the debasing din of yah boo sucks politics or even the leisurely three-hour speeches of Gladstone's time.

The essential requirement is better staffing. On an early visit to the US, I was struck by how easy it is for constituents to put issues and questions to senators and congressmen. Large staffs give congressmen a wider reach than that afforded to Members of Parliament, who must deal with too much personally. To put a case to a staffer is to feed it into the congressman's machine, get an answer and have it dealt with. It should be the same here. That means bigger and more expert staffs to make MPs more effective.

The ideal is a professional parliamentary staff attached in teams to individual Members and supplemented by them with their own personal staffs and work experience kids from the constituency. This will give each Member a wider reach, a greater capability to develop their interests, and a better research capacity. All that leads to a more powerful and professional Parliament surrounded by a university of government.

Employment of spouses and offspring to keep money in the family shouldn't be part of this professionalisation. The Independent Parliamentary Standards Authority was right to try to stop it, but it felt obliged to continue an exemption for existing employment, allowing two fifths of Members to employ spouses or other relatives, often at inflated salaries. This is bad for the morale of other staff. It undermines the independence and effectiveness of the team and should be phased out. Marriage is a partnership, but spousal support is best recognised by paying an allowance and generous travel rights, rather than fiddling them onto the books. Parliamentary work is professional, not marriage guidance. Neither Parliament not constituencies have a right to expect two for the price of one.

We should also stop MPs holding outside jobs and consultancies. This has always gone on and Parliament has been and still is a useful second income for the law and the City. Brian Walden, the Labour MP I'd admired at Oxford, took a job as the highest-paid bookies' runner, as a lobbyist for the bookmakers, and this political bribery increased as the lobbying industry grew, businesses became more political and inadequate parliamentary salaries made MPs greedy for outdoor relief. The excuse was that it keeps them in touch with the real world. The reality is that it keeps them in better touch with money.

No MP can serve their constituents and do the job effectively if they also work for someone else. Democracy is damaged when companies and causes can buy influence and respect, and Parliament declines if it is felt that MPs are for sale. In fact, they're not worth buying and Parliament should be a full-time job, not a platform for self-enrichment. That destroys public trust and changes the imperatives of Members. Simply requiring MPs to register their incomes and interests is not enough. Far more sensible to pay MPs a much bigger salary, make the job full-time and ban outside earnings and employment. This need not cover journalism or media appearances, but must stop payments for speeches, which become an indirect form of bribery. Feed speakers, by all means – some people like rubber chickens – but neither pay them to sing for it nor allow them to get retainers for rehashing the literary efforts of some hack researcher with some decline in the grammar.

Recent reforms of Parliament have given more power to backbenchers. They now have their own debates, selected weekly by a backbench committee and a second chamber in Westminster Hall which provides the opportunity for overflow yammering. We have reduced the power of opposition to hold up government, by programming bills to stop filibustering hold-ups in committee, but this weakens the obstructive power of opposition. Changing the hours to start earlier and cut out all-night sittings was intended to give Members more free 'family' time. In fact, it merely sent MPs home to watch TV or indulge in more nefarious activities, which weakened the collegiate atmosphere (as well as the gossip and plotting) that built up as Members were detained for divisions. By Thursday, the nation's political hothouse is largely deserted.

We should work MPs harder by a four-day week with compulsory attendance and end the frequent breaks, particularly the long summer break, which is really an excuse for longer holidays and escapism rather than diligent attendance on the constituency. That may burn them out quicker by shorter but better-rewarded tenures, but there is an enormous amount of extra work to be done if Parliament is to protect the citizens in the face of our complex society dominated by powerful monoliths and privatised functions, all keener on profit than on service. Only MPs can do it.

Harder work should mean more Members. Misguidedly, the Conservatives proposed a reduction from 650 to 600, as if it was legitimate to save money on democracy. The idea is wrong-headed. It takes a peculiar view of democracy to cut back the elected chamber while increasing the appointed one, the House of Lords, to over 800. This piece of parliamentary vandalism would reduce the range of choice for ministerial appointments, boost the workload of the backbenchers and increase the power of the executive. The cut should be reversed. The only case for change is an increase in the number to 700. With no federal division of legislative power and no elective second chamber, Britain is under-legislatored compared to other countries, having fewer legislators per capita than in federal systems or those with two elective chambers. Unless we move to a system of elected regional governments (as we should), we need more MPs to run a more effective committee system and provide the service that constituents have a right to expect.

It makes no sense to reduce the talent pool for the selection of ministers at time when the growing exodus of ability to better jobs outside is already draining it. We need a larger House in which people come in younger but stay for shorter periods, so that it can act as a training ground for talent. This would create a situation in which able young people see a period of service in the Commons as a gateway to other opportunities. Gyles Brandreth, an involuntary departee who went on to better things, enjoyed being an MP and thought it had helped him to understand politics in a way only a Member can. Others could benefit from that training as they spread it out into the community.

MPs should be better trained. They should get a first year of intensive education in economics, administration and governance to learn the job and understand the system and its problems. Running a complex society and a difficult economy require different skills than the old public school training for running an empire. We prescribe better training and skilling for the workers. Why not for MPs?

Having more MPs serving smaller constituencies would allow them to better fulfil their new role. It's particularly necessary to develop the select committee system, which has been the most successful reform of my period in Parliament. Long urged by political scientists, the reform was sneaked in by Norman St John-Stevas as Leader of the House in 1979. Opposed by traditionalists such as Michael Foot and Dennis Skinner because it took the primacy away from a chamber which had long since lost it, the fourteen select committees, each covering the field of one department, gradually found their feet, gained confidence and began to assert their authority by enquiring into failures, departmental policies and problems.

The most effective is the oldest, the Public Accounts Committee, served by the 800 staff of the National Audit Office, who research the problems and prepare the documentation on which the committee can then report. This hasn't stopped 'Think Big' follies such as HS2, Trident, Hinkley Point C or useless aircraft carriers, but it has created an awareness of their dangers, provided safeguards to check overspends and allowed the PAC to draw the lessons. That's the way all the select committees should go.

Already a powerful force, under Margaret Hodge's active chairmanship from 2010, the PAC extended its inquiries into tax evasion by major multinationals, the failures of privatised agencies, and abuses in the health service and the free schools, highlighting serious problems for the government to address. Similarly, the Treasury Committee showed the way by demonstrating the illogicality of monetarism and requiring reform of the banks, as did the Business Committee by unveiling the greed and incompetence with which Carillion had been run; the Culture, Media and Sport Committee revealed the extent of media phone-hacking; the Work and Pensions Committee put Sir Philip Green in the pillory over his treatment of BHS; while the first parliamentary criticism of the effects of austerity came from several of the departmental committees. All this has been a huge advance in the relevance of Parliament. It put more information into the public arena, forced reluctant regulators to act and informed public opinion about the issues in a way that would have been quietly covered up by the chapocracy.

Time now to move forward from these pioneer efforts. By building on them, we can increase the relevance of Parliament and enable it not only to question executive power but to call all power to account. In an elective dictatorship, Parliament's only direct power is to bring the executive down. Most of the time it can't do that, even when the majority is small. In a complex modern society, power is dispersed and should be made accountable at its many levels. Citizens find it difficult to assert their rights, protect themselves against abuses and contest the decisions made by ever larger units wielding ever more power, whether companies, multinationals, banks and financial institutions, local authorities, agencies or the state. Markets strengthen the strong and fail the weak and need to be continuously checked, rebalanced and regulated. A nation claiming to be a good place to do business is a good place for business to do the people. Capitalism is not virtuous.

Companies, banks and big accountancy houses lie, cheat and cut corners in ways they then attempt to conceal by advertising and PR. They can't be left free to do as they please to boost profits.

After the Great Depression, European democracies had seen the answer to the problems of capitalism as nationalisation, while the US saw it as strong regulation. Now, with public ownership out of fashion and so much privatised, we need to follow the USA's lead. The only protection of the citizen and small business now is effective regulation, with regulators reporting to and supervised by Parliament and working under the aegis of a select committee. This would bring the authority of Parliament to bear. By questioning the holders of power, the select committees can give MPs and the public the opportunity to evaluate the performance of the elite, the monoliths and the government. It can rip away the veil of confidentiality and secrecy under which the machine conceals its follies and failures.

The USA has effective regulation, but in Britain its structures are immature, complicated (audit has seven regulators), weak, and often captured by the regulated. The lawyers regulate the lawyers and the accountants the accountants, and they usually find in favour of their members. When chaps regulate chaps, they give chaps the benefit of the doubt and the ordinary citizen has all too little power of redress. The law is too cumbersome, liable to be manipulated by money and deep pockets, and has priced itself out of the range of the ordinary citizen. The regulators are feeble (and too complicated), the media too fickle, and whistle-blowers are unprotected.

This is not good enough in a society dominated by big multinationals, huge companies and institutions, and enormous concentrations of power. All commit themselves to the public service and run big advertising budgets to assert their pristine purity and virtue, but in the last analysis banks that are too big to fail and professional service providers that are too big to be accountable owe their main allegiance to profit, which means a better return to their partners and group management rather than to the public service. The result is scandals like LIBOR manipulation, mis-selling, poor auditing and crushing the small for the profit of the big. Only an institutionalised system of regulation backed by the power and invigilation of Parliament can protect the people in that situation.

That suggests more select committees, each covering a particular area of policy, with stronger regulators reporting to them and empowered by them. Such a framework would protect the people, expose abuses, make power accountable and open up the obscure processes of government by making far more information available to the media and the public. The powerless need a public defender. Only Parliament can provide it.

We can bring Parliament to the people by establishing regional Grand Committees, holding their meetings in the regions they cover and giving open access to citizens, businesses and organisations to make representations, discuss their problems and be involved in solving them. In the last days of the Labour government, Yorkshire regional MPs held what amounted to a mini-Parliament in Barnsley Town Hall, where we performed like grown-ups. It attracted little local interest because it was a one-off and it wasn't even reported in the *Yorkshire Post*, which by that time was too cash-strapped to send a reporter, but the Public Accounts Committee's meeting in Whitehaven on the specific problem of nuclear waste and decommissioning was a major success, indicating that regular local meetings of select and regional committees can make Parliament more relevant to the people.

The days are long gone when steady growth allowed fair distribution of spending and an efficient civil service could be relied on to ensure fairness. Today's is a zero-sum society. Causes and needs compete and the civil service is a harassed, over-strained, defensive body rather than the Rolls-Royce machine it used to be. Once, it provided considered policy advice to ministers. Now, with the neoliberal revolution, the balance has changed. In the neoliberal era, ministers have the policy roadmaps in their own heads, so the first-class brains of the civil service are reduced to providing second-class defences for third-rate policies. The man in Whitehall doesn't always know best, as Douglas Jay claimed, but he does know a damn sight better than ministers pressured by vested interests and guided by political prejudice.

Only Parliament can ensure a degree of fairness and protection for the public. It can give the people a say in what has become a more political programme. It can also provide for better legislation if the select committees hear representations on legislative proposals in their area, shape the legislation in advance, then review the law in operation in the light of two years of experience.

This regulatory role should become more important than the old legislative role. This is now the parliamentary salt mines and more difficult to improve. Yet it could be made more sensitive by holding pre-hearings on bills to allow objections to be made, then to discuss changes. Most legislation will remain a party responsibility, but all should be subject to a legislative review after two years of application to hear objections and assess whether the bill is achieving its purpose – processes which are particularly necessary where legislation has been rushed through in an emotional spasm, like the Dangerous Dogs Act, which prolonged the lives of several dangerous dogs over arcane arguments as to whether they were pitbull terriers or not. (Give a dog a bad name and some vet will dispute it. For a fee.) All this means more strain for the parliamentary workforce, but this could be eased by involving members of the second chamber in the processes of consideration and review. Nice to give them something useful to do.

One further reform is more controversial. The British political elite have always resisted proportional representation, even though it is the norm in most other countries. Elected Members think the system that elected them is the best in the world, and political parties like the power the elective dictatorship usually gives them, even if it's the power to make horrendous mistakes. Much of the time, the two-party system, sustained by the first-past-the-post electoral system, has worked adequately, if not well. Today, much has changed. Respect for politicians has declined and there is a growing feeling of impotent anger, particularly among areas and people who feel they have been left behind. The parties are divided between Brexiteers and Remainers, left and right, populists and elitists, in ways they haven't been before, and those divisions aren't going to fade away after Brexit, because the old pretences of Cabinet solidarity and party unity are less relevant to a more complex, better-educated society. People are voting tactically on a bigger scale and the electorate appears disinclined to give a majority to either main party. The result is a shambles, not firm government, and that shambles is going to go on because we'll never have glad, confident Churchill again. Only proportional representation can make such a fissiparous situation workable and make Parliament more representative of our more diverse nation.

PR would give every vote an equal value, give every voter an investment in Parliament in the form of representation there, make Parliament more genuinely representative and give it more credibility. By making coalitions more likely, and putting the politicians on a shorter leash, it would ensure that decisions are reached by compromise and negotiation, not by diktat. There is no guarantee of better outcomes, but it would certainly produce a government more acceptable to the nation. Coalitions prevented most European countries from following Mrs Thatcher's onslaught on the post-war settlement. Even in the US, where powers are separated, they avoided austerity because no one had the power to impose it, with the result that, as Senator Daniel Patrick Moynihan put it, 'Reagan borrowed a trillion dollars from the Japanese and threw a party.'

All this will be seen as a change too far by a political elite anxious to keep power in its own hands. Yet it would increase the power of the citizens, as we need to do in a better-educated consumer democracy, where people won't tolerate being treated like sheep. That would be helped by allowing them to vote for the party that comes closest to their preferences. It would increase the power of MPs, who are stronger when their votes have to be won, not just counted. It would create the more sensitive and effective democracy appropriate to a better-educated electorate living in a more complex society. This can only happen if the political elite accepts that our present structures are no longer trusted and can't deliver what the nation wants. The people want more power. The parliamentarians are looking for a more useful role. Both needs can be better accommodated with proportional representation. As on so many issues, we should learn from New Zealand, which voted for PR against the opposition of the politicians and later voted to keep it because it was working well.

CHAPTER FIFTEEN

BECOMING IRRELEVANT

I didn't realise it at the time, but the 2010 election was the start of my downfall. It was an enormous disappointment because my vote had fallen by 5,000, from 47 per cent to 33 per cent, bringing my majority down to 714. The fall was largely due to national trends, Labour's loss of support (and government) and the Lib Dem surge, with Cleggmania pushing their share of the vote up to 22 per cent, but the surprise was the rise in the Tory vote, up 6 per cent thanks to the national swing and the energetic efforts of Victoria Ayling, the first Tory candidate who had nursed the constituency and worked hard to win it.

She deserved better from her party, because an ungrateful Tory Party rewarded Victoria for her success by removing her from the official candidates list, for no reason I could understand, with the result that she defected to UKIP, which was in much closer accord with her strong anti-European views. But the main effect of her success was on me. The size of their majority has a psychological effect on the self-confidence of Members. When I'd had the support of over half of Grimsby's voters in 2001, and nearly half in 2005, it was a boost to my self-confidence. Now that I was down to a third, I was uneasy.

Something was wrong and I didn't know what. For some reason, Grimsby's feelings had changed. I was getting out of tune with the people I represented, the worst thing that can happen to an MP.

Yet there was also a benefit. Neither I nor the Labour Party had realised that North East Lincolnshire was no longer a safe seat to be safely neglected but was becoming a marginal area. The Conservatives had won Cleethorpes with Martin Vickers, a hard-working MP devoted to his constituency, while Grimsby had become marginal. When we'd had two Labour MPs it had been a struggle to get anything out of the Labour government, but the new balance of power meant that the Tory government became more attentive to our needs. Prior to the election, all the local Labour MPs had worked hard to get the tolls slashed on the Humber Bridge, which had become the most expensive crossing in the country. The most we'd got out of Labour was a review of the charges. Ian Cawsey, MP for Brigg & Goole, and I had objected strongly to a Valuation Office Agency proposal to charge retrospective rates to the port employers, which would have bankrupted them. The agency, the minister and Prime Minister Gordon Brown were all obdurate. The rates were due and must be paid. Imagine my joy, then, when the Tories came in and promptly slashed the bridge tolls and wrote off the retrospective rates. 'How did you do it?' I asked Bob Neill, the Tory minister who'd backed our campaign in opposition. 'Buggered if I know,' he replied, but a Treasury official later told me that it was a simple matter of extending the debt, which was in any case hypothetical. Just as in 1931 when the Tories went off gold, which Labour had painfully defended, Sidney Webb ruefully reflected, 'Nobody told us we could do that.' Labour was still deferential to orthodoxies which the Tories have the self-confidence to ignore.

The result of becoming marginal was that Vickers and I in

partnership got a better deal and a better response from the coalition than two Labour MPs had got from the Blair and Brown governments. I kept quiet about this, but the lesson is obvious: become a marginal seat. Safe ones may have more confident (and longer-sitting) MPs, but marginal ones get more from government. Grimsby hadn't done well for being so loyal to Labour.

It was a disillusioning lesson to learn, and I certainly didn't want Grimsby to learn it, but Labour hadn't been faithful to its roots. Yet Ed Miliband as our new leader didn't seem disposed to learn from that failure. Nor did he see that anything needed to be done for the neglected areas of the north and the smaller towns like Grimsby. In fact, his whole aim seemed to be to make it younger, more feminine and more metropolitan trendy, all of which made oldies like me largely irrelevant.

There was no great debate about party policy and what kind of party we should be, as there had been when we'd lost office in 1979. Then, a crop of books and tracts had offered different routes to socialism, new ideas and new policies. Now, public relations replaced thinking, PLP meetings became intolerant of dissent and the lefties stopped attending. I felt isolated and out of date. The only group that still discussed ideas and policies was the Campaign Group. It was stimulating but small and, with Diane Abbott as secretary, badly organised. If the revolution ever comes, the Campaign Group won't be there. Diane will have forgotten to book the room. The Campaign Group was ostracised as hard left but was really an oldies' trip down memory lane, far from the nest of Trotskyites the Blairites felt it to be.

I joined it and, though soft in my own politics, I felt more at home there than standing around waiting for nothing to happen, but it was in fact the final stage of my long day's journey into irrelevance. Nothing seemed less relevant in Miliband's new world than the old and the left, huddled round to cheer each other up. Ideas were dying. Mine were getting out of date and, as the party looked for salvation in youth and freshness, I had little to offer and no prospects to look forward to.

There comes a moment in every MP's life when it's time to go, and a later time when he or she realises it. Both were approaching. Some can't wait to get out. Some realise that their duty is done and go while they can get out gracefully. Too many try to hang on and don't realise it at all, though usually their constituency parties realise it for them and they're out, nilly if not willy. I came into none of these categories. I'd drifted in, drifted on, and eventually I drifted out.

I'd been there too long, though it didn't seem that long to me. The average length of service for retired MPs is around eighteen years, higher in safe seats, lower in the marginals, though the lucky ones who go on winning elections can develop the assumption that they'll carry on for ever. I'd done that. I never gave retirement a thought and never wanted another job. I was doing the job, and I thought I was doing it well, serving Grimsby to the best of my abilities and, I hoped, its satisfaction. Why think about stepping down?

The answer was a disease diagnosed quickly by competitors but more difficult to self-diagnose: age. Inside, you feel twenty-five, the same dynamic young Lochinvar who'd been elected, though in fact I'd been an already middle-aged Lochinvar in 1977. But as you come near shuffling-off point, others see an ageing figure who walks more slowly, has less to contribute and is much less interesting or relevant. When the media begin to describe you as a 'veteran' and young ladies stand in the Tube to offer you their place, it's time to realise that your time is up.

I was reaching that stage in a politician's life cycle when parliamentary life becomes a routine, the old excitement fades and new stimuli, new excitements, new challenges aren't coming along in the way they used to. The first symptom is that you're of less interest to the media. They prefer the immature babble of youths who've just been elected, even though they have little of interest to say. Journalists talk to 'veterans' only if they're desperate. Invitations to lunch drop off, as do invitations to the Spectator awards, to cup finals or even to the Chelsea Flower Show, or other occasions you don't particularly want to go to.

The five years of the Con–Lib coalition were the start of my decline, as well as that of the Lib Dems. We were both on our way out, though they went more quickly and were more surprised than I. Their new partnership with the Tories had made them responsible for illiberal policies which they'd have abused loudly before power lured. I continued to oppose them as I'd done under Thatcher but was disorientated by going back to the futilities of opposition in Parliament's game of musical chairs. Some weeks after the change, I wandered into the government Whips' Office looking for the Chief Whip, to find strange people behind the desks. Pictures of Mrs Thatcher had replaced those of Labour leaders. It took me several minutes to realise we'd changed sides. Dozy bugger.

I'd already been hit by the expenses scandal. I'd been able to dismiss the first round of overspends with jokes about buying whisky because my wife was an alcoholic, or biscuits because they were made in Yorkshire (which led to presents of biscuits from Grimsby fishermen), but the second round of deeper dredging revealed that Barclays Bank had put an increase in my mortgage on a repayment basis. I'd asked that it be on the same basis as the existing mortgage but since then they'd transferred mortgage business to the Woolwich, which had ignored my instructions, so public funding had been paying off part of the capital. I protested my innocence and grudgingly repaid £11,000, but folk always believe that there's no smoke in politics without a raging bush fire, so I was viewed as being as guilty as hell.

The expenses scandal, which hit nearly half of all Members, was the last stage in the long decline of respect for MPs as governments failed to solve the economic problems and austerity punished the people. More people came to surgery because problems multiplied, but at the same time more abuse poured in and the new opportunities of the internet in general and Twitter in particular made it easier to abuse the Member of Parliament, the council and the party. What should have been a new opportunity to keep in touch with the electorate became a cudgel to bash the nearest available surrogate for government. More criticism arrived, particularly about expenses but also about anything else that took the fancy of a discontented nation. I should have ignored it, but I couldn't, so the result was depression and despair. My jokey offer for people who complained about my staff toilet being repainted at public expense to come in and use it was treated as a guilty plea, not a public convenience. No one believed that I could be so careless as not to read bank statements, though my real crime was actually worse. I couldn't understand them.

Grimsby electors and the party no longer seemed as enthusiastic as they had been. My TV shine had worn off. People in Zimmer frames still recognised me, but my age was beginning to show, more to others than to me. In 2010, one elector had told me that he wouldn't vote for me because I was likely to die on the job. I resented his frankness, but it jolted me as I realised that I wasn't quite the exciting, young, dynamic presence I thought myself to be.

After a time, 'Good old Austin' becomes 'That bastard's too old'. Life went on but now it was dragging me behind as I began to realise my age for the first time. Politicians try to show themselves as 'with it' by trotting out the names of their favourite pop group. Now I'd never heard of the names and had only Bob Dylan and Joan Baez to offer. I'd laced the names of television characters into speeches to show the common touch, but no one now knew who Amy Turtle was. *Crossroads* had finished years before. As for jokes for after-dinner speeches, it became clear that the ones I'd stolen from Ken Dodd about mothers-in-law, homosexuals, epileptics, Irishmen and Pakistanis, which had got roars of laughter in the '70s, were not so much funny as politically disastrous. I began to feel like a prehistoric monster speaking an archaic language. Thank God none of the invigilators of political correctness ever discovered my three Yorkshire joke books!

Having learned nothing and forgotten nothing, the Conservatives reverted to the failed policies of the '80s. Been there, opposed that, but now with less energy. Our new leader, Ed Miliband, neither rose to the occasion nor inspired us. He didn't give us the same impetus as Tony Blair had, and preferred to change the decor by making Labour fresher, younger and more fashionable, a vision which clearly didn't include me. Nor did I like Ed Balls's strategy of winning respectability by promising to eliminate the deficit. An accommodation too far and not my cup of Labour, which has to be about spending or it fails. Yet when I said so, people were shocked and fellow members of the Campaign Group didn't support me. Balls's buddies objected and Ed glowered. Safer to shut up and conform than rock the boat or question whether it can float.

I stopped attending Prime Minister's Questions, which had been reduced to ever lower levels by David Cameron's slick nastiness and occasional petulance. Another mistake. PMQs is a bonding process and an opportunity to keep up with the issues. Not attending compounded my isolation. I still made speeches attacking Osborne's wrong-headed austerity, but my Keynesian criticisms of cuts, overvaluation and the euro folly weren't welcomed in a party struggling to present itself as responsible and conservative, with a small, smiling 'c'.

I was reaching my sell-by date. When I attacked Liam Byrne, the Home Office minister, for brutally ignoring my protests and deporting a Pakistani family who'd made a good contribution in Grimsby, the Chief Whip called me in for a dressing-down, with a note-taker ready to write my repentance. His pad remained as blank as his expression. When *The Independent* quoted me as saying I was ashamed to support a party carrying out dawn raids on asylum seekers, a fellow Labour MP invited me to 'fuck off' if I didn't like it.

Finally I collapsed. I was getting slower but not knowing why. I began to set off early for votes so as to avoid holding up my colleagues in the inevitable last-minute rush as I climbed ponderously up the back stairs. En route, I collapsed onto the hard stone flags. I damaged my head and beauty as I fell – thank heavens, in a way, because the shock to my head restarted my heart. Colleagues had to climb over my bleeding body to get to the division but fortunately a medically trained policeman came to my rescue and saved my life.

It turned out I had a leaky heart valve, but because of my head injuries I was taken to King's College Hospital, as head injuries usually are. They had a marvellous coronary team who performed two open-heart operations and implanted a defibrillator. I'd been saved by the NHS, who sent me back to Parliament as the first bionic MP: plastic spine, defibrillator, false teeth and hearing aids.

My first intimation of mortality. I realised suddenly that my time was drawing to a close and began to think, as I never had before, that it was time to go. That trend of thought grew stronger when I returned from a long period in hospital to find that no one had missed me, either in Grimsby, where my wonderful office staff were running the constituency better than if I'd been there, or in Westminster, where the few 'get well' cards had gone to the wrong hospital.

Labour was under the delusion that it now had a prospect of power, mainly because the coalition was so bad rather than because we were so brilliant. They were wrong, of course, because, as my old friend Professor Richard Rose pointed out to me, the Tories could do the dirty on their Lib Dem colleagues and steal their seats, but I shared the delusion and would clearly be nothing but a possible museum exhibit if we came to power. As a sick, possibly senile oldie, I would clearly play no part in any bright new dawn or in the youthful world Ed thought he'd soon be building. Unless they needed a doorman in Downing Street or someone to polish Ed's shoes, and even then there were better and more youthful lickers, whereas I'd probably have found difficulty in doing even those menial jobs.

I resumed work. People told me I looked well, which is what they say to oldies. The media began to give me the 'Don't call us, we'll call you' routine, and I was too proud to call back. I tried to pretend nothing had happened, and I could because the staff in my Grimsby office served the constituency as if it still had an MP. Sue, whom I'd taken over when my neighbour Shona McIsaac had lost the Cleethorpes seat, handled the party and local authority matters; Joyce Benton, who'd been with me for yonks, organised me in her efficient fashion; and Jo Hammond was brilliant at defending the interests of constituents, who were being increasingly bullied under austerity's grudging care. Their energy and skill compensated for the decline in mine. They were the best MP's office in the country, so effective that if other Members had had similar teams we could have managed without any need for MPs at all.

At Westminster, I was kept active and involved by my chairman-
ships in the many all-party groups I'd accumulated: the NUJ Group,
Trading Standards and Consumer Affairs, Fisheries, the Debating
Group and the Photography Group, where I'd organised the annual
exhibition and had persuaded new sponsors to come as our old ones
went bankrupt. I'd joined this early on and taken it over from Roland
Boyes, a brilliant photographer who proposed that the members
should smuggle cameras into the chamber and, at a given signal (from
him), rise and photograph each other. This seemed barmy at the time,
though it's become commonplace with new Members after 2015 taking
photos and selfies in the chamber with their mobile phones. Shocking!
(Though they do have better-looking Members since 2015.)

The Public Accounts Committee, on which I'd managed to get a
place after long years of exclusion, was a major consolation. It was
backroom work that took an increasing amount of time and effort
but was, for me, the most exciting and fascinating part of the job and
became even more so after 2010, when Margaret Hodge took over
the chairmanship and led us into areas of corporate governance, tax
evasion and the excessive power of the Big Four accountancy houses
where I was keen to go.

Many MPs prefer throwing eggs in the chamber to the detail of
committee work, but the PAC is an opportunity to apply a more forensic analysis to major problems, grill officials (most of whom were
less impressive than I'd expected) and make major recommendations
to improve the failing governmental machine and check its overspends
and clumsy failures. Margaret was open to new approaches and Prem
Sikka and I encouraged her to enquire into abuses of power and tax
evasion and avoidance by big multinationals, the Big Four and Britain's powerful tax evasion industry. Prem would watch the committee

proceedings on TV and email me questions and suggestions, a pioneering venture which should be developed. I was less successful on my own because I was getting deaf, so I could ask brilliant questions but not hear the reply. My follow-ups weren't exactly at Marr levels and certainly not as quick.

Useful work and a solace for the old, but largely behind the scenes and out of the headlines. In front of them, I was becoming disposable. Desperate to capture a dynamic image, Ed and his advisers wanted a younger profile for the party. Old, white has-beens were a wart on its youthful face (and remained so until Jeremy Corbyn became leader). They spoiled the party's pretty picture and were more querulous (I called it wise) and inclined to live in the past. The national party had taken control of selections in an effort to keep out ideologues and idiots, but rather than going for quality and intelligence, this control was then used to bring in loyalists and pretty up the PLP by imposing more women and driving out the oldies. Like me.

I saw this as the wrong treatment for Grimsby. The town was a marginal seat where the threat now came from UKIP, not the Tories. Grimsby was strongly hostile to the EU because of what it had done to fishing, which made the UKIP threat more manageable with an anti-European MP, but less so if Labour imposed a young, trendy, enthusiastically European candidate on our staid, more traditional electorate. I wanted the party to be aware of the threat to its heartlands. It took them for granted. I also wanted an independent-minded constituency to be given a noisy, independent-minded MP to fight for it rather than a party hack.

Wise parties overseas impose age limits on MPs and usually require retirement at seventy. It's hypocritical to say it after thirty-eight years of service, but we should too. Better to pick mature, more experienced people as MPs, work them hard and then boot them out to take up a new career after two parliaments, rather than have them sit around hoping for a job, a knighthood or a peerage. Parliaments shouldn't be bed blocked because people are living longer and pompous pillocks hang on with nowhere else to go.

I was beginning to feel that I was a bed blocker too, but still resented suggestions that I should go. They were few, but I'd be eighty-five by the end of the next parliament and the Grimsby party didn't seem too enthused when I told them that Gladstone had been eighty-two when he formed his last government and US Congressman Wilbur Mills had taken up with a stripper, Fanne Foxe, after thirty-five years of service. This might have enthused the shrinking population of local strippers, but was badly received by a party that didn't care about strippers but was beginning to feel my age.

Having reconciled myself to retirement, I wanted to go with whatever dignity is available to geriatric MPs. I had two major concerns. The first was the future of my brilliant staff, who had served me well and Grimsby better. They deserved to carry on. The second was my hope for a good, strong replacement who'd be a credit to Grimsby.

I consulted both the Chief Whip and the leader about retirement, half hoping they'd say, 'Don't go, Austin, we'll love you for ever.' Margaret Hodge said that. They didn't. Not only were they assuming that I would go, but they had already made plans for my successor and proposed to select her by an all-women shortlist (AWS).

Anna Yearley, Ed's political secretary, prepared the way. She came to both meetings and gently explained that I might, at my age, feel that the best available replacement was another man, but the chauvinist north was backward in selecting women and therefore had to have all-women shortlists. Grimsby would set the example. Though she didn't say it, she had the perfect replacement in mind, in the person of an attractive Grimsby-born apparatchick who'd been compliance secretary for the Labour Party in London but had gone north to work for Unison. There she'd joined the Grimsby Labour Party, where she stood out for her attractiveness and youth. It would have been nice to be told what was planned for my funeral. Surrounding MPs, the regional organisation and Ed's coterie were, but I was kept in the dark. Mustn't grumble. Though, being a politician, I do. Parties are brutal creatures. Nick Budgen had pointed out that since the fate of an MP is to be betrayed by his leader, he might at least be betrayed elegantly. The Tories could manage that. Charm isn't on Labour's agenda, however.

At Ed's request, I postponed an announcement which was now being taken for granted. Other evictions came first in the master plan of polishing up the party, which eventually led to the biggest exodus for a long time. I had to go along with him, but I baulked at the insistence on an all-women shortlist. This wasn't because I was anti-women – we do need a better gender balance in Parliament and all-women shortlists are a legitimate way of getting it. But not necessarily for Grimsby, which wasn't a metropolitan trendy town. It would undermine local party democracy and, more important, restrict the range of choice for my successor.

Constituencies like change after a long tenure: lefties are replaced by righties or vice versa, age by youth, constituency servants by ministrables. So there was no reason to assume that the Grimsby Labour Party would want yet another Oxford college fellow, as the past three MPs had been, or a loud-mouthed exhibitionist like the last one. Yet I did hope for quality and stature and I knew that in previous AWS selections only small numbers of candidates had come forward because the pool of eligible women keen to get into Parliament isn't yet as large as it should be to provide a real choice.

I was right. In the event, only three women came forward, including the heir designate and Shona McIsaac, the former MP for Cleethorpes (who'd also been selected on an AWS). A number of able candidates, including an excellent former MP and two people who later became heads of Oxford colleges, were excluded, either because they weren't women (and not prepared to designate themselves as such) or because they were warned off a selection that was already sewn up.

But airing my doubts was construed as a chauvinist attack on women and attracted loud abuse from feminists, as another retiring MP, Mike Wood, had warned me it would. After all, it is up to the local party to accept or reject the restriction of choice. They could say 'no', as the chairman of the Grimsby party wanted to do, though they'd then have to suffer the consequences, which were likely to be more of me. I'd protested to Ed, the Chief Whip and to a national executive who knew nothing about Grimsby's feelings and needs, all in vain. It was like asking the Pope not to be Catholic, and when it became clear that the Grimsby party, and particularly the women, were perfectly happy to have an AWS, I gave in. It wasn't a battle worth fighting if the party didn't want to fight it.

My wife, less easily persuaded than I, worked hard to get more women to apply. She succeeded in finding only one, an excellent candidate who ran the Electoral Reform Society but had the disadvantage (for Grimsby) of being brown. She ran the chosen one a close race but lost, so the heir designate took over. Meanwhile my reservations meant that I left as an out-of-date chauvinist, fit only to be chucked into the dustbin of history, an image I managed to reinforce by clumsy mistakes.

I hadn't realised that discarded MPs are fair game for the media, and jokes about women were completely out of bounds. Youth was all, and I didn't have it. Silence is golden for MPs on their way to the exit. Stupidly, I'd got into the habit of tweeting, the last resort of the geriatric. Conservative MP Louise Mensch had decided to leave Parliament and go to New York, citing a desire to spend more time with her family. Her husband, meanwhile, had told an interviewer that she had stepped down partly out of a fear of losing to Labour. From the train as I travelled south, I tweeted a clumsy joke that this ardent feminist was really leaving because her husband wanted her to. Abuse poured in. By the time my train reached London, I'd received demands from both the Chief Whip and Ed Miliband that I should eat humble pie and withdraw this monstrous slur. I didn't, but was then pursued round the building by Ed's enforcer. I hid.

The farce was repeated when I tweeted that the Pfizer takeover of Astra Zeneca was industrial rape. More outrage. Did I not realise the horror of rape and the sufferings of women who'd been raped? Again, instructions from the Chief Whip to withdraw and apologise. I asked whether Labour MPs were allowed to read Pope's 'Rape of the Lock', but no one seemed to know what that was. Finally, an even bigger torrent was unleashed when I made the mistake of criticising all-women shortlists. In the new world, as in the Communist show trials in 1938, sin requires confession and punishment. Criticising AWSs was an attack on women, feminism and probably civilisation.

Invited on *Newsnight* to repent, I had to sit there vainly trying to extenuate my crime while Stella Creasy and Kirsty Wark chuntered on, denouncing me and men generally. Stella is an excellent MP and a powerful campaigner but talks so fast she's incomprehensible and will never knowingly allow herself to be interrupted. Kirsty impartially agreed at some length. I was reduced to sitting on a penitent's stool in a regional newsroom vainly waving my arms in a desperate attempt to get a word in, which only reinforced feminist feelings that I was a pathetic chauvinist who couldn't even defend himself when confronted by two brave women in the main studio in London.

I was too old to learn the language, or to realise that the new rules forbade mentions of Hitler, opposition to AWSs and any criticism of women. All were symptoms of chauvinist dementia, a worse crime than liking Tories, which I was also accused of because I cooperated with some on anti-EU campaigns.

I compounded these crimes when *The Independent* headlined me as saying that 'even if we selected a raving alcoholic sex paedophile we wouldn't lose Grimsby'. I had said it, as a joke. I thought I'd told them that, but on their transcript of the interview there was a long gap during which I'd raved on but they claimed not to have heard me because of a fault in the connection. When I protested, I got a lecture from the editor pointing out that responsible journalism and their duty to the truth required them to publish. I should have known that in modern journalism anything you say can be taken down and used against you under the excuse that it's a crusade for truth.

Clearly my retirement was not going to be a sad farewell and a gold watch. I announced it on YouTube, which annoyed the authorities in a palace which doesn't like being used for political purposes. Labour List chronicled my offences, put me down as an 'attention seeker' and said, 'Withdrawing the whip for attacking the party would be an unsuitable solution – that's a slippery slope that no one should encourage the party to embark on – but frankly he should have received such a punishment for previous offences.' My neighbour in Hull East, Karl Turner, kindly wrote to tell me:

You're a joke, Austin. That's very sad to see but it's becoming increasingly apparent. You think it clever to attack us. It's not clever and you've had plenty out of the party. I am reluctant to pull you up publicly because you love the attention so very much. If you can't say anything supportive just keep your opinion to yourself.

He didn't sign it 'Yours fraternally'. I published the letter in the press as an example of our mutual admiration. No use getting upset or depressed, though I was, but it would have been daft to give them any more excuses for heaping faggots on the pyre (or even making a joke about faggots).

It was all over. The selection of my replacement was like Hobson's choice with Hobson excluded for being male. The chosen one was backed by the regional party, who excluded my three children, Grimsby Labour Party members for thirty years, from the ballot (with no offer of a refund of their contributions). Melanie Onn was duly selected as my successor. I took photographs of the triumph and left the rejoicing party celebrating. My era was over. Melanie improved on my vote in the election and proved to be a vigorous local MP, much better at reviving the local party than I'd been. She reached the front bench after a few weeks, which I hadn't managed in four decades, and was so good at raising money that she made a profit on her first two elections. Sadly, she refused to keep on any of my brilliant staff or take over my files. Forty years of work were carted off to Hull University Library to fascinate future generations of historians.

It was time to shuffle off the Grimsby coil with as much dignity as I could muster. Labour's transition arrangements ensured that wasn't a lot. I consoled myself with the thought that I'd done my best for Grimsby, and it would be less than best if I'd gone on doing it.

Rather than conduct a state funeral in which I'd provide the corpse, my supporters organised a big send-off dinner for everyone who's no one in Grimsby. Helen Clark, the former Labour Prime Minister of New Zealand, came, spoke and sang 'Pokarekare Ana', which moved me to tears. Linda made a great film extolling the town and its prospects to cheer everyone up. Off we went. I was sad to leave Grimsby, but mainly I regretted that my staff were unemployed. They deserved better.

No farewell letter from Ed Miliband, though I had hoped he might give me the Ed stone for my garden. No gold watch from the party, though I did get a lovely tribute from Defend Council Housing and a smashing painting of the docks (plus a glittery pair of braces) from the Grimsby party. *Sic transit Austin*. All that work, and all that public spending to make me a better MP, down the drain.

CHAPTER SIXTEEN

IS THERE LIFE AFTER PARLIAMENT?

For the big boys and a few girls there is. All political careers end in failure, though it can be a beautifully decorated and comfortable one in the House of Lords. Clement Attlee said of his own retirement:

> Few thought he was even a starter
> There were many who thought themselves smarter
> But he ended PM
> CH and OM
> An earl and a knight of the garter.

He deserved all of it, though his successors in our more mercenary age have declined the trimmings and the ermine and gone straight into the money mines to dig a few millions to comfort their failure.

It's different for backbenchers. Their careers end on the dump. My own career had begun with promise, drifted into irrelevance and ended in oblivion. For me and for all who toil on the back benches of political life, the end is sad. Unlike the sentimental songs about 'the leaving of Liverpool' or 'leaving on a jet plane', leaving Parliament is sharp, abrupt and as emotional as toast popping out of the toaster. You're the corpse in a funeral as silent and swift as the burial of Sir John Moore at Corunna, though not quite as memorable. When Leon Trotsky retired from the revolution in Russia, his reward was an ice pick to the head. That doesn't happen in Britain, but you're equally dead.

The past is another party and another parliament. So are you, and they want you out with as much speed and as little fuss as is appropriate for politicians. Two days max. Your office is needed for someone else. So is the constituency to which you've devoted so much attention and effort. As for your once and former colleagues and 'friends', Parliament works on the principle that in death and departure, there is hope (for everyone else).

Alan Clark remarked that MPs enjoy nothing so much as the execution of a colleague. You've made them happy by opting for the next best thing: retirement. They won't thank you for it. There's little courtesy left in the Commons and they're too busy dividing up the spoils to bother about you. So you have to be shuffled off the board to become just another name on the long list of MPs going back to the thirteenth century, which no one reads. There's more ceremony and regret, and far better rewards, when contestants leave the *Big Brother* house, and at least they get an opportunity to spill the beans on the folk they're leaving. You don't. You're more likely to face a garbled list of accusations, ranging from telling dirty jokes to admiring a woman MP's legs. Much is made of inappropriate touching, though no one ever touched me, and there are even claims of satanic witchcraft in Dolphin Square, with a little child murder and a lot of rape for afters. Put your head down, zip up your mouth and trousers and say nowt, though in my case the lack of accusations was really an indication of how unimportant I'd been.

I did get a few consoling letters from other mavericks such as Tam

Dalyell and Ann Widdecombe, and farewells from some of the organisations I'd helped (the nicest from the Trots' nest of Defend Council Housing), but not a word from Ed Miliband or the Labour Party, either nationally or regionally (though they kept writing to me as they now do to all party members, asking if I'd like to stand for Whitby or Calder Valley or anywhere). Been there, done that. No word came from the GMB, or my fellow fighters for freedom, truth and justice.

One minute you're a man of destiny, striding purposefully down the corridors of power, a VIP in restaurants, vying for your custom, and in the health service, which is particularly keen to keep you alive if you're a Labour MP. You're lobbied by interest groups, consulted by pollsters (who pay you for thoughts you don't have) and treated with respect by people and pressure groups daft enough to think you have some power.

The *Grimsby Gazette* prints your press releases announcing that you've managed to ensure the No. 18 bus runs on time. You're in demand for television and radio interviews, if only to balance some Tory fool or be outbid on everything by a passing Liberal, the party that can promise anything because it will never have the chance to deliver. If you can manage to find something striking to say, or talk fashionable rubbish, you may get the honour of being shouted at by Andrew Neil or heckled by John Humphrys or even embalmed by Michael Cockerell.

All this because you were a junior member (pro tem) of the political class you're now leaving. When you go, you lose it all. You're chucked out to be forgotten, into a changed world where you must catch up with everything you've neglected in the long scrabble of politics: culture, family, pets, garden, even the neighbours. The world may once have been your oyster. Now you've got to shell out for everything you once got for free.

It's changed. What had previously been free – travel, computers, housing, overseas visits and the beautifully bound (and unread) volumes of Hansard (saleable now only as room decor) – must now be paid for, at prices which have rocketed while you've been cosseted by the state. Where you'd once had staff to do anything you wanted – to research obscure facts, or bring cups of tea, gossip and the news about who Eric Joyce has bopped or George Galloway sued – now everything is DIY, even talking to the wife and family you've neglected for so long.

You're out. With you goes the huge accumulation of papers, reports you've never read, mementos from overseas visits, souvenirs of this or that forgotten election campaign, or fight for justice for people whose names you don't recognise, or compensation you didn't get, minutes of vital meetings which achieved nothing, and information about governments, home and abroad, which have been dumped or shot. It's all packed in boxes and sent after you, even though you've nowhere to put it and no desire to ever look at it again.

You must leave the constituency for which you've worked so hard for so little gratitude for so long. Your party wants you bound and gagged, so that you don't spill the beans on the past few decades. The constituency party would rather forget you ever represented it because they've now selected someone different and much better, and the new Member wants to show how much difference their greater youth, energy and charm can achieve for a constituency which has been neglected for yonks. All the organisations that had once been begging for you to attend their coffee mornings, handicraft sales and fêtes suddenly fall silent. Even the ones for whom you've suffered every possible humiliation, from being slapped in the face (repeatedly) with a wet haddock to arriving last, sweaty and panting, in their sponsored runs, neither tell you what's happened to the money you've helped raise nor hold out any prospect of you benefiting from it.

Mrs Thatcher had the status, and the bossy personality, to attempt back-seat driving. You have neither, and it's humiliating to tread sour grapes or try to justify your life's work. It's all ephemeral. People now want something new and different and no one wants to know about you. They've had enough. They just want you to go silently to the bourn from which no traveller returns. If possible, to follow Napoleon into exile. Not necessarily as far away as St Helena. That may be too accessible now they've built the airport.

You're Mr or Ms Nobody, re-entering a strange new world which has changed unrecognisably while you've been running round in small political circles. You're Rip Van Winkle dressed in a suit and tie, as people used to be, head filled with the facts, feel and faces of thirty years ago, all now irrelevant, and desperately trying to catch up with a new world you don't quite understand.

It's no use demanding 'Don't you know who I am?' They don't. You aren't. Some say 'Didn't you used to be…' but then tail off because they're not sure what, either because they're senile or because they think you're someone they vaguely remember from the *News of the World*. You're no longer a figure of stature, just another shuffling pensioner babbling about something they don't quite remember or understand but know they didn't like.

For the first time in years there's time to reflect. For mere backbench MPs, that isn't on success or acclaim. My triumphs were few enough with Grimsby still in decline, the north drained, equality less and the economy less able to lay golden eggs. All that makes gloating impossible and no one loves those who claim to have been right before the catastrophe, because they see such a claim as underlining their own stupidity before it. My successes were too few to fill much thinking time, which provided more space and time to think about the reasons I failed, though I knew them well enough already.

When I went into Parliament, I got three pieces of advice. In the Strangers' bar, a disconsolate Geordie said, 'You're that chap who does that TV programme, aren't you?'

'*Don't Ask Me?*' said I.

'Well, I am and I like it,' he said. 'You shouldn't do it.'

Michael White, at that time *The Guardian*'s humorous sketchwriter, but a serious man with an inner Norman Shrapnel, told me off for trying to be funny. 'Don't make jokes. It's a sure way to fail in politics.'

Joe Ashton, the man who got me into politics, read the draft of *Four Years in the Death of the Labour Party* and said, 'Don't publish it, for Christ's sake. They'll never forgive you.'

All three were wise men. All three were right. I ignored them all and suffered the consequences for thirty years.

The fact is I was a loner who'd come in too late and didn't particularly want to climb another ladder. Slippery-pole climbing wasn't my game and no fun. I'd much rather watch others do it and try to explain their failures while I devoted my own efforts to pursuing hares all over the landscape, doing television and cooking on too many ovens. All that was more interesting than committing myself body and soul to politics, to getting on or to becoming rich. MPs who aren't bothered are a rare commodity and regarded by their fellow Members with a mixture of bemusement and contempt. They're safe to be ignored.

I was nice. Sadly, that's no virtue in politics or in any other jungle, and these days it's no longer necessary even in life. In any case niceness is the enemy of awkwardness, which, as Tam Dalyell had shown, is vital for dissenters. Yet, looking back, it seems clear that I'd tried too hard to be a commentator rather than a participant, not realising that pundits shouldn't do politics. Prophets are without honour in their own party and they're no bloody use in the scrum. Thinking too much about the shape of the ball means fumbling it. I didn't make a good disciple and had found no one I wanted to disciple to, except other loners like Denis Healey, Peter Shore and Bryan Gould, who'd all died or deserted.

I tried to take solace in the thought that the age had failed me rather than me failing it. After I'd come into Parliament on the ebb tide of social democracy, the tide began to flow the other way and I'd arrived just in time for Margaret Thatcher's coronation and the triumph of everything I opposed: finance, greed, wealth and markets. From being part of a Keynesian consensus I'd gradually become a minor but quavering voice in a chorus of dissent that no one listened to. Politics, which had still been a respectable occupation in the '70s, had become a minority sport and as attractive as drug smuggling or porn peddling. In thinking that the world had failed, not me, I was clearly falling back on the old political trick of blaming other people for my own failure. That made reminiscence a little easier.

I reflected on all this. As an inveterate moralist, I thought I should. But not for too long. My wife had pointed out most of my mistakes and failures already, at some length. I was no longer in political life, so why look or feel perpetually miserable? I was me, not Tony Blair. I didn't have to devote my life to refighting the Iraq War. Or anything else.

My faults were mine and were reflections of my personality, but because I was a backbencher I never had much power, so why should I carry any burden of blame for anything? My virtues had had all the impact of a eunuch in a harem, so why not assume that my faults had been equally impotent? If we hadn't built Jerusalem, that was more the fault of Tony and Gordon, along with Mrs Thatcher's demolition crew. I absolved myself of any responsibility for either.

In any case, at my stage of life faults won't be corrected and failures are irredeemable, so there's little point in wasting time or money either in thinking about them or in trying to explain that I'd really been right all along. Those at the top of the pole are far better at doing that and have far more need to. For the rest of us in the political game, it's better to look on the bright side than play Hitler in his bunker. Too much Götterdaämmerung makes Jack a dull boy.

There are some benefits to pulling out of Parliament. While you've been in it, the world has been rebalanced to give a better deal to the baby boomers (that's you, even though you never boomed in your life). The world has showered them with capital gains on their houses and shifted the costs of their health care and sheltered accommodation, whether in the Lords or the Grimsby senior citizens centre, onto the younger generation to teach them respect. Life may be worse for those at the bottom of the heap, but for those at the top, even if they're visitors not residents, it's bearable.

Now you're out of Parliament you're no longer a brainless sheep to be herded round at the will of party, constituency or causes. There's no longer a clamour of demands and commitments. You're your own master, free do anything you want within, or without, reason. He may not have realised it at the time but Sir Shortly Floorcross's 1945 cry 'We are the masters now' can only be realised on leaving Parliament. You have. And you are.

Brush away the tears. The pressure and stress of living two lives, one in the constituency and another in Westminster, the tightly timetabled trudges from one useless meeting to another and the wait for votes to decide nothing is suddenly lifted. There's no longer a vital need to campaign for getting Grimsby on the signposts of the M1, in the hope that someone will want to go there. There's the blessed relief of not having to trek down and back up the A1 to London every week, battling through clogged-up rush hours at one end, to arrive bleary and late at night to a deserted town at the other, having passed en route and remembered the site of every crash, breakdown and off-road skid you've had over the years. Who could miss the delights of Doncaster railway station in the rain or the invigorating diesel fumes of London's permanent traffic jams?

The joys of retirement are widely proclaimed in adverts and an out-pouring of books on the fun of approaching death. Retirement is said to bring a new fulfilment as the start of a happy second life of cruise ships, travel to the sun, whizzing up and down on Stannah stair lifts, even a new sexual bliss with the aid of a little Viagra and a lot of waiting.

It's all a bit exaggerated, but you can take up opportunities to cook, paint or practise t'ai chi (or is it lychee?), look over your stamp collection or take up fretwork. You can put your name down for an allotment if some other codger dies. You can take up knitting, though you'll find that needles which once cost ten pence now are imported and cost £5. These are opportunities you've never had (and probably never wanted) before. There's also the chance to read and time to think, neither of which you had when you could do anything about it. Now you're one of the spectators, not a player. That can be a little frustrating. Politics have gone so seriously wrong without you to talk sense into the idiots who've taken over from you that it's sickening to watch.

You're your own master. Just in time to discover that you're not sure what you want to do and are less capable physically of doing it. Sadly, for most retirees, this picture of golden years for silver heads is a myth to conceal the aimless drift of a pensioner's life, rotting their brains with daytime TV, reliving through it decades of programmes they never saw. Or suffering in medical waiting rooms and hospital beds from pre-existing conditions which suddenly blossom once the pressure is taken off.

At home, retired MPs can sit in their easy chairs (less comforta-ble than the library's) trying to remember better times while getting under the feet of a spouse who's suddenly become more powerful, more demanding and certainly more bossy than the whips used to be. The household's balance of power has shifted spousewards. After years of subordination and admiring silence for every platitude MPs utter, retirement allows spouses (no longer spice) to take revenge and change from accessory to boss. Don't ask 'Who is the master now?' It ain't you.

The immediate test of retirement is whether you become peer or pensioner. Rewarded at £360 a day, a peerage is the sign that you're still marginally in the game, even if it only seems that way to fellow peers. In the Lords, you're kept warm in ermine, there are capacious sofas to sleep on and you can mix with the great and the dud, discarded Liberals, all perfectly preserved, along with high rollers daft enough to have donated over £200,000 to the Tories to sit on the Aldermanic bench of life and be paid for lamenting that the country has gone to the dogs.

If you aren't sent to this parliamentary retirement home (and you won't be if you've ever joked that Tony Blair might have been wrong or Ed Miliband is a pillock), then clearly your party doesn't want you. You're no one. If you get there, they'll know you're a super-creep and possible grandmaster of the old English art of arselikhan and therefore not worth listening to. If you don't, they'll know that your party would prefer you to be concrete booted in the river, so they have no need to listen to you either.

Civilian oldies join pensioners' clubs. In Grimsby, retired dockers and fishermen used to hold regular get-togethers to talk about old times. Nothing like that for MPs. They have an organisation run by the dullest of survivors which brings together, for a small fee, MPs who never particularly liked each other to reminisce about how well they got on together. Retired parliamentarians need myths to live by to justify their work. Yet they know each other too well to believe them, and old hatreds linger, it's just that they're less able to fight them. The deputy governor of Wandsworth told me that when two Labour MPs were sent to his prison, one refused to share a cell with the other, 'that left-wing bastard'. The organisation's newsletter is filled with obituaries (saying *nihil nisi* shovelfuls of *bonum* about each of the not-very-dear departed). It carries rambling reminiscences which you know can't possibly be true. It meets in London, where no one in their right mind would want to go. Unless they're paid, and you're not.

Former Members are allowed visiting rights to parts of the palace at times when no one else wants to go there, but if they do visit, existing Members are usually too busy to talk to them. You can watch proceedings on television but only to see a lot of people you no longer recognise doing what you used to do better. Watching TV, you can no longer exercise your thighs by bobbing up and down to get called, or raise your blood pressure in the way Question Time used to. You can't heckle or throw in clever interjections, either. Switch to another channel before you burst into tears.

It may make you happy to think you could do better than the present lot, with the country in so much of a mess. It's certainly true, but no one cares. Ex-Labour MPs have the satisfaction of knowing that if they'd stayed they could have been in the shadow Cabinet for a week or two, and former Tories will know they'd have been a better Prime Minister than Theresa the Terrible. But wishful thinking is no use. Let's face it, who cares? They didn't before. Why should they now?

The worst thing about keeping up with your old world is seeing what a mess your successors are making of it since your wise influence has been removed. No nous, this new lot. The same old insolvable problems are being tackled by new idiots, who'll fail in the same old way. Speeches are read like sixth-form essays, ministers fratch, parties split and argue, and the whole caboodle is viewed with so much contempt by the public that you'll think it better to keep quiet about the fact that you ever had anything to do with it. Better keep quiet too about the fact that it was all so much better in your day, because it shows you've been part of the system. Try to speak out and no one will report it. Go on Twitter and you'll be deluged with abuse and called a dinosaur, demented or a doddering idiot who should never have been elected in the first place and was probably drummed out for fiddling expenses. It's a frustrating life for someone who's not used to shutting up, but Valium is the better part of discretion.

The media are flooded with appeals for donations to save wild animals, distressed gentlefolk, battered wives and starving children. Ex-MPs, more ex than most exes, get no such support. At the time of writing there are 954 of them at loose in the world but no charity protects or helps them. Most people wonder why they're not put in the stocks or whipped.

Americans exes keep their titles. Once a senator always a senator – or a congressman or a governor. There, grey hair is allowed on television and even viewed as a sign of wisdom, not rigor mortis.

In Australia, New Zealand and Canada, the once Honourable keep the title, however little they've done to deserve it. In Britain, those who've quietly betrayed their constituents for decades become knights, and those appointed to the Privy Council can continue to be Right Honourable, even though they're neither and have never even attended the farce. But why bother? Grimsby is placarded with plaques commemorating openings by Rt Hon. Austin Mitchell, but I never bothered to tell them I wasn't either and they wouldn't have known what I was talking about if I had. I just accepted the promotion in modest silence, knowing they couldn't afford to repaint the plaque. In a country in such a mess as ours, any kind of title is a sign that you may be responsible. Better just wear sackcloth and ashes and subside gracefully into being just another pensioner and not even an esquire.

Besides, telling people you've been an MP reminds them that you've been a total waste of large sums of the public's money. Millions have been spent on training MPs, supporting them, carting them round the country and the world, providing housing, libraries, computer staffs and travel to make them better Members of Parliament. On retirement, several million pounds which have been spent to make Members better MPs is all thrown away. Do you really want to remind anyone of that?

The constitutions of other countries announce that all people are equal. In Britain they never have been, and ex-MPs are less equal than most. Those who've managed to scrabble and claw their way to the top of the greasy pole can write books to tell the world how they did it, and give speeches for large sums to gullible groups of Americans and Chinese who don't know what a mess they've made back home. Some Tories fall back on the mattress capitalism provides for its minions by taking up business jobs as advisers, lobbyists and directors to add a touch of status to dodgy companies and lobby for their nefarious purposes, though rarely on the George Osborne scale. Labour MPs are a glut on the market. Which could be why some of them spend so much parliamentary time accumulating property for retirement.

The smart ones jump ship early on. Those who haven't been smart enough to do that are thrown onto a market that doesn't want them. No reprocessing is available at this late stage and it's a bit late for cosmetic surgery. The Washington Speakers Bureau has lost their address. So has every one of those local organisations who once clamoured for MP orations to fill time. The most the retired backbencher gets, if they're really unlucky, is an invitation to some pensioners' club fifty miles away to talk about 'the funny side of Parliament (no politics please)' with a PS warning that they are unable to pay travelling expenses.

Those with a strong exhibitionist streak can do telly. Michael Portillo took to the trains and succeeded brilliantly. Others go on reality shows keen to make a fool of anyone for a fat fee. Ann Widdecombe bravely appeared in the *Big Brother* house and on *Strictly Come Dancing*. Ed Balls danced into show-biz and really enjoyed it. Edwina Currie appeared on everything that's going, though she wasn't offered a part on *Celebrity Love Island*. Media managers haven't yet devised a *Strictly Come Politics* show for other exes to appear on, but it would only have featured a pillory and an audience well supplied with tomatoes. That might not have been a big enough draw, even for Channel 4.

A very few retire to riches. Tony Blair owned thirty-seven properties in 2016 worth a total of £427 million, but compare that with David Cameron huddled in a £14,000 caravan writing his memoirs. The prospects for you, Mr or Ms Average Ex-MP, tainted as you are with politics, distrusted by party and people and clapped out by service, are not bright. You can write. No one will publish it. Offer advice, but no one wants to take it. Tweet even on a Trumpian scale, like Denis MacShane, who tweets for Europe, but no one will read or retweet them. Everywhere you're liable to be dismissed as a geriatric whose time has not only gone but never came in the first place. You're just a pre-loved (and not very much loved, at that) MP, well past your sell-by date, who's not prepared to do the decent thing by kicking the bucket and therefore must hang around quietly waiting for the Grim Reaper to call, as the Speaker once did, while wondering if he'll look like Norman Tebbit.

It's like leaving school without the tears and sentiment. Had Your Chips, not Mr Chips. A few masochists try to get back for a second chance to fail. The unwise complain, like Jamie Reed, who said on

leaving Parliament, 'I arrived with a healthy contempt for its culture, behaviours and practices; I leave with the knowledge that this
contempt was correct.' This will earn a paragraph in *The Sun*, but everywhere else it merely generates amazement at the stupidity of anyone
who has put up with it for so long.

Some write alibiographies to dispute the verdict of history and
prove that they were right all along, but that's a luxury allowed only to
the top people. Some even self-publish, which is an expensive way of
producing books for no one to read, fit only to be given away. For the
rest, there may be opportunities in window cleaning, and experience at
canvassing could come in useful for door-to-door brush sales.

You won't be poor. The parliamentary pension isn't bad by the
standards of 1957, as the *Daily Mail* never ceases to remind everyone.
But sinking into obscurity, being plunged into silence and generally
ignored is a terrible fate for those who've devoted their whole lives
to attention seeking, pretending to be powerful, and pontificating on
everything that comes to hand. When even the spouse (or, as we used
to call her, the wife) doesn't want to hear, it's time to shut up.

The only consolation is that as a member of a failed and reviled political
class, now viewed as dishonest, incompetent and corrupt, who've devoted
their lives to committees which achieve nothing and hanging around for
votes which decide nothing, you can at least have a rest. Let someone else
take the blame for ruining what was once a perfectly nice little country.

Ex-MP syndrome is a medical condition. Call it post-parliamentary
triste, it's been well diagnosed by Dame Jane Roberts, who interviewed
the ejectees of 2015 (a record year for discards) and concluded that:

> most had experienced a period of what, at best, was described as dis-
> location. Many had initially struggled to find a new narrative about

who they were and what they did … It had been a time of emotional turmoil with a profound sense of personal failure. Many felt deeply angry at the lack of acknowledgement from the political party they had served so loyally. [Say that again, Dame Jane.] There was a deep sense of frustration that there was so little interest in the skills, knowledge and experience gained in political office.

Bang on the nail, though it may have something to do with the collapse of respect of politics as well as the high pretensions and low prospects of its practitioners.

I was lucky. I felt no great desire to go back and I didn't miss either the dusty corridors of non-existent power or the phoney pomposities of Parliament. I found myself able to do things I'd had no time for before, like reading, thinking and understanding. Even though I now had to pay for the press and television, I could get to know more about what was going on than I had gossiping in the tea room or working in my office. I was liberated from hectic overwork, boring committees, the joys of the A1 and the endless political treadmill. It was nice to be my own master, not someone else's sheep.

I was even more lucky that my departure from Parliament was followed by the thrill of the battle of Brexit. Unable to decide what to do, but overconfident in their indispensability, the politicians handed power back to the people with a referendum they were sure would ratify their wisdom. Angered by three decades of cuts, stagnant living standards, deindustrialisation and austerity, the people used this unaccustomed power to express their view on Europe, decades of neo-liberalism, globalisation and austerity.

The referendum needed a debate. As one of the few survivors of that rare breed, once abounding, but now nearing extinction, the

Labour Eurosceptic, I was suddenly in demand to provide a balance to overconfident Euro-enthusiasts and disgruntled Tories, by supplying a Labour fig leaf for those insane enough to want to leave the Franco-German Condominium. This produced a series of invitations to speak on the same platform as Tories and even UKIP at meetings all over the north, repeating arguments against the EU that I'd been making for years but no one had previously heard.

I was greeted enthusiastically by Tories I'd disliked and opposed for years, but shunned by Labour colleagues who were mostly (and sanctimoniously) on the other side. My friend Bob Marshall-Andrews was so enthusiastic about the EU that he deserted Labour to join the Lib Dems, though he excluded me from his Euro-enthusiastic fulminations against the Brexiters in his old stomping ground for extenuating reasons:

> You represented the lantern-jawed, sturdy fishermen of England, who had good reason to complain. That is a long way from the monstrously tattooed, drunken, racist xenophobic, lumpen BNPers it was my privilege to serve in Medway. They are now in full cry to crush the saboteurs and hunt down the enemies of the people.

I wrote back to thank him for finding me guilty but insane and offered to defend him from the tumbrils (for a small fee). Blair wouldn't have done more to help this renegade QC, even though Bob was agreeing with him for the first time in history.

The Brexit campaign was the best fun I'd had for years. I enjoyed telling Eurosceptics all over the north what they wanted to hear. It was marvellous to harangue large audiences who were with me rather than sitting there in stony-faced silence as Labour audiences had. Even more wonderfully, the campaign ended in triumph. Victory was a strange new phenomenon. It had never happened to me before. I was as euphoric as any politician is ever allowed to be.

It was in fact a peasants' revolt rather than a triumph for my arguments, but it was good to see it, gratifying to have participated in the struggle and even more so to have achieved something after years of political struggle. It was also a victory more important than Brexit. Given the EU's intransigence and the weakness of an insecure government in negotiating, withdrawal will be messy and difficult. But the vote was also one against the neoliberal policies followed by both parties over the decades I'd toiled so unsuccessfully against them on the back benches. It demonstrated the unhappiness of the British people with the state to which three decades of neoliberalism, austerity, public service failure, static incomes and increasing inequality had reduced them.

In doing that, the referendum forced policy change. Austerity was dropped as a policy of strength through suffering. Government was forced to spend, or to promise future spending, to alleviate the glaring problems produced by the cuts in public services like health, housing and education, and in local government, where authorities were at the end of their tether. Glaring abuses in tax avoidance and evasion, excessive financial power, and casualisation and underpayment in the gig economy stood revealed and were tentatively tackled. The Tory government promised to give priority to those just about managing (the JAM folk) rather than to wealth and power, and Labour shook off its inferiority complex and began to look to more radical policies, realising that its job is to deliver betterment, not to dilute neoliberalism. In all this, the vote achieved much of what I'd struggled for so long and so vainly.

Its real importance was not to take us out of the European Union but to end the long march down Dead-End Street. No thanks to me, and thirty years too late, but Slick Dave and Malevolent George were booted out. The pound fell to slightly more competitive levels, the path to the necessary reconstruction and rebalancing was opened and both parties were forced to realise that eliminating debt is not the be all and end all of government, but leads to a poorer, meaner and less happy society. No honour for me, nor for the few others who had warned in vain, but a sense of quiet satisfaction does soothe political impotence.

For me, it was the turning point I'd hoped for since 1979. The people had achieved what the politicians had failed to. Just as in New Zealand two decades before they'd taken their revenge in the only way open to them: by referendum. Perhaps that's the only way change can come in our complacent, conservative country, but it's a shame that it took so long and that so much damage was done before it came. Winning is rare in the political game. But it's nice all the same.

It's not, though, the key to belated acclaim. After the referendum, invitations to speak dried up as if I'd been a personal friend of Jimmy Savile. *The Guardian* lost every article I sent them (as it had before, but now without explanation or reply). The BBC, which had used me as a tame Brexiteer throughout the campaign, once it was over immediately replaced me with a Muslim to keep up their other diversty targets.

I took solace by going to New Zealand to teach a summer school at Canterbury University. There, I fell back in love with a country I should never have left in the first place. It too had been damaged by neoliberalism, applied there by the Labour Party in which I'd retained membership just in case I failed to make it in Britain. The People's Paradise had been quicker to reject neoliberalism, and had taken their revenge by bringing in proportional representation, putting the politicians on a short leash to stop future rushes to folly. The result was contentment and a country at ease with its politicians.

My visit to New Zealand was enjoyable, but all good things must come to an end, as Tony Blair said. I returned home to an Alan Bennett lifestyle of pottering, reminiscing and going to funerals. That's the lot of the retired MP on the scrapyard of life.

No swan song. No regrets. I've tried. I've failed, as all politicians must. But I've done my best. Being a maverick is more interesting and useful than climbing the slippery pole, which means I've enjoyed a pretty unenjoyable job more than most. Both roles demand the same single-minded, obsessive drive, as well as the same total commitment to the political arts of working, fighting and fiddling; the difference is whether these traits are used for public benefit or personal advancement. Politics is not for the faint-hearted and it's no use going into them unless you're committed full-time and obsessively, whether to your cause or to yourself. Such total devotion was beyond me. I was a better observer than player and wanted to live a life as well as play the game. So it's best just to say I've done my best to advance people, party and Grimsby, and though I've achieved little for any of them, I've not let them down. And I've had fun in the process.

I've enjoyed it. Most of it. Now there's damn all I can do about any of it, except sit and watch a new generation go through the same dances and fail in their turn against the inertia of the system. It's their time not mine now. Though trying the old solutions to the old problems is said to be a sign of madness, it's also very British, and now it's someone else's time to do it. Mine is to watch. Ex-MPs whose strutting time is over must, like chimney sweepers, come to dust. For me, as Roy Orbison said, 'It's over. It's over. It's oooooooover.'

ACKNOWLEDGEMENTS

Those who rise to the top in politics have ghosts more skilled than they to help them write their autobiographies. Most spectacularly, Winston Churchill had a powerful team of historians, advisers and researchers working on his marvellous outpourings. The backbencher entering alibi-land, in print as in life, must struggle on alone.

Which doesn't mean that he or she doesn't owe a thousand debts, both for support in four decades of happy mavericking and for the harder struggle of putting ego to paper. I certainly do, both for a career that couldn't have been accomplished without the support, the indulgence and the acquiescence of a host of consenting others, and for a book that would never have emerged without the work of people far more skilled at their craft than I.

My thanks, therefore, to the electors of Grimsby, taciturn but lovely each and every one of them, whether they voted for me or not, for their patience and tolerance, and to the Grimsby Labour Party, who put up with me and endured decades of my jejune monthly lectures without apparent derangement. Best of luck too to my successor, Melanie Onn.

My thanks to the companions who supported me on my maverick

journey (the few, not the many), particularly to Bryan Gould, John Mills, Helen Clark, Michael Meacher (RIP), John McDonnell, Kelvin Hopkins, Prem Sikka, Eileen Short and anyone else whose name I've missed out but who should be inscribed on my war memorial.

MP is a title but its power depends on its backing team. By their staffs shall ye know them and mine were the best. Joyce Benton, Jo Hammond, Pat Murray (RIP), Dawn Seaton (RIP), Anne Tate and Sue Turner deserve the medal of honour from Grimsby, while Adrian Barker, Micky Chittenden (RIP), Harbakhsh (Tim) Grewal, Matt Kay, Joy Millward (Mrs Banksy) and Nick Toon kept me on my feet in London along with a series of American and Hull students, several of whom have gone on to greater things. I owe them all.

Those who turned my egomaniac ramblings into an approximation to literature were my friend Martin Levene; Iain Dale, who encouraged me to publish; and his wonderful team at Biteback, particularly Olivia Beattie, who edited it with skill and charm. Our friend Ian Bloom read it through his legal glasses to save me from the litigious powerful.

It wouldn't have materialised without my wife, Linda McDougall, pushing me on, demonstrating the wonder of computers and imposing a discipline of which I'm personally incapable.

To the rest of my burgeoning family I can only offer my apologies for the neglect they've endured while I deprived myself of the pleasure of helping them to grow up and trying to grow up with them. Sorry. Politicians don't deserve families.

Needless to say after this roll call of honour, the photos and the remaining faults are mine. The worst part of being a maverick is not so much the loneliness of the long-distance runner, but that you've no one else to blame.

Have fun. I did, as I tried to do my duty, rather than pursue power, place or pecuniary success. I can't call it a successful career, since so many of the problems I pointed to haven't been dealt with and most of the dangers I lamented have materialised, or even got worse. I don't think I was wrong, just out of some very dodgy times. I still have the backbencher's only consolation in life: I did my best. I did my duty as I saw it and I still managed to have fun in a very unfunny world. What more can any maverick ask?

Austin Mitchell
Sowerby
West Yorkshire